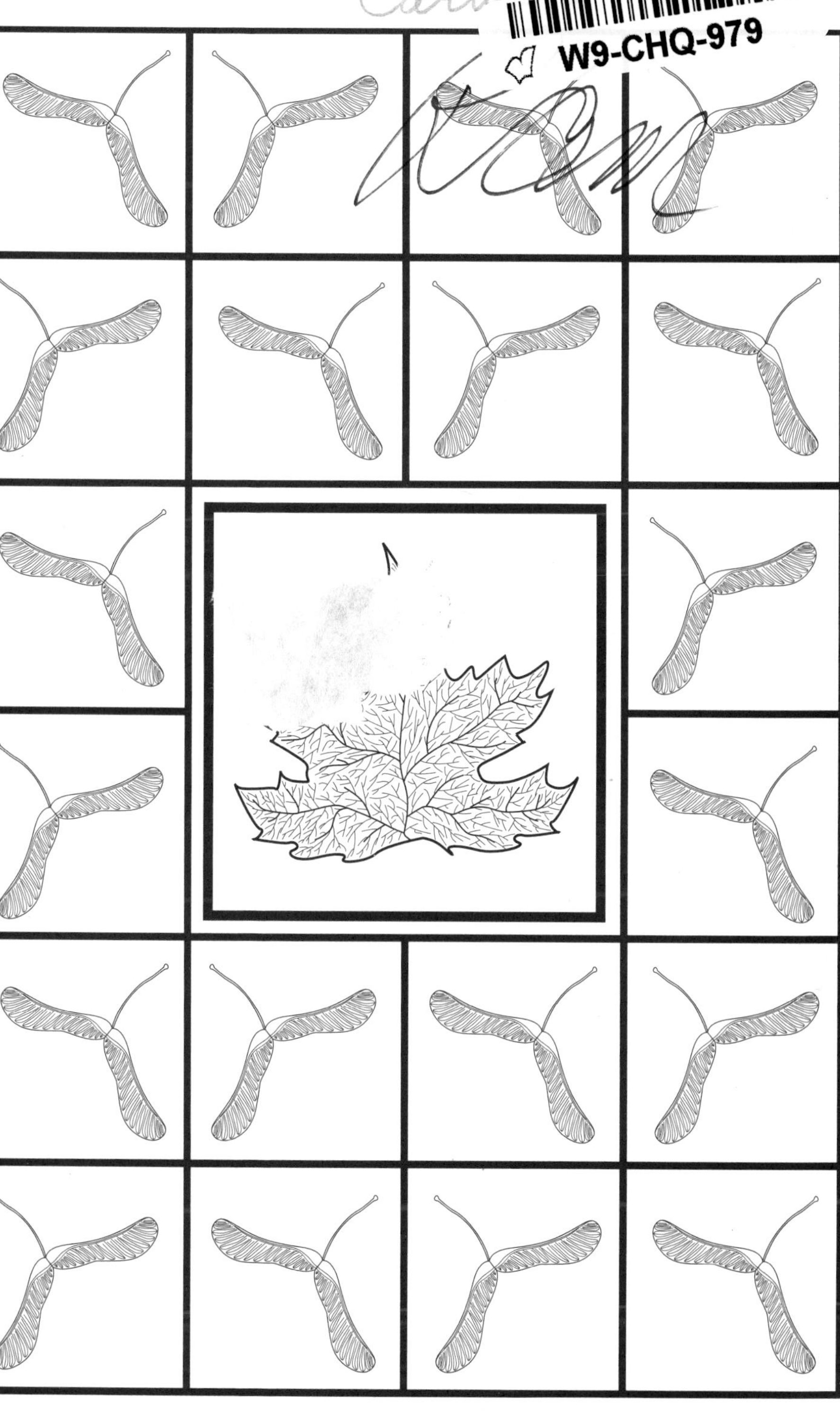

PETER, THE CHIEF.

THE LIBRARY OF ENTERTAINING KNOWLEDGE.

THE

BACKWOODS OF CANADA:

BEING

LETTERS FROM THE WIFE OF AN EMIGRANT OFFICER,

ILLUSTRATIVE OF THE DOMESTIC ECONOMY OF BRITISH AMERICA.

PROSPERO

TORONTO
2000

The Backwoods of Canada:
Being Letters from the Wife of an Emigrant Officer,
Illustrative of the Domestic Economy of British America

This edition first published by
Prospero Books in 2000
from the 1836 Charles Knight edition

Canadian Cataloguing in Publication Data

Traill, Catharine Parr, 1802-1899
The Backwoods of Canada:
being the letters from the wife of an emigrant officer,
illustrative of the domestic economy of British America

(Prospero Canadian Collection)
Facsim. reprint.
Originally published: London: C. Knight, 1836.
(The library of entertaining knowledge).
ISBN 1-55267-143-7

1. Traill, Catharine Parr, 1802-1899 - Correspondence.
2. Frontier and pioneer life - Ontario.
3. Ontario - Description and travel.
4. Ontario - Social life and customs.
I. Title. II. Series.

FC3067.2.T72 2000 917.1304'2 C00-931933-6
F1057.T76 2000

Prospero Books
90 Ronson Drive, Toronto, Ontario, Canada
M9W 1C1

Printed on acid free paper

Printed and bound in Canada

CONTENTS.

ILLUSTRATIONS.

UNDER THE SUPERINTENDENCE OF THE SOCIETY FOR THE DIFFUSION OF USEFUL KNOWLEDGE.

THE LIBRARY

OF

ENTERTAINING KNOWLEDGE

BACKWOODS OF CANADA.

INTRODUCTION.

AMONG the numerous works on Canada that have been published within the last ten years, with emigration for their leading theme, there are few, if any, that give information regarding the domestic economy of a settler's life, sufficiently minute to prove a faithful guide to the person on whose responsibility the whole comfort of a family depends—the mistress, whose department it is "to haud the house in order."

Dr. Dunlop, it is true, has published a witty and spirited pamphlet, "The Backwoodsman," but it does not enter into the routine of feminine duties and employment, in a state of emigration. Indeed, a woman's pen alone can describe half that is requisite to be told of the internal management of a domicile in the backwoods, in order to enable the outcoming female emigrant to form a proper judgment of the trials and arduous duties she has to encounter.

"Forewarned, forearmed," is a maxim of our forefathers, containing much matter in its pithy brevity; and, following its spirit, the writer of the following pages has endeavoured to afford every possible information to the wives and daughters of emigrants of the higher class who contemplate seeking a home amid our Canadian wilds. Truth has been conscientiously her object in the work, for it were cruel to write in flattering terms calculated to deceive emigrants into the belief that the land to which they are transferring their families, their capital, and their hopes, a land flowing with milk and honey, where comforts and affluence may be obtained with little exertion. She prefers honestly representing facts in their real and true light, that the female part of the emigrant's family may be enabled to look them firmly in the face; to find a remedy in female ingenuity and expediency for some difficulties; and, by being properly prepared, encounter the rest with that high-spirited cheerfulness of which well-educated females often give extraordinary proofs. She likewise wishes to teach them to discard every thing exclusively pertaining to the artificial refinement of fashionable life in England; and to point out that, by devoting the money consumed in these incumbrances to articles of real use, which cannot be readily obtained in Canada, they may enjoy the pleasure of superintending a pleasant, well-ordered home. She is desirous of giving them the advantage of her three years' experience, that they may properly apply every part of their time, and learn to consider that every pound or pound's worth belonging to any member of an out-coming emigrant's family, ought to be sacredly considered as *capital*, which must make proper returns either as the means of bringing increase in the shape of income, or, what is still better, in healthful domestic comfort.

These exhalations in behalf of utility in preference to artificial personal refinement, are not so needless as the English public may consider. The emigrants to British America are no longer of the rank of life that formerly left the shores of the British Isles. It is not only the poor husbandmen and artisans, that move in vast bodies to the west, but it is the enterprising English capitalist, and the once affluent landholder, alarmed at the difficulties of establishing numerous families in independence, in a country where every profession is overstocked, that join the bands that Great Britain is pouring forth into these colonies! Of what vital importance is it that the female members of these most valuable colonists should obtain proper information regarding the important duties they are undertaking; that they should learn beforehand to brace their minds to the task, and thus avoid the repinings and discontent that is apt to follow unfounded expectations and fallacious hopes!

It is a fact not universally known to the public, that British officers and their families are usually denizens of the backwoods; and as great numbers of unattached officers of every rank have accepted grants of land in Canada, they are the pioneers of civilization in the wilderness, and their families, often of delicate nurture and honourable descent, are at once plunged into all the hardships attendant on the rough life of a bush-settler. The laws that regulate the grants of lands, which enforce a certain time of residence, and certain settlement duties to be performed, allow no claims to absentees when once the land is drawn. These laws wisely force a superiorly-educated man with resources of both property and intellect, to devote all his energies to a certain spot of uncleared land. It may easily be supposed that no persons would encounter these hardships who have not a young family to establish in the healthful ways of independence. This family renders the residence of such a head still more valuable to the colony; and the half-pay officer, by thus leading the advanced guard of civilization, and bringing into these rough districts gentle and well-educated females, who soften and improve all around them by *mental* refinements, is serving his country as much by founding peaceful villages and pleasant homesteads in the trackless wilds, as ever he did by personal courage, or military stratagem, in times of war.

It will be seen, in the course of this work, that the writer is as earnest in recommending ladies who belong to the higher class of settlers to cultivate all the mental resources of a superior education, as she is to induce them to discard all irrational and artificial wants and mere useless pursuits. She would willingly direct their attention to the natural history and botany of this new country, in which they will find a never-failing source of amusement and instruction, at once enlightening and elevating the mind, and serving to fill up the void left by the absence of those lighter feminine accomplishments, the practice of which are necessarily superseded by imperative domestic duties. To the person who is capable of looking abroad into the beauties of nature, and adoring the Creator through his glorious works, are opened stores of unmixed pleasure, which will not permit her to be dull or unhappy in the loneliest part of our Western Wilderness. The writer of these pages speaks from experience, and would be pleased to find that the simple sources from which she has herself drawn pleasure, have cheered the solitude of future female sojourners in the backwoods of Canada.

As a general remark to all sorts and conditions of settlers, she would observe, that the struggle up the hill of Independence is often a severe one, and it ought not to be made alone. It must be aided and encouraged by the example and assistance of an active and cheerful partner. Children should be taught to appreciate the devoted love that has induced their parents to overcome the natural reluctance felt by all persons to quit for ever the land of their forefathers, the scenes of their earliest and happiest days, and to become aliens and wanderers in a distant country,—to form new ties and new friends, and begin, as it were, life's toilsome march anew, that their children may be placed in a situation in which, by industry and activity, the substantial comforts of life may be permanently obtained, and a landed property handed down to them, and their children after them.

Young men soon become reconciled to this country, which offers to them that chief attraction to youth,—great personal liberty. Their employments are of a cheerful and healthy nature ; and their amusements, such as hunting, shooting, fishing, and boating, are peculiarly fascinating. But in none of these can their sisters share. The hardships and difficulties of the settler's life, therefore, are felt peculiarly by the female part of the family. It is with a view of ameliorating these privations that the following pages have been written, to show how some difficulties may be best borne and others avoided. The simple truth, founded entirely on personal knowledge of the facts related, is the basis of the work; to have had recourse to fiction might have rendered it more acceptable to many readers, but would have made it less useful to that class for whom it is especially intended. For those who, without intending to share in the privations and dangers of an emigrant's life, have a rational curiosity to become acquainted with scenes and manners so different from those of a long-civilized country, it is hoped that this little work will afford some amusement, and inculcate some lessons not devoid of moral instruction.

THE

BACKWOODS OF CANADA.

Letter I.

Departure from Greenock in the Brig *Laurel*.—Fitting-up of the Vessel.—Boy Passenger.—Sea Prospect.—Want of Occupation and Amusement.—Captain's Goldfinch.

Brig *Laurel*, July 18, 1832.

I RECEIVED your last kind letter, my dearest mother, only a few hours before we set sail from Greenock. As you express a wish that I should give you a minute detail of our voyage, I shall take up my subject from the time of our embarkation, and write as inclination prompts me. Instead of having reason to complain of short letters, you will, I fear, find mine only too prolix.

After many delays and disappointments, we succeeded at last in obtaining a passage in a fast-sailing brig, the *Laurel*, of Greenock; and favourable winds are now rapidly carrying us across the Atlantic.

The *Laurel* is not a regular passenger-ship, which I consider an advantage, for what we lose in amusement and variety we assuredly gain in comfort. The cabin is neatly fitted up, and I enjoy the luxury (for such it is, compared with the narrow berths of the state cabin) of a handsome sofa, with crimson draperies, in the great cabin. The state cabin is also ours. We paid fifteen pounds each for our passage to Montreal. This was high, but it includes every expense; and, in fact, we had no choice. The only vessel in the river bound for Canada, was a passenger-ship, literally swarming with emigrants, chiefly of the lower class of Highlanders.

The only passengers besides ourselves in the *Laurel* are the captain's nephew, a pretty yellow-haired lad, about fifteen years of age, who works his passage out, and a young gentleman who is going out as clerk in a merchant's house in Quebec. He seems too much wrapped up in his own affairs to be very communicative to others; he walks much, talks little, and reads less; but often amuses himself by singing as he paces the deck, "Home, sweet home," and that delightful song by Camoens, "Isle of beauty." It is a sweet song, and I can easily imagine the charm it has for a home-sick heart.

I was much pleased with the scenery of the Clyde; the day we set sail was a lovely one, and I remained on deck till nightfall. The morning light found our vessel dashing gallantly along, with a favourable breeze, through the north channel; that day we saw the last of the Hebrides, and before night lost sight of the north coast of Ireland. A wide expanse of water and sky is now our only prospect, unvaried by any object save the distant and scarcely to be traced outline of some vessel just seen at the verge of the horizon, a speck in the immensity of space, or sometimes a few sea-fowl. I love to watch these wanderers of the ocean, as they rise and fal with the rocking billows, or flit about our vessel; and often I wonder whence they came, to what distant shore they are bound, and if they make the rude wave their home and resting-place during the long day and dark night; and then I recall to mind the words of the American poet, Bryant,—

> "He who from zone to zone
> Guides through the boundless air their certain flight,
> In the long way that I must tread alone
> Will guide my steps aright."

Though we have been little more than a week on board, I am getting weary of the voyage. I can only compare the monotony of it to being weather-bound in some country inn. I have already made myself acquainted with all the books worth reading in the ship's library; unfortunately, it is chiefly made up with old novels and musty romances.

When the weather is fine I sit on a bench on the deck, wrapped in my cloak, and sew, or pace the deck with my husband, and talk over plans for the future, which in all probability will never be realized. I really do pity men who are not actively employed: women have always their needle as a resource against the overwhelming weariness of an idle life; but where a man is confined to a small space, such as the deck and cabin of a trading vessel, with nothing to see, nothing to hear, nothing to do, and nothing to read, he is really a very pitiable creature.

There is one passenger on board that seems perfectly happy, if one may judge from the liveliness of the songs with which he greets us whenever we approach his cage. It is "Harry," the captain's goldfinch—"the *captain's mate*," as the sailors term him. This pretty creature has made no fewer than twelve voyages in the *Laurel*. "It is all one to him whether his cage is at sea or on land, he is still at home," said the captain, regarding his little favourite with an air of great affection, and evidently gratified by the attention I bestowed on his bird.

I have already formed a friendship with the little captive. He never fails to greet my approach with one of his sweetest songs, and will take from my fingers a bit of biscuit, which he holds in his claws till he has thanked me with a few of his clearest notes. This mark of acknowledgment is termed by the steward, "saying grace."

If the wind still continues to favour us, the captain tells us we shall be on the banks of Newfoundland in another week. Farewell for the present.

LETTER II.

Arrival off Newfoundland.—Singing of the Captain's Goldfinch previous to the discovery of Land.—Gulf of St. Laurence.—Scenery of the River St. Laurence.—Difficult navigation of the River.—French Fisherman engaged as a Pilot.—Isle of Bic.—Green Island.—Regular Pilot engaged.—Scenery of Green Island.—Gros Isle.—Quarantine Regulations.—Emigrants on Gros Isle.—Arrival off Quebec.—Prospect of the City and Environs.

Brig *Laurel*, River St. Laurence,
August 6, 1832.

I LEFT off writing, my dear mother, from this simple cause,—I had nothing to say. One day was but the echo, as it were, of the one that preceded it; so that a page copied from the mate's log would have proved as amusing, and to the full as instructive, as my journal, provided I had kept one during the last fortnight.

So barren of events has that time been that the sight of a party of bottle-nosed whales, two or three seals, and a porpoise, possibly on their way to a dinner or tea party at the North Pole, was considered an occurrence of great importance. Every glass was in requisition as soon as they made their appearance, and the marine monsters were well nigh stared out of countenance.

We came within sight of the shores of Newfoundland on the 5th of August, just one month from the day we took our last look of the British isles. Yet though the coast was brown, and rugged, and desolate, I hailed its appearance with rapture. Never did any thing seem so refreshing and delicious to me as the land breeze that came to us, as I thought, bearing health and gladness on its wings.

I had noticed with some curiosity the restless activity of the captain's bird some hours previous to "land" being proclaimed from the look-out station. He sang continually, and his note was longer, clearer, and more thrilling than heretofore; the little creature, the captain assured me, was conscious of the difference in the air as we approached the land. "I trust almost as much to my bird as to my glass," he said, "and have never yet been deceived."

Our progress was somewhat tedious after we entered the gulf. Ninety miles across is the entrance of this majestic river; it seems an ocean in itself. Half our time is spent poring over the great chart in the cabin, which is constantly being rolled and unrolled by my husband to gratify my desire of learning the names of the distant shores and islands which we pass.

We are without a pilot as yet, and the captain being a cautious seaman is unwilling to risk the vessel on this dangerous navigation; so that we proceed but slowly on our voyage.

August 7.—We were visited this morning by a beautiful little bird, not much larger than our gold-crested wren. I hailed it as a bird of good omen—a little messenger sent to bid us welcome to the New World, and I felt almost a childish joy at the sight of our little visitor. There are happy moments in our lives when we draw the greatest pleasure from the most trifling sources, as children are pleased with the most simple toy.

From the hour we entered the gulf a perceptible

change had taken place in all on board. The captain, a man of grave, quiet manners, grew quite talkative. My husband was more than usually animated, and even the thoughtful young Scotchman became positively an entertaining person. The crew displayed the most lively zeal in the performance of their duty, and the goldfinch sung cheerily from dawn till sunset. As for me Hope was busy in my heart, chasing from it all feelings of doubt or regret that might sadden the present or cloud the future.

I am now able to trace distinctly the outline of the coast on the southern side of the river. Sometimes the high lands are suddenly enveloped in dense clouds of mist, which are in constant motion, rolling along in shadowy billows, now tinted with rosy light, now white and fleecy, or bright as silver, as they catch the sunbeams. So rapid are the changes that take place in this fog-bank, that perhaps the next time I raise my eyes I behold the scene changed as if by magic. The misty curtain is slowly drawn up, as if by invisible hands, and the wild, wooded mountains partially revealed, with their bold rocky shores and sweeping bays. At other times the vapoury volume dividing, moves along the valleys and deep ravines, like lofty pillars of smoke, or hangs in snowy draperies among the dark forest pines.

I am never weary of watching these fantastic clouds; they recall to me the pleasant time I spent in the Highlands, among the cloud-capped hills of the north.

As yet, the air is cold, and we experience frequent squalls of wind and hail, with occasional peals of thunder; then again all is serene and bright, and the air is filled with fragrance, and flies, and bees, and birds come flitting past us from the shore.

August 8.—Though I cannot but dwell with feelings of wonder and admiration on the majesty and power of this mighty river, I begin to grow weary of its immensity, and long for a nearer view of the shore; but at present we see nothing more than long lines of pine-clad hills, with here and there a white speck, which they tell me are settlements and villages to the south; while huge mountains divested of verdure bound our view on the north side the river. My admiration of mountainous scenery makes me dwell with more interest on this side the river, and I watch the progress of cultivation among these rugged and inhospitable regions with positive pleasure.

During the last two days we have been anxiously looking out for a pilot to take us up to Quebec. Various signals have been fired, but hitherto without success; no pilot has condescended to visit us, so we are somewhat in the condition of a stage without a coachman, with only some inexperienced hand to hold the reins. I already perceive some manifestations of impatience appearing among us, but no one blames the captain, who is very anxious about the matter; as the river is full of rocks and shoals, and presents many difficulties to a person not intimately acquainted with the navigation. Besides, he is answerable for the safety of the ship to the underwriters, in case he neglects to take a pilot on board.

* * * * * * *

While writing the above I was roused by a bustle on deck, and going up to learn the cause was informed that a boat with the long looked-for pilot had put off from the shore; but, after all the fuss and bustle, it proved only a French fisherman, with a poor ragged lad, his assistant. The captain with very little difficulty persuaded Monsieur Paul Breton to pilot us as far as Green Island, a distance of some hundred miles higher up the river, where he assured us we should meet with a regular pilot, if not before.

I have some little difficulty in understanding Monsieur Paul, as he speaks a peculiar dialect; but he seems good-natured and obliging enough. He tells us the corn is yet green, hardly in ear, and the summer fruits not yet ripe, but he says, that at Quebec we shall find apples and fruit in plenty.

As we advance higher up the river the country on both sides begins to assume a more genial aspect. Patches of verdure, with white cottages, are seen on the shores and scattered along the sides of the mountains; while here and there a village church rears its simple spire, distinguished above the surrounding buildings by its glittering vane and bright roof of tin. The southern shores are more populous but less picturesque than those of the north, but there is enough on either side to delight the eye.

This morning we anchored off the Isle of Bic, a pretty low island, covered with trees and looking very pleasant. I felt a longing desire to set my foot on Canadian ground, and must own I was a little disappointed when the captain advised me to remain on board, and not attempt to make one of the party that were preparing to go on shore: my husband seconded the captain's wish, so I contented myself with leaning over the ship's side and feasting my eyes on the rich masses of foliage as they waved to and fro with the slight breeze that agitated them. I had soon reason to be thankful that I had not followed my own wayward will, for the afternoon proved foggy, and on the return of the boat I learned that the ground was swampy just where the party landed, and they sunk over their ankles in water. They reported the island to be covered knee-deep with a most luxuriant growth of red clover, tall trees, low shrubs, and an abundance of wild flowers.

That I might not regret not accompanying him, my husband brought me a delightful bouquet, which he had selected for me. Among the flowers were fragrant red roses, resembling those we call Scotch burnet-leaved, with smooth shining leaves and few if any thorns; the blue flower called Pulmonaria or Lungwort, which I gathered in the Highlands; a sweet pea, with red blossoms and wreaths of lovely pale green foliage; a white orchis, the smell of which was quite delicious. Besides these were several small white and yellow flowers, with which I was totally unacquainted. The steward furnished me with a china jar and fresh water, so that I shall have the pleasure of a nosegay during the rest of the voyage. The sailors had not forgotten a green bough or two to adorn the ship, and the bird cage was soon as bowery as leaves could make it.

Though the weather is now very fine, we make but slow progress; the provoking wind seems determined to blow from every quarter but the right. We float up with the flood tide, and when the tide fails cast anchor, and wait with the best grace we can till it is time to weigh anchor again. I amuse myself with examining the villages and settlements through the captain's glass, or watching for the appearance of the white porpoises tumbling among the waves. These creatures are of a milky whiteness, and have nothing of the disgusting look of the black ones. Sometimes a seal pops its droll head up close beside our vessel, looking very much like Sinbad's little old man of the sea.

It is fortunate for me that my love of natural history enables me to draw amusement from objects that are deemed by many unworthy of attention. To me they present an inexhaustible fund of interest. The simplest weed that grows in my path, or the fly that flutters about me, are subjects for reflection, admiration, and delight.

We are now within sight of Green Island. It is the largest, and I believe one of the most populous, we have passed. Every minute now seems to increase the beauty of the passage. Far as the eye can reach you see the shore thronged with villages and farms in one continuous line. On the southern side all are gay and glittering with the tin roofs on the most important buildings; the rest are shingles, whitewashed. This I do not like so well as the plain shingled roofs; the whiteness of the roofs of the cottages and homesteads have a glaring effect, and we look in vain for that relief to the eye that is produced by the thatched or slated roofs. The shingles in their natural state soon acquire the appearance of slates, and can hardly be distinguished from them. What would you say to a rose-coloured house, with a roof of the same gaudy hue, the front of the gay edifice being garnished with grass-green shutters, doors, and verandah. No doubt the interior is furnished with corresponding taste. There is generally one or more of these *smart* buildings in a Canadian village, standing forth with ostentatious splendour above its more modest brethren.

August 11.—Just below Green Island we took on board a real pilot, who, by the way, I do not like half so well as Monsieur Paul. He is a little bit pragmatical, and seems evidently proud of his superior knowledge of the river. The good-natured fisherman relinquished his post with a very good grace, and seems already excellent friends with his more able rival. For my part I was very sorry when the new pilot came on board; the first thing he did was to hand us over a pamphlet, containing regulations from the Board of Health at Quebec respecting the cholera, which is raging, he tells us, like a fearful plague both at that place and Montreal.

These regulations positively forbid the captain and the pilot to allow any person, whether of the crew or passengers, to quit the vessel until they shall have passed examination at the quarantine ground, under the risk of incurring a severe penalty.

This was very annoying; as the captain, that very morning, had proposed taking us on shore at a lovely spot called Crane Island, to spend the afternoon, while we waited for the return of the tide, at the house of a Scotch gentleman, the owner of the prettiest settlement I had yet seen, the buildings and grounds being laid out with great taste.

The situation of this island is of itself very beautiful. Around it are the waters of the St. Laurence, bearing on its mighty current the commerce of several nations: in the foreground are the populous and lively settlements of the southern shores, while behind and far far above it rise the lofty range of mountains to the north, now studded with rural villages, pleasant farms, and cultivated fields. The island itself showed us smooth lawns and meadows of emerald verdure, with orchards and corn-fields sloping down to the water's edge. After a confinement of nearly five weeks on board, you may easily suppose with what satisfaction we contemplated the prospect of spending a few hours on this inviting spot.

We expect to reach the quarantine ground (Gros Isle) this evening, where the pilot says we shall be detained three days. Though we are all in good health, yet, having sailed from an infected port, we shall be detained on the quarantine ground, but not allowed to land.

August 12.—We reached Gros Isle yesterday evening. It is a beautiful rocky island, covered with groves of beech, birch, ash, and fir-trees. There are several vessels lying at anchor close to the shore; one bears the melancholy symbol of disease, the yellow flag; she is a passenger-ship, and has the small-pox and measles among her crew. When any infectious complaint appears on board, the yellow flag is hoisted, and the invalids conveyed to the cholera-hospital or wooden building, that has been erected on a rising bank above the shore. It is surrounded with palisadoes and a guard of soldiers.

There is also a temporary fort at some distance from the hospital, containing a garrison of soldiers, who are there to enforce the quarantine rules. These rules are considered as very defective, and in some respects quite absurd, and are productive of many severe evils to the unfortunate emigrants*.

When the passengers and crew of a vessel do not exceed a certain number, they are not allowed to land under a penalty, both to the captain and the offender; but if, on the contrary, they should exceed the stated number, ill or well, passengers and crew must all turn out and go on shore, taking with them their bedding and clothes, which are all spread out on the shore, to be washed, aired, and fumigated, giving the healthy every chance of taking the infection from the invalids. The sheds and buildings put up for the accommodation of those who are obliged to submit to the quarantine laws, are in the same area as the hospital.

Nothing can exceed the longing desire I feel to be

* It is to be hoped that some steps will be taken by Government to remedy these obnoxious laws, which have repeatedly entailed those very evils on the unhappy emigrants that the Board of Health wish to avert from the colony at large.

Many valuable lives have been wantonly sacrificed by placing the healthy in the immediate vicinity of infection, besides subjecting them to many other sufferings, expenses, and inconvenience, which the poor exile might well be spared.

If there must be quarantine laws—and I suppose the evil is a necessary one—surely every care ought to be taken to render them as little hurtful to the emigrant as possible.

allowed to land and explore this picturesque island; the weather is so fine, and the waving groves of green, the little rocky bays and inlets of the island, appear so tempting; but to all my entreaties the visiting surgeon who came on board returned a decided negative.

A few hours after his visit, however, an Indian basket, containing strawberries and raspberries, with a large bunch of wild flowers, was sent on board for me, with the surgeon's compliments.

I amuse myself with making little sketches of the fort and the surrounding scenery, or watching the groups of emigrants on shore. We have already seen the landing of the passengers of three emigrant ships. You may imagine yourself looking on a fair or crowded market, clothes waving in the wind or spread out on the earth, chests, bundles, baskets, men, women, and children, asleep or basking in the sun, some in motion busied with their goods, the women employed in washing or cooking in the open air, beside the wood fires on the beach; while parties of children are pursuing each other in wanton glee rejoicing in their newly-acquired liberty. Mixed with these you see the stately form and gay trappings of the sentinels, while the thin blue smoke of the wood fires, rising above the trees, heightens the picture and gives it an additional effect. On my husband remarking the picturesque appearance of the scene before us to one of the officers from the fort who had come on board, he smiled sadly, and replied, "Believe me, in this instance, as in many others, 'tis distance lends enchantment to the view." Could you take a nearer survey of some of those very picturesque groups which you admire, I think you would turn away from them with heart sickness; you would there behold every variety of disease, vice, poverty, filth, and famine—human misery in its most disgusting and saddening form. Such pictures as Hogarth's pencil only could have pourtrayed, or Crabbe's pen described.

August 14.—We are once more under weigh, and floating up the river with the tide. Gros Isle is just five-and-twenty miles below Quebec, a favourable breeze would carry us up in a few hours; as it is we can only make a little way by tacking from side to side when we lose the tide. I rather enjoy this way of proceeding, as it gives one a close view of both sides the river, which narrows considerably as we approach nearer towards Quebec. To-morrow, if no accident happens, we shall be anchored in front of a place rendered interesting both by its historical associations and its own native beauty of situation. Till to-morrow, then, adieu.

I was reckoning much on seeing the falls of Montmorenci, which are within sight of the river; but the sun set, and the stars rose brilliantly before we approached within sound of the cataract; and though I strained my eyes till they were weary of gazing on the dim shadowy scene around me, I could distinguish nothing beyond the dark masses of rock that forms the channel through which the waters of the Montmorenci rush into the St. Laurence.

At ten last night, August the 15th, the lights of the city of Quebec were seen gleaming through the distance like a coronet of stars above the waters. At half-past ten we dropped anchor opposite the fort, and I fell asleep dreaming of the various scenes

Falls of Montmorenci.

through which I had passed. Again I was destined to be disappointed in my expectations of going on shore. The visiting surgeon advised my husband and me by no means to land, as the mortality that still raged in the town made it very hazardous. He gave a melancholy description of the place. "Desolation and woe and great mourning—Rachel weeping for her children because they are not," are words that may well be applied to this city of the pestilence.

Nothing can be more imposing than the situation of Quebec, built on the sides and summit of a magnificent rock, on the highest point of which (Cape Diamond) stands the fortress overlooking the river, and commanding a most superb view of the surrounding scenes. I did, indeed, regret the loss of this noble prospect, the equal of which I suppose I shall never see. It would have been something to have thought on and recalled in after years, when buried in the solitude of the Canadian woods.

The opposite heights, being the Point Levi side, are highly picturesque, though less imposing than the rock on which the town stands. The bank is rocky, precipitous, and clothed with trees that sweep down to the water's edge, excepting where they are cleared away to give place to white cottages, gardens, and hanging orchards. But, in my opinion, much less is done with this romantic situation than might be effected if good taste were exercised in the buildings, and on the disposal of the ground. How lovely would such a spot be rendered in England or Scotland. Nature here has done all, and man but little, excepting sticking up some ugly wooden cottages, as mean as they are tasteless. It is, however, very possible there may be pretty villas and houses higher up, that are concealed from the eye by the intervening groves.

The river is considered to be just a mile across from Point Levi to the landing-stairs below the custom-house in Quebec; and it was a source of amusement to me to watch the horse ferry-boats that ply between the two shores. The captain told me there were not less than twelve of these comical-looking machines. They each have their regular hours, so that you see a constant succession going or returning. They carry a strange assortment of passengers; well and ill-dressed; old and young; rich and poor; cows, sheep, horses, pigs, dogs, fowls, market-baskets, vegetables, fruit, hay, corn, anything and everything you will see by turns.

The boat is flat, railed round, with a wicker at each end to admit the live and dead stock that go or are taken on board; the centre of the boat (if such it can be called) is occupied by four lean, ill-favoured hacks, who walk round and round, as if in a threshing machine, and work the paddles at each side. There is a sort of pen for the cattle.

I am told there is a monument erecting in honour of Wolfe, in the governor's garden, looking towards the St. Laurence, and to be seen from Point Levi: the inscription has not yet been decided upon*.

* Since the period in which the author visited Quebec, Wolfe's monument has been completed. Lord Dalhousie, with equal good feeling and good taste, has united the names of the rival heroes Wolfe and Montcalm in the dedication of

The captain has just returned from the town. He very kindly brought on board a basket of ripe apples for me, besides fresh meat, vegetables, bread, butter, and milk. The deck is all bustle with custom-house officers, and men unloading a part of the ship's freight, which consists chiefly of rum, brandy, sugar, and coals, for ballast. We are to leave Quebec by five o'clock this evening. The *British America*, a superb steam-vessel of three decks, takes us in tow as far as Montreal. I must now say farewell.

the pillar—a liberality of feeling that cannot but prove gratifying to the Canadian French, while it robs the British warrior of none of his glory.

The monument was designed by Major Young of the 97th Regiment. To the top of the surbase is fourteen feet from the ground; on this rests a sarcophagus, seven feet three inches high, from which rises an obelisk forty-two feet eight inches in height, aud the apex is two feet one inch. The dimensions of the obelisk at the base are six feet by four feet eight inches. A prize medal was adjudged to J. C. Fisher, LL.D. for the following inscription on the sarcophagus:—

Mortem virtus communem
Famam Historia
Monumentum Posteritas
Dedit.

On the surbase is an inscription from the pen of Dr. Mills, stating the fact of the erection of the monument at the expense of Lord Dalhousie, Governor of Lower Canada, to commemorate the death of Wolfe and Montcalm, Sept. 13 and 14, 1759. Wolfe fell on the field; and Montcalm, who was wounded by the single gun in the possession of the English, died on the next day after the battle.

Letter III.

Departure from Quebec.—Towed by a Steam-vessel.—Fertility of the Country.—Different Objects seen in sailing up the River.—Arrival off Montreal.—The Rapids.

Brig *Laurel*, St. Laurence, below Montreal,
August 17, 1832.

It was after sunset, and a glorious evening, when we left Quebec, which we did in company with a fine steam-vessel, whose decks and gallery were crowded with passengers of all descriptions. A brave sight she was to look upon; ploughing the bright waters which foamed and sung beneath her paddles; while our brig, with her white sails, followed like a butterfly in her wake. The heavens were glowing with the richest tints of rose and saffron, which were reflected below on the bosom of the river; and then came forth the stars, in the soft blue ether, more brilliant than ever I saw them at home, and this, I suppose, I may attribute to the superior purity of the atmosphere. My husband said this evening resembled the sunsets of Italy.

Our voyage has proved a very pleasant one; the weather moderately warm, and the air quite clear. We have within the last few days emerged from a cold, damp atmosphere, such as we often experience in Britain in the spring, to a delightful summer, moderated by light breezes from the river.

The further we advance up the country the more fertile it appears. The harvest is ripening under a more genial climate than that below Quebec. We see fields of Indian corn in full flower: it is a stately-looking crop, with its beautiful feathery top tinted with a rich purple hue, below which tufts of pale green silk are waving in the breeze. When fully ripe they tell me it is beautiful to see the golden grain bursting from its silvery sheath; but that it is a crop liable to injury from frost, and has many enemies, such as bears, racoons, squirrels, mice, fowls, &c.

We saw several fields of tobacco along the banks of the river, which looked healthy and flourishing. I believe tobacco is cultivated to some extent in both provinces; but the Canadian tobacco is not held in such high esteem as that of Virginia.

There is a flourishing and very pretty town situated at the junction of the Richelieu river with the St. Laurence, formerly called Sorel, now called Fort William Henry. The situation is excellent. There are several churches, a military fort, with mills, and other public buildings, with some fine stone houses. The land, however, in the immediate vicinity of the town seems very light and sandy.

I was anxious to obtain a near view of a log-house or a shanty, and was somewhat disappointed in the few buildings of this kind that I saw along the banks of the river. It was not the rudeness of the material so much as the barn-like form of the buildings of this kind, and the little attention that was paid to the picturesque, that displeased me. In Britain even the peasant has taste enough to plant a few roses or honeysuckles about his door or his casement, and there is the little bit of garden enclosed and neatly kept; but here no such attempt is made to ornament the cottages. We saw no smiling orchard or grove to conceal the bare log walls; and as to the little farm-houses, they are uglier still, and look so pert and ungraceful stuck upon the bank close to the water's edge.

Further back a different style of building and cultivation appears. The farms and frame-houses are really handsome places, and in good taste, with clumps of trees here and there to break the monotony of the clearing. The land is nearly one unbroken level plain, apparently fertile and well farmed, but too flat for fine scenery. The country between Quebec and Montreal has all the appearance of having been under a long state of cultivation, especially on the right bank of the river. Still there is a great portion of forest standing which it will take years of labour to remove.

We passed some little grassy islands on which there were many herds of cattle feeding. I was puzzling myself to know how they got there, when the captain told me it was usual for farmers to convey their stock to these island pastures in flat-bottomed boats, or to swim them, if the place was fordable, and leave them to graze as long as the food continued good. If cows are put on an island within a reasonable distance of the farm, some person goes daily in a canoe to milk them. While he was telling me this, a log-canoe with a boy and a stout lass with tin pails, paddled across from the bank of the river, and proceeded to call together their herd.

We noticed some very pleasant rural villages to the right as we advanced, but our pilot was stupid, and could not, or would not, tell their names. It was Sunday morning, and we could just hear the quick tinkling of the church bells, and distinguish long lines of caleches, light waggons, with equestrians and pedestrians hastening along the avenue of trees that led to the churchyard; besides these, were boats and canoes crossing the river, bound to the same peaceful haven.

In a part of the St. Laurence, where the channel is rendered difficult by shoals and sand-banks, there occur little lighthouses, looking somewhat like miniature watermills, on wooden posts, raised above the flat banks on which they are built. These droll little huts were inhabited, and we noticed a merry party, in their holiday clothes, enjoying a gossip with a party in a canoe below them. They looked clean and smart, and cheerful enough, but I did not envy them their situation, which I should think far from healthy.

Some miles below Montreal the appearance of the country became richer, more civilized, and populous; while the distant line of blue mountains, at the verge of the horizon, added an interest to the landscape. The rich tint of ripened harvest formed a beautiful contrast with the azure sky and waters of the St. Laurence. The scenery of the river near Montreal is of a very different character to that below Quebec; the latter possesses a wild and rugged aspect, and its productions are evidently those of a colder and less happy climate. What the former loses in grandeur and picturesque effect, it gains in fertility of soil and warmth of temperature. In the lower division of the province you feel that the industry of the inhabitants is forcing a churlish soil for bread; while in the upper, the land seems willing to yield her increase to a moderate exertion. Remember, these are merely the cursory remarks of a passing traveller, and founded on no personal experience.

There was a feeling of anxiety and dread upon our minds that we would hardly acknowledge to each other as we drew near to the city of the pestilence, as if ashamed of confessing a weakness that was felt; but no one spoke on the subject. With what unmixed delight and admiration at any other time should we have gazed on the scene that opened upon us.

The river here expands into a fine extensive basin, diversified with islands, on the largest of which Montreal is situated.

The lofty hill from which the town takes its name rises like a crown above it, and forms a singular and magnificent feature in the landscape, reminding me of some of the detached hills in the vicinity of Inverness.

Opposite to the Quebec suburbs, just in front of the rapids, is situated the island of St. Helens, a spot of infinite loveliness. The centre of it is occupied by a grove of lofty trees, while the banks, sloping down to the water, seem of the most verdant turf. The scene was heightened by the appearance of the troops which garrison the island.

The shores of the river, studded with richly cultivated farms; the village of La Prairie, with the little island of St. Ann's in the distance; the glittering steeples and roofs of the city, with its gardens and villas,—looked lovely by the softened glow of a Canadian summer sunset.

The church bells ringing for evening prayer, with the hum of voices from the shore, mingled not inharmoniously with the rush of the rapids.

These rapids are caused by a descent in the bed of the river. In some places this declination is gradual, in others sudden and abrupt. Where the current is broken by masses of limestone or granite rock, as at the Cascades, the Cedars, and the Long Sault, it creates whirlpools and cataracts. But the rapids below Montreal are not of this magnificent character, being made perceptible only by the unusual swiftness of the water, and its surface being disturbed by foam, and waving lines and dimples. In short, I was disappointed in my expectation of seeing something very grand; and was half angry at these pretty-behaved quiet rapids, to the foot of which we were towed in good style by our faithful consort the *British America*.

As the captain is uncertain how long he may be detained at Montreal, I shall send this letter without further delay, and write again as soon as possible.

Letter IV.

Landing at Montreal.—Appearance of the Town.—Ravages of the Cholera.—Charitable Institutions in Montreal.—Catholic Cathedral.—Lower and Upper Town.—Company and Conversation at the Hotel.—Writer attacked with the Cholera.—Departure from Montreal in a Stage-coach.—Embark at Lachine on board a Steam-vessel.—Mode of travelling alternately in Steam-vessels and Stages.—Appearance of the Country.—Manufactures.—Ovens at a distance from the Cottages.—Draw-wells.—Arrival at Cornwall.—Accommodation at the Inn.—Departure from Cornwall, and Arrival at Prescott.—Arrival at Brockville.--Ship-launch there.—Voyage through Lake Ontario.—Arrival at Cobourg

Nelson Hotel, Montreal, August 21.

Once more on terra firma, dearest mother: what a strange sensation it is to tread the land once again, free from the motion of the heaving waters, to which I was now, in truth, glad to bid farewell.

By daybreak every creature on board was up and busily preparing for going on shore. The captain himself obligingly escorted us, and walked as far with us as the hotel, where we are at present lodged.

We found some difficulty in getting on shore, owing to the badness of the landing. The river was full of floating timbers, between which it required some skill to guide the boat. A wharf is now being built—not before it was needed*.

We were struck by the dirty, narrow, ill-paved or unpaved streets of the suburbs, and overpowered by the noisome vapour arising from a deep open fosse that ran along the street behind the wharf. This ditch seemed the receptacle for every abomination,

* Some excellent wharfs have since been completed.

and sufficient in itself to infect a whole town with malignant fevers*.

I was greatly disappointed in my first acquaintance with the interior of Montreal; a place of which travellers had said so much. I could compare it only to the fruits of the Dead sea, which are said to be fair and tempting to look upon, but yield only ashes and bitterness when tasted by the thirsty traveller †.

I noticed one peculiar feature in the buildings along the suburb facing the river—that they were mostly furnished with broad wooden balconies from

* This has since been arched over. A market has been erected above it.

† The following description of Montreal is given by M'Gregor in his British America, vol. ii. p. 504:—"Betwixt the royal mountain and the river, on a ridge of gentle elevation, stands the town. Including the suburbs, it is more extensive than Quebec. Both cities differ very greatly in appearance; the low banks of the St. Laurence at Montreal want the tremendous precipices frowning over them, and all that grand sublimity which characterizes Quebec.

"There are no wharfs at Montreal, and the ships and steamers lie quietly in pretty deep water, close to the clayey and generally filthy bank of the city. The whole of the lower town is covered with gloomy-looking houses, having dark iron shutters; and although it may be a little cleaner than Quebec, it is still very dirty; and the streets are not only narrow and ill-paved, but the footpaths are interrupted by slanting cellar-doors and other projections."

"It is impossible (says Mr. Talbot, in his Five Years' Residence) to walk the streets of Montreal on a Sunday or holiday, when the shops are closed, without receiving the most gloomy impressions; the whole city seems one vast prison;"—alluding to the window-shutters and outer doors of iron, that have been adopted to counteract the effects of fire.

the lower to the upper story; in some instances they surrounded the houses on three sides, and seemed to form a sort of outer chamber. Some of these balconies were ascended by flights of broad stairs from the outside.

I remember when a child dreaming of houses so constructed, and fancying them very delightful; and so I think they might be rendered, if shaded by climbing shrubs, and adorned with flowers, to represent a hanging-garden or sweet-scented bowery walk. But nothing of this kind gladdened our eyes as we toiled along the hot streets. Every house of public resort was crowded from the top to the bottom with emigrants of all ages, English, Irish, and Scotch. The sounds of riotous merriment that burst from them seemed but ill-assorted with the haggard, careworn faces of many of the thoughtless revellers.

The contrast was only too apparent and too painful a subject to those that looked upon this show of outward gaiety and inward misery.

The cholera had made awful ravages, and its devastating effects were to be seen in the darkened dwellings and the mourning habiliments of all classes. An expression of dejection and anxiety appeared in the faces of the few persons we encountered in our walk to the hotel, which plainly indicated the state of their minds.

In some situations whole streets had been nearly depopulated; those that were able fled panic-stricken to the country villages, while others remained to die in the bosom of their families.

To no class, I am told, has the disease proved so fatal as to the poorer sort of emigrants. Many of these, debilitated by the privations and fatigue of a long voyage, on reaching Quebec or Montreal indulged in every sort of excess, especially the dangerous one of intoxication; and, as if purposely paving the way to certain destruction, they fell immediate victims to the complaint.

In one house eleven persons died, in another seventeen; a little child of seven years old was the only creature left to tell the woful tale. This poor desolate orphan was taken by the nuns to their benevolent institution, where every attention was paid that humanity could suggest.

The number both of Catholic and Protestant benevolent societies is very great, and these are maintained with a liberality of principle that does honour to both parties, who seem indeed actuated by a fervent spirit of Christian charity.

I know of no place, not even excepting London itself, where the exercise of benevolent feelings is more called for than in these two cities, Quebec and Montreal. Here meet together the unfortunate, the improvident, the helpless orphan, the sick, the aged, the poor virtuous man, driven by the stern hand of necessity from his country and his home, perhaps to be overtaken by sickness or want in a land of strangers.

It is melancholy to reflect that a great number of the poorest class of emigrants that perished in the reign of the cholera have left no trace by which their sorrowing anxious friends in the old country may learn their fate. The disease is so sudden and so violent that it leaves no time for arranging worldly matters; the sentinel comes, not as it did to Hezekiah, "Set thine house in order, for thou shalt die, and not live."

The weather is sultry hot, accompanied by frequent thunder-showers, which have not the effect one would expect, that of cooling the heated atmosphere. I experience a degree of languor and oppression that is very distressing, and worse than actual pain.

Instead of leaving this place by the first conveyance for the upper province, as we fully purposed doing, we find ourselves obliged to remain two days longer, owing to the dilatoriness of the custom-house officers in overlooking our packages. The fact is that everything and everybody are out of sorts.

The heat has been too oppressive to allow of my walking much abroad. I have seen but little of the town beyond the streets adjacent to the hotel: with the exception of the Catholic Cathedral, I have seen few of the public buildings. With the former I was much pleased: it is a fine building, though still in an unfinished state, the towers not having been carried to the height originally intended. The eastern window, behind the altar, is seventy feet in height by thirty-three in width. The effect of this magnificent window from the entrance, the altar with its adornments and paintings, the several smaller altars and shrines, all decorated with scriptural designs, the light tiers of galleries that surround the central part of the church, the double range of columns supporting the vaulted ceiling, and the arched windows, all combine to form one beautiful whole. What most pleased me was the extreme lightness of the architecture, though

I thought the imitation of marble, with which the pillars were painted, coarse and glaring. We missed the time-hallowing mellowness that age has bestowed on our ancient churches and cathedrals. The grim corbels and winged angels that are carved on the grey stone, whose very uncouthness tells of time gone by when our ancestors worshipped within their walls, give an additional interest to the temples of our forefathers. But, though the new church at Montreal cannot compare with our York Minster, Westminster Abbey, and others of our sacred buildings, it is well worthy the attention of travellers, who will meet with nothing equal to it in the Canadas.

There are several colleges and nunneries, a hospital for the sick, several Catholic and Protestant churches, meeting-houses, a guard-house, with many other public edifices.

The river-side portion of the town is entirely mercantile. Its narrow, dirty streets and dark houses, with heavy iron shutters, have a disagreeable appearance, which cannot but make an unfavourable impression on the mind of a British traveller. The other portion of the town, however, is of a different character, and the houses are interspersed with gardens and pleasant walks, which looked very agreeable from the windows of the ball-room of the Nelson Hotel. This room, which is painted from top to bottom, the walls and ceiling, with a coarse imitation of groves and Canadian scenery, commands a superb view of the city, the river, and all the surrounding country, taking in the distant mountains of Chamblay, the shores of St. Laurence, towards La Prairie, and the rapids above and below the island of St. Anne's. The royal mountain (Mont Real), with its wooded sides, its rich scenery, and its city with its streets and public buildings, lie at your feet: with such objects before you the eye may well be charmed with the scenery of Montreal.

We receive the greatest attention from the master of the hotel, who is an Italian. The servants of the house are very civil, and the company that we meet at the ordinary very respectable, chiefly emigrants like ourselves, with some lively French men and women. The table is well supplied, and the charges for board and lodging one dollar per day each*.

I am amused with the variety of characters of which our table is composed. Some of the emigrants appear to entertain the most sanguine hopes of success, appearing to foresee no difficulties in carrying their schemes into effect. As a contrast to these there is one of my countrymen, just returned from the western district on his way back to England, who entreats us by no means to go further up this horrid country, as he emphatically styles the Upper Province, assuring us he would not live in it for all the land it contained.

He had been induced, by reading Cattermole's pamphlet on the subject of Emigration, to quit a good farm, and gathering together what property he possessed, to embark for Canada. Encouraged by the advice of a friend in this country, he purchased a lot of wild land in the western district; "but, sir," said he, addressing my husband with much vehemence, "I found

* This hotel is not of the highest class, in which the charge is a dollar and a half per day.—Ed.

I had been vilely deceived. Such land, such a country—I would not live in it for all I could see. Why, there is not a drop of wholesome water to be got, or a potato that is fit to eat. I lived for two months in a miserable shed they call a shanty, eaten up alive with mosquitoes. I could get nothing to eat but salted pork, and, in short, the discomforts are unbearable. And then all my farming knowledge was quite useless—people know nothing about farming in this country. Why, it would have broken my heart to work among the stumps, and never see such a thing as a well-ploughed field. And then," he added, in a softer tone, "I thought of my poor wife and the little one. I might, for the sake of bettering my condition, have roughed out a year or so myself, but, poor thing, I could not have had the heart to have brought her out from the comforts of England to such a place, not so good as one of our cow-houses or stables, and so I shall just go home; and if I don't tell all my neighbours what sort of a country this is they are all crazing to throw up their farms and come to, never trust a word of mine again."

It was to no purpose that some persons present argued with him on the folly of returning until he had tried what could be done: he only told them they were fools if they staid an hour in a country like this; and ended by execrating those persons who deceived the people at home by their false statements, who sum up in a few pages all the advantages, without filling a volume with the disadvantages, as they might well do.

"Persons are apt to deceive themselves as well as to be deceived," said my husband; "and having once fixed their minds on any one subject, will only read and believe those things that accord with their wishes."

This young man was evidently disappointed in not finding all things as fair and pleasant as at home. He had never reflected on the subject, or he could not have been so foolish as to suppose he would encounter no difficulties in his first outset, in a settlement in the woods. We are prepared to meet with many obstacles, and endure considerable privations, though I dare say we may meet with many unforeseen ones, forewarned as we have been by our Canadian friend's letters.

Our places are taken in the stage for Lachine, and, if all is well, we leave Montreal to-morrow morning. Our trunks, boxes, &c. are to be sent on by the forwarders to Cobourg.—*August* 22.

Cobourg, August 29.—When I closed my last letter I told you, my dear mother, that we should leave Montreal by sunrise the following day; but in this we were doomed to be disappointed, and to experience the truth of these words: "Boast not thyself of to-morrow, for thou knowest not what an hour may bring forth." Early that very morning, just an hour before sunrise, I was seized with the symptoms of the fatal malady that had made so many homes desolate. I was too ill to commence my journey, and, with a heavy heart, heard the lumbering wheels rattle over the stones from the door of the hotel.

I hourly grew worse, till the sister of the landlady, an excellent young woman, who had previously shown me great attention, persuaded me to send for a physician; and my husband, distracted at seeing me in such agony, ran off to seek for the best medical aid. After some little delay a physician was found. I was then in extreme torture; but was relieved by bleeding, and by the violent fits of sickness that ensued. I will not dwell minutely on my sufferings, suffice to say, they were intense; but God, in his mercy, though he chastened and afflicted me, yet gave me not over unto death. From the females of the house I received the greatest kindness. Instead of fleeing affrighted from the chamber of sickness, the two Irish girls almost quarrelled which should be my attendant; while Jane Taylor, the good young woman I before mentioned, never left me from the time I grew so alarmingly ill till a change for the better had come over me, but, at the peril of her own life, supported me in her arms, and held me on her bosom, when I was struggling with mortal agony, alternately speaking peace to me, and striving to soothe the anguish of my poor afflicted partner.

The remedies applied were bleeding, a portion of opium, blue pill, and some sort of salts—not the common Epsom. The remedies proved effectual, though I suffered much from sickness and headache for many hours. The debility and low fever that took place of the cholera, obliged me to keep my bed some days. During the two first my doctor visited me four times a day; he was very kind, and, on hearing that I was the wife of a British officer emigrating to the Upper Province, he seemed more than ever interested in my recovery, evincing a sympathy for us that was very grateful to our feelings. After a weary confinement of several days, I was at last pronounced in a sufficiently convalescent state to begin my journey, though still so weak that I was scarcely able to support myself.

The sun had not yet risen when the stage that was to take us to Lachine, the first nine miles of our route, drove up to the door, and we gladly bade farewell to a place in which our hours of anxiety had been many, and those of pleasure few. We had, however, experienced a great deal of kindness from those around us, and, though perfect strangers, had tasted some of the hospitality for which this city has often been celebrated. I omitted, in my former letter, telling you how we formed an acquaintance with a highly respectable merchant in this place, who afforded us a great deal of useful information, and introduced us to his wife, a very elegant and accomplished young woman. During our short acquaintance, we passed some pleasant hours at their house, much to our satisfaction.

I enjoyed the fresh breeze from the river along the banks of which our road lay. It was a fine sight to see the unclouded sun rising from behind the distant chain of mountains. Below us lay the rapids in their perturbed state, and there was the island of St. Anne's, bringing to our minds Moore's Canadian boat song: "We'll sing at Saint Anne's our parting hymn."

The bank of the St. Laurence, along which our road lay, is higher here than at Montreal, and clothed with brushwood on the summit, occasionally broken with narrow gulleys. The soil, as near as I could see, was sandy or light loam. I noticed the wild vine for the first time twining among the saplings. There were raspberry bushes, too, and a profusion of that tall yellow flower we call Aaron's golden rod, a *solidago*, and the white love-everlasting, the same that the chaplets are made of by the French and Swiss girls to adorn the tombs of their friends, and which they call *immortelle* ; the Americans call it life-everlasting ; also a tall purple-spiked valerian, that I observed growing in the fields among the corn, as plentiful as the bugloss is in our light sandy fields in England.

At Lachine we quitted the stage and went on board a steamer, a fine vessel elegantly fitted up with every accommodation. I enjoyed the passage up the river exceedingly, and should have been delighted with the journey by land had not my recent illness weakened me so much that I found the rough roads very unpleasant. As to the vehicle, a Canadian stage, it deserves a much higher character than travellers have had the candour to give it, and is so well adapted for the roads over which it passes that I doubt if it could be changed for a more suitable one. This vehicle is calculated to hold nine persons, three back, front, and middle ; the middle seat, which swings on broad straps of leather, is by far the easiest, only you are liable to be disturbed when any of the passengers choose to get out.

Certainly the travelling is arranged with as little trouble to the traveller as possible. Having paid your fare to Prescott you have no thought or care. When you quit the steam-boat you find a stage ready to receive you and your luggage, which is limited to a certain proportion. When the portage is passed (the land carriage), you find a steam-vessel ready, where you have every accommodation. The charges are not immoderate, considering the comforts you enjoy.

In addition to their own freight, the steamers generally tow up several other vessels. We had three Durham boats at one time, beside some other small craft attached to us, which certainly afforded some variety, if not amusement.

With the exception of Quebec and Montreal, I must give the preference to the Upper Province. If not on so grand a scale, the scenery is more calculated to please, from the appearance of industry and fertility it displays. I am delighted, in travelling along the road, with the neatness, cleanliness, and comfort of the cottages and farms. The log-house and shanty rarely occur, having been supplanted by pretty frame-houses, built in a superior style, and often painted white-lead colour or a pale pea-green. Around these habitations were orchards, bending down with a rich harvest of apples, plums, and the American crab, those beautiful little scarlet apples so often met with as a wet preserve among our sweetmeats at home.

You see none of the signs of poverty or its attendant miseries. No ragged, dirty, squalid children, dabbling in mud or dust; but many a tidy, smart-looking lass was spinning at the cottage-doors, with bright eyes and braided locks, while the younger girls were seated on the green turf or on the threshold, knitting and singing as blithe as birds.

There is something very picturesque in the great spinning-wheels that are used in this country for spinning the wool, and if attitude were to be studied among our Canadian lasses, there cannot be one more becoming, or calculated to show off the natural advantages of a fine figure, than spinning at the big wheel. The spinster does not sit, but walks to and fro, guiding the yarn with one hand while with the other she turns the wheel.

I often noticed, as we passed by the cottage farms, hanks of yarn of different colours hanging on the garden or orchard fence to dry; there were all manner of colours, green, blue, purple, brown, red, and white. A civil landlady, at whose tavern we stopped to change horses, told me these hanks of yarn were first spun and then dyed by the good wives, preparatory to being sent to the loom. She showed me some of this home-spun cloth, which really looked very well. It was a dullish dark brown, the wool being the produce of a breed of black sheep. This cloth is made up in different ways for family use.

"Every little dwelling you see," said she, "has its lot of land, and, consequently, its flock of sheep; and, as the children are early taught to spin, and knit, and help dye the yarn, their parents can afford to see them well and comfortably clothed.

"Many of these very farms you now see in so thriving a condition were wild land thirty years ago, nothing but Indian hunting-grounds. The industry of men, and many of them poor men, that had not a rood of land of their own in their own country, has effected this change."

I was much gratified by the reflection to which this good woman's information gave rise. "We also are going to purchase wild land, and why may not we see our farm, in process of time," thought I, "equal these fertile spots. Surely this is a blessed country to which we have emigrated," said I, pursuing the pleasing idea, "where every cottage abounds with the comforts and necessaries of life."

I perhaps overlooked at that time the labour, the difficulties, the privations to which these settlers had been exposed when they first came to this country. I saw it only at a distance of many years, under a high state of cultivation, perhaps in the hands of their children or their children's children, while the toil-worn parent's head was low in the dust.

Among other objects my attention was attracted by the appearance of open burying-grounds by the road-side. Pretty green mounds, surrounded by groups of walnut and other handsome timber trees, contained the graves of a family, or may be, some favoured friends slept quietly below the turf beside them. If the ground was not consecrated, it was hallowed by the tears and prayers of parents and children.

These household graves became the more interesting to me on learning that when a farm is disposed of to a stranger, the right of burying their dead is generally stipulated for by the former possessor.

You must bear with me if I occasionally weary you with dwelling on trifles. To me nothing that bears the stamp of novelty is devoid of interest. Even the clay-built ovens stuck upon four legs at a little distance from the houses were not unnoticed in passing. When there is not the convenience of one of these ovens outside the dwellings, the bread is baked in large iron pots—"*bake-kettles*" they are termed. I have already seen a loaf as big as a peck measure baking on the hearth in one of these kettles, and tasted of it, too; but I think the confined steam rather imparts a peculiar taste to the bread, which you do not perceive in the loaves baked in brick or clay ovens. At first I could not make out what these funny little round buildings, perched upon four posts, could be; and I took them for bee-hives till I spied a good woman drawing some nice hot loaves out of one that stood on a bit of waste land on the road-side, some fifty yards from the cottage.

Besides the ovens every house had a draw-well near it, which differed in the contrivance for raising the water from those I had seen in the old country. The plan is very simple:—a long pole, supported by a post, acts as a lever to raise the bucket, and the water can be raised by a child with very trifling exertion. This method is by many persons preferred to either rope or chain, and from its simplicity can be constructed by any person at the mere trouble of fixing the poles. I mention this merely to show the ingenuity of people in this country, and how well adapted all their ways are to their means*.

We were exceedingly gratified by the magnificent appearance of the rapids of the St. Laurence, at the cascades of which the road commanded a fine view from the elevation of the banks. I should fail in my attempt to describe this grand sheet of turbulent

* The plan is pursued in England and elsewhere, and may be seen in the market-gardens on the western suburb of London. It can only be done when the water is near the surface. —Ed.

water to you. Howison has pictured them very minutely in his work on Upper Canada, which I know you are well acquainted with. I regretted that we could not linger to feast our eyes with a scene so wild and grand as the river here appears; but a Canadian stage waits for no one, so we were obliged to content ourselves with a passing sight of these celebrated rapids.

We embarked at Couteau du Lac, and reached Cornwall late the same evening. Some of the stages travel all night, but I was too much fatigued to commence a journey of forty-nine miles over Canadian roads that night. Our example was followed by a widow lady and her little family.

We had some difficulty in obtaining a lodging, the inns being full of travellers; here, for the first time, we experienced something of that odious manner ascribed, though doubtless too generally, to the American. Our host seemed perfectly indifferent as to the comfort of his guests, leaving them to wait on themselves or go without what they wanted. The absence of females in these establishments is a great drawback where ladies are travelling. The women keep entirely out of sight, or treat you with that offensive coldness and indifference that you derive little satisfaction from their attendance.

After some difficulty in obtaining sight of the landlady of the inn at Cornwall, and asking her to show me a chamber where we might pass the night, with a most ungracious air she pointed to a door, which opened into a mere closet, in which was a bed divested of curtains, one chair, and an apology for a wash-stand. Seeing me in some dismay at the sight of this uninviting domicile, she laconically observed there was that or none, unless I chose to sleep in a four-bedded room, which had three tenants in it,—and those gentlemen. This alternative I somewhat indignantly declined, and in no very good humour retired to my cabin, where vile familiars to the dormitory kept us from closing our weary eye-lids till the break of day.

We took an early and hasty breakfast, and again commenced our journey. Here our party consisted of myself, my husband, a lady and gentleman with three small children, besides an infant of a month old, all of whom, from the eldest to the youngest, were suffering from hooping-cough; two great Cumberland miners, and a French pilot and his companion,—this was a huge amphibious-looking monster, who bounced in and squeezed himself into a corner seat, giving a knowing nod and comical grin to the driver, who was in the secret, and in utter defiance of all remonstrance at this unlooked-for intrusion, cracked his whip with a flourish, that appeared to be reckoned pretty considerably smart by two American travellers that stood on either side the door at the inn, with their hats not in their hands nor yet on their heads, but slung by a black ribbon to one of their waistcoat buttons, so as to fall nearly under one arm. This practice I have seen adopted since, and think if Johnny Gilpin had but taken this wise precaution he might have saved both hat and wig.

I was dreadfully fatigued with this day's travelling, being literally bruised black and blue. We suffered much inconvenience from the excessive heat of the day, and could well have dispensed with the company of two out of the four of our bulky companions.

We reached Prescott about five the same afternoon, where we met with good treatment at the inn; the female servants were all English, and seemed to vie with each other in attention to us.

We saw little in the town of Prescott to interest or please. After an excellent breakfast we embarked on board the *Great Britain*, the finest steamer we had yet seen, and here we were joined by our new friends, to our great satisfaction.

At Brockville we arrived just in time to enjoy what was to me quite a novel sight,—a ship-launch. A gay and exciting scene it was. The sun shone brilliantly on a concourse of people that thronged the shore in their holiday attire; the church bells rang merrily out, mingling with the music from the deck of the gaily painted vessel that, with flags and streamers, and a well-dressed company on board, was preparing for the launch.

To give additional effect, a salute was fired from a temporary fort erected for the occasion on a little rocky island in front of the town. The schooner took the water in fine style, as if eager to embrace the element which was henceforth to be subject to her. It was a moment of intense interest. The newly launched was greeted with three cheers from the company on board the *Great Britain*, with a salute from the little fort, and a merry peal from the bells, which were also rung in honour of a pretty bridè that came on board with her bridegroom on their way to visit the falls of Niagara.

Brockville is situated just at the entrance of the lake of the Thousand Islands, and presents a pretty appearance from the water. The town has improved rapidly, I am told, within the last few years, and is becoming a place of some importance.

The shores of the St. Laurence assume a more rocky and picturesque aspect as you advance among its thousand islands, which present every variety of wood and rock. The steamer put in for a supply of fire-wood at a little village on the American side the river, where also we took on board five-and-twenty beautiful horses, which are to be exhibited at Cobourg and York for sale.

There was nothing at all worthy of observation in the American village, unless I except a novelty that rather amused me. Almost every house had a tiny wooden model of itself, about the bigness of a doll's house, (or baby-house, I think they are called,) stuck up in front of the roof or at the gable end. I was informed by a gentleman on board, these baby-houses, as I was pleased to call them, were for the swallows to build in.

It was midnight when we passed Kingston, so of course I saw nothing of that "key to the lakes," as I have heard it styled. When I awoke in the morning the steamer was dashing gallantly along through the waters of the Ontario, and I experienced a slight sensation of sickness.

When the waters of the lake are at all agitated, as they sometimes are, by high winds, you might imagine yourself upon a tempest-tossed sea.

The shores of the Ontario are very fine, rising in

waving lines of hill and dale, clothed with magnificent woods, or enlivened by patches of cultivated land and pretty dwellings. At ten o'clock we reached Cobourg.

Cobourg, at which place we are at present, is a neatly built and flourishing village, containing many good stores, mills, a banking-house, and printing-office, where a newspaper is published once a week. There is a very pretty church and a select society, many families of respectability having fixed their residences in or near the town.

To-morrow we leave Cobourg, and shall proceed to Peterborough, from which place I shall again write and inform you of our future destination, which will probably be on one of the small lakes of the Otanabee.

LETTER V.

Journey from Cobourg to Amherst.—Difficulties to be encountered on first settling in the Backwoods.—Appearance of the Country.—Rice Lake.—Indian Habits.—Voyage up the Otanabee.—Log-house, and its Inmates. —Passage-boat.—Journey on foot to Peterborough.

Peterborough, Newcastle District,
September 9, 1832.

WE left Cobourg on the afternoon of the 1st of September in a light waggon, comfortably lined with buffalo robes. Our fellow-travellers consisted of three gentlemen and a young lady, all of whom proved very agreeable, and willing to afford us every information respecting the country through which we were travelling. The afternoon was fine—one of those rich mellow days we often experience in the early part of September. The warm hues of autumn were already visible on the forest trees, but rather spoke of ripeness than decay. The country round Cobourg is well cultivated, a great portion of the woods having been superseded by open fields, pleasant farms, and fine flourishing orchards, with green pastures, where abundance of cattle were grazing.

The county gaol and court-house at Amherst, about a mile and a half from Cobourg, is a fine stone edifice, situated on a rising ground, which commands an extensive view over the lake Ontario and surrounding scenery. As you advance further up the country, in the direction of the Hamilton or Rice Lake plains, the land rises into bold sweeping hills and dales.

The outline of the country reminded me of the hilly part of Gloucestershire; you want, however, the charm with which civilization has so eminently adorned that fine county, with all its romantic villages, flourishing towns, cultivated farms, and extensive downs, so thickly covered with flocks and herds. Here the bold forests of oak, beech, maple, and bass-wood, with now and then a grove of dark pine, cover the hills, only enlivened by an occasional settlement, with its log-house and zig-zag fences of split timber: these fences are very offensive to my eye. I look in vain for the rich hedge-rows of my native country. Even the stone fences in the north and west of England, cold and bare as they are, are less unsightly. The settlers, however, invariably adopt whatever plan saves time, labour, and money. The great law of expediency is strictly observed;—it is borne of necessity. Matters of taste appear to be little regarded, or are, at all events, after-considerations.

I could see a smile hover on the lips of my fellow-travellers on hearing of our projected plans for the adornment of our future dwelling.

"If you go into the backwoods your house must necessarily be a log-house," said an elderly gentleman, who had been a settler many years in the country. "For you will most probably be out of the way of a saw-mill, and you will find so much to do, and so many obstacles to encounter, for the first two or three years, that you will hardly have opportunity for carrying these improvements into effect.

"There is an old saying," he added, with a mixture of gravity and good humour in his looks, "that I used to hear when I was a boy, 'first creep* and then go. Matters are not carried on quite so easily here as at home; and the truth of this a very few weeks' acquaintance with the *bush*, as we term all unbroken forest land, will prove. At the end of five years you may begin to talk of these pretty improvements and elegancies, and you will then be able to see a little what you are about."

"I thought," said I, "every thing in this country was done with so much expedition. I am sure I have heard and read of houses being built in a day." The old gentleman laughed.

"Yes, yes," he replied, "travellers find no difficulty in putting up a house in twelve or twenty-four hours, and so the log-walls can be raised in that time or even less; but the house is not completed when the outer walls are up, as your husband will find to his cost."

"But all the works on emigration that I have read," replied I, "give a fair and flattering picture of a settler's life; for, according to their statements, the difficulties are easily removed."

"Never mind books," said my companion, "use your own reason. Look on those interminable forests, through which the eye can only penetrate a few yards, and tell me how those vast timbers are to be removed, utterly extirpated, I may say, from the face of the earth, the ground cleared and burnt, a crop

* Derived from infants crawling on all-fours before they have strength to walk.

sown and fenced, and a house to shelter you raised, without difficulty, without expense, and without great labour. Never tell me of what is said in books, written very frequently by tarry-at-home travellers. Give me facts. One honest, candid emigrant's experience is worth all that has been written on the subject. Besides, that which may be a true picture of one part of the country will hardly suit another. The advantages and disadvantages arising from soil, situation, and progress of civilization, are very different in different districts: even the prices of goods and of produce, stock and labour, vary exceedingly, according as you are near to, or distant from, towns and markets."

I began to think my fellow-traveller spoke sensibly on the subject, with which the experience of thirteen years had made him perfectly conversant. I began to apprehend that we also had taken too flattering a view of a settler's life as it must be in the backwoods. Time and our own personal knowledge will be the surest test, and to that we must bow. We are ever prone to believe that which we wish.

About halfway between Cobourg and the Rice Lake there is a pretty valley between two steep hills. Here there is a good deal of cleared land and a tavern: the place is called the "Cold Springs." Who knows but some century or two hence this spot may become a fashionable place of resort to drink the waters. A Canadian Bath or Cheltenham may spring up where now Nature revels in her wilderness of forest trees.

We now ascended the plains—a fine elevation of land—for many miles scantily clothed with oaks, and

Rice Grounds

here and there bushy pines, with other trees and shrubs. The soil is in some places sandy, but varies, I am told, considerably in different parts, and is covered in large tracks with rich herbage, affording abundance of the finest pasture for cattle. A number of exquisite flowers and shrubs adorn these plains, which rival any garden in beauty during the spring and summer months. Many of these plants are peculiar to the plains, and are rarely met with in any other situation. The trees, too, though inferior in size to those in the forests, are more picturesque, growing in groups or singly, at considerable intervals, giving a sort of park-like appearance to this portion of the country. The prevailing opinion seems to be, that the plains laid out in grazing or dairy farms would answer the purpose of settlers well; as there is plenty of land that will grow wheat and other corn-crops, and can be improved at a small expense, besides abundance of natural pasture for cattle. One great advantage seems to be, that the plough can be introduced directly, and the labour of preparing the ground is necessarily much less than where it is wholly covered with wood.

There are several settlers on these plains possessing considerable farms. The situation, I should think, must be healthy and agreeable, from the elevation and dryness of the land, and the pleasant prospect they command of the country below them, especially where the Rice Lake, with its various islands and picturesque shores, is visible. The ground itself is pleasingly broken into hill and valley, sometimes gently sloping, at other times abrupt and almost precipitous.

An American farmer, who formed one of our party at breakfast the following morning, told me that these plains were formerly famous hunting-grounds of the Indians, who, to prevent the growth of the timbers, burned them year after year; this, in process of time, destroyed the young trees, so as to prevent them again from accumulating to the extent they formerly did. Sufficient only was left to form coverts; for the deer resort hither in great herds for the sake of a peculiar tall sort of grass with which these plains abound, called deer-grass, on which they become exceedingly fat at certain seasons of the year.

Evening closed in before we reached the tavern on the shores of the Rice Lake, where we were to pass the night; so that I lost something of the beautiful scenery which this fine expanse of water presents as you descend the plains towards its shores. The glimpses I caught of it were by the faint but frequent flashes of lightning that illumined the horizon to the north, which just revealed enough to make me regret I could see no more that night. The Rice Lake is prettily diversified with small wooded islets: the north bank rises gently from the water's edge. Within sight of Sully, the tavern from which the steam-boat starts that goes up the Otanabee, you see several well-cultivated settlements; and beyond the Indian village the missionaries have a school for the education and instruction of the Indian children. Many of them can both read and write fluently, and are greatly improved in their moral and religious conduct. They are well and comfortably clothed, and have houses to live in. But they are still too much attached to their wandering habits to become good and industrious settlers. During certain seasons they leave the village, and encamp themselves in the woods along the borders of those lakes and rivers that present the most advantageous hunting and fishing-grounds.

The Rice Lake and Mud Lake Indians belong, I am told, to the Chippewas; but the traits of cunning and warlike ferocity that formerly marked this singular people seem to have disappeared beneath the milder influence of Christianity.

Certain it is that the introduction of the Christian religion is the first greatest step towards civilization and improvement; its very tendency being to break down the strong-holds of prejudice and ignorance, and unite mankind in one bond of social brotherhood. I have been told that for some time drunkenness was unknown, and even the moderate use of spirits was religiously abstained from by all the converts. This abstinence is still practised by some families; but of late the love of ardent spirits has again crept in among them, bringing discredit upon their faith. It is indeed hardly to be wondered at, when the Indian sees those around him that call themselves Christians, and who are better educated, and enjoy the advantages of civilized society, indulging to excess in this degrading vice, that he should suffer his natural inclination to overcome his

Christian duty, which might in some have taken no deep root. I have been surprised and disgusted by the censures passed on the erring Indian by persons who were foremost in indulgence at the table and the tavern; as if the crime of drunkenness were more excusable in the man of education than in the half-reclaimed savage.

There are some fine settlements on the Rice Lake, but I am told the shores are not considered healthy, the inhabitants being subject to lake-fevers and ague, especially where the ground is low and swampy. These fevers and agues are supposed by some people to originate in the extensive rice-beds which cause a stagnation in the water; the constant evaporation from the surface acting on a mass of decaying vegetation must tend to have a bad effect on the constitution of those that are immediately exposed to its pernicious influence.

Besides numerous small streams, here called *creeks*, two considerable rivers, the Otanabee and the Trent, find an outlet for their waters in the Rice Lake. These rivers are connected by a chain of small lakes, which you may trace on any good map of the province. I send you a diagram, which has been published at Cobourg, which will give you the geography of this portion of the country. It is on one of these small lakes we purpose purchasing land, which, should the navigation of these waters be carried into effect, as is generally supposed to be in contemplation, will render the lands on their shores very advantageous to the settlers; at present they are interrupted by large blocks of granite and lime-

Sleigh-driving.

stone, rapids, and falls, which prevent any but canoes or flat-bottomed boats from passing on them, and even these are limited to certain parts, on account of the above-named obstacles. By deepening the bed of the river and lakes, and forming locks in some parts and canals, the whole sweep of these waters might be thrown open to the Bay of Quinte. The expense, however, would necessarily be great; and till the townships of this portion of the district be fully settled, it is hardly to be expected that so vast an undertaking should be effected, however desirable it may be.

We left the tavern at Rice Lake, after an unusual delay, at nine o'clock. The morning was damp, and a cold wind blew over the lake, which appeared to little advantage through the drizzling rain, from which I was glad to shroud my face in my warm plaid cloak, for there was no cabin or other shelter in the little steamer than an inefficient awning. This apology for a steam-boat formed a considerable contrast with the superbly-appointed vessels we had lately been passengers in on the Ontario and the St. Laurence. But the circumstance of a steamer at all on the Otanabee was a matter of surprise to us, and of exultation to the first settlers along its shores, who for many years had been contented with no better mode of transport than a scow or a canoe for themselves and their marketable produce, or through the worst possible roads with a waggon or sleigh.

The Otanabee is a fine broad, clear stream, divided into two mouths at its entrance to the Rice Lake by a low tongue of land, too swampy to be put under cultivation. This beautiful river (for such I consider it to be) winds its way between thickly-wooded banks, which rise gradually as you advance higher up the country.

Towards noon the mists cleared off, and the sun came forth in all the brilliant beauty of a September day. So completely were we sheltered from the wind by the thick wall of pines on either side, that I no longer felt the least inconvenience from the cold that had chilled me on crossing the lake in the morning.

To the mere passing traveller, who cares little for the minute beauties of scenery, there is certainly a monotony in the long and unbroken line of woods, which insensibly inspires a feeling of gloom almost touching on sadness. Still there are objects to charm and delight the close observer of nature. His eye will be attracted by fantastic bowers, which are formed by the scarlet creeper (or Canadian ivy) and the wild vine, flinging their closely-entwined wreaths of richly tinted foliage from bough to bough of the forest trees, mingling their hues with the splendid rose-tipped branches of the soft maple, the autumnal tints of which are unrivalled in beauty by any of our forest trees at home.

The purple clusters of the grape, by no means so contemptible in size as I had been led to imagine, looked temptingly to my longing eyes, as they appeared just ripening among these forest bowers. I am told the juice forms a delicious and highly-flavoured jelly, boiled with sufficient quantity of sugar; the seeds are too large to make any other preparation

Silver Pine.

of them practicable. I shall endeavour, at some time or other, to try the improvement that can be effected by cultivation. One is apt to imagine where Nature has so abundantly bestowed fruits, that is the most favourable climate for their attaining perfection with the assistance of culture and soil.

The waters of the Otanabee are so clear and free from impurity that you distinctly see every stone-pebble or shell at the bottom. Here and there an opening in the forest reveals some tributary stream, working its way beneath the gigantic trees that meet above it. The silence of the scene is unbroken but by the sudden rush of the wild duck, disturbed from its retreat among the shrubby willows, that in some parts fringe the left bank, or the shrill cry of the kingfisher, as it darts across the water. The steam-boat put in for a supply of fire-wood at a clearing about half-way from Peterborough, and I gladly availed myself of the opportunity of indulging my inclination for gathering some of the splendid cardinal flowers that grew among the stones by the river's brink. Here, too, I plucked as sweet a rose as ever graced an English garden. I also found, among the grass of the meadow-land, spearmint, and, nearer to the bank, peppermint. There was a bush resembling our hawthorn, which, on examination, proved to be the cockspur hawthorn, with fruit as large as cherries, pulpy, and of a pleasant tartness not much unlike to tamarinds. The thorns of this tree were of formidable length and strength. I should think it might be introduced with great advantage to form live fences; the fruit, too, would prove by no means contemptible as a preserve.

As I felt a great curiosity to see the interior of a log-house, I entered the open door-way of the tavern, as the people termed it, under the pretext of buying a draught of milk. The interior of this rude dwelling presented no very inviting aspect. The walls were of rough unhewn logs, filled between the chinks with moss and irregular wedges of wood to keep out the wind and rain. The unplastered roof displayed the rafters, covered with moss and lichens, green, yellow, and grey; above which might be seen the shingles, dyed to a fine mahogany-red by the smoke which refused to ascend the wide clay and stone chimney, to curl gracefully about the roof, and seek its exit in the various crannies and apertures with which the roof and sides of the building abounded.

The floor was of earth, which had become pretty hard and smooth through use. This hut reminded me of the one described by the four Russian sailors that were left to winter on the island of Spitzbergen. Its furniture was of corresponding rudeness; a few stools, rough and unplaned; a deal table, which, from being manufactured from unseasoned wood, was divided by three wide open seams, and was only held together by its ill-shaped legs; two or three blocks of grey granite placed beside the hearth served for seats for the children, with the addition of two beds raised a little above the ground by a frame of split cedars. On these lowly couches lay extended two poor men, suffering under the wasting effects of lake-fever. Their yellow bilious faces strangely contrasted with the gay patchwork-quilts that covered them. I felt much concerned for the poor emigrants, who told me they had not been many weeks in the country when they were seized with the fever and ague. They both had wives and small children, who seemed very miserable. The wives also had been sick with ague, and had not a house or even shanty of their own up; the husbands having fallen ill were unable to do anything; and much of the little money they had brought out with them had been expended in board and lodging in this miserable place, which they dignified by the name of a tavern. I cannot say I was greatly prepossessed in favour of their hostess, a harsh, covetous woman. Besides the various emigrants, men, women, and children, that lodged within the walls, the log-house had tenants of another description. A fine calf occupied a pen in a corner; some pigs roamed grunting about in company with some half-dozen fowls. The most attractive objects were three snow-white pigeons, that were meekly picking up crumbs, and looking as if they were too pure and innocent to be inhabitants of such a place.

Owing to the shallowness of the river at this season, and to the rapids, the steam-boat is unable to go up the whole way to Peterborough, and a scow or row-boat, as it is sometimes termed—a huge, unwieldy, flat-bottomed machine—meets the passengers at a certain part of the river, within sight of a singular pine-tree on the right bank; this is termed the

"Yankee bonnet," from the fancied resemblance of the topmost boughs to a sort of cap worn by the Yankees, not much unlike the blue bonnet of Scotland.

Unfortunately, the steamer ran aground some four miles below the usual place of rendezvous, and we waited till near four o'clock for the scow. When it made its appearance, we found, to our discomfort, the rowers (eight in number, and all Irishmen) were under the exciting influence of a cag of whiskey, which they had drunk dry on the voyage. They were moreover exasperated by the delay on the part of the steamer, which gave them four miles additional heavy rowing. Beside a number of passengers there was an enormous load of furniture, trunks, boxes, chests, sacks of wheat, barrels of flour, salt, and pork, with many miscellaneous packages and articles, small and great, which were piled to a height that I thought very unsafe both to goods and passengers.

With a marvellous ill grace the men took up their oars when their load was completed, but declared they would go on shore and make a fire and cook their dinners, they not having eaten any food, though they had taken large potations of the whiskey. This measure was opposed by some of the gentlemen, and a fierce and angry scene ensued, which ended in the mutineers flinging down their oars, and positively refusing to row another stroke till they had satisfied their hunger.

Perhaps I had a fellow-feeling for them, as I began to be exceedingly hungry, almost ravenous, myself, having fasted since six that morning; indeed, so faint was I, that I was fain to get my husband to procure me a morsel of the coarse uninviting bread that was produced by the rowers, and which they ate with huge slices of raw pickled pork, seasoning this unseemly meal with curses "not loud but deep," and bitter taunts against those who prevented them from cooking their food like *Christians*.

While I was eagerly eating the bit of bread, an old farmer, who had eyed me for some time with a mixture of curiosity and compassion, said, "Poor thing: well, you do seem hungry indeed, and I dare say are just out from the *ould* country, and so little used to such hard fare. Here are some cakes that my woman (*i. e.* wife) put in my pocket when I left home; I care nothing for them, but they are better than that bad bread; take 'em, and welcome." With these words he tossed some very respectable home-made seed-cakes into my lap, and truly never was anything more welcome than this seasonable refreshment.

A sullen and gloomy spirit seemed to prevail among our boatmen, which by no means diminished as the evening drew on, and "the rapids were near." The sun had set, and the moon and stars rose brilliantly over the still waters, which gave back the reflection of this glorious multitude of heavenly bodies. A sight so passing fair might have stilled the most turbulent spirits into peace; at least so I thought, as, wrapped in my cloak, I lean't back against the supporting arm of my husband, and looking from the waters to the sky, and from the sky to the waters, with delight and admiration. My pleasant reverie was, however, soon ended, when I suddenly felt the boat touch the rocky bank, and heard the boatmen protesting they would go no further that night. We were nearly three miles below Peterborough, and how I was to walk this distance, weakened as I was by recent illness and fatigue of our long travelling, I knew not. To spend the night in an open boat, exposed to the heavy dews arising from the river, would be almost death. While we were deliberating on what to do, the rest of the passengers had made up their minds, and taken the way through the woods by a road they were well acquainted with. They were soon out of sight, all but one gentleman, who was bargaining with one of the rowers to take him and his dog across the river at the head of the rapids in a skiff.

Imagine our situation, at ten o'clock at night, without knowing a single step of our road, put on shore to find the way to the distant town as we best could, or pass the night in the dark forest.

Almost in despair, we entreated the gentleman to be our guide as far as he went. But so many obstacles beset our path in the form of newly-chopped trees and blocks of stone, scattered along the shore, that it was with the utmost difficulty we could keep him in sight. At last we came up with him at the place appointed to meet the skiff, and, with a pertinacity that at another time and in other circumstances we never should have adopted, we all but insisted on being admitted into the boat. An angry growling consent was extorted from the surly Charon, and we hastily entered the frail bark, which seemed hardly calculated to convey us in safety to the opposite shores.

I could not help indulging in a feeling of indescribable fear, as I listened to the torrent of profane invective that burst forth continually from the lips of the boatman. Once or twice we were in danger of being overset by the boughs of the pines and cedars which had fallen into the water near the banks. Right glad was I when we reached the opposite shores; but here a new trouble arose: there was yet more untracked wood to cross before we again met the skiff which had to pass up a small rapid, and meet us at the head of the small lake, an expansion of the Otanabee a little below Peterborough. At the distance of every few yards our path was obstructed by fallen trees, mostly hemlock, spruce, or cedar, the branches of which are so thickly interwoven that it is scarcely possible to separate them, or force a passage through the tangled thicket which they form.

Had it not been for the humane assistance of our conductor, I know not how I should have surmounted these difficulties. Sometimes I was ready to sink down from very weariness. At length I hailed, with a joy I could hardly have supposed possible, the gruff voice of the Irish rower, and, after considerable grumbling on his part, we were again seated.

Glad enough we were to see, by the blazing light of an enormous log-heap, the house of our friend. Here we received the offer of a guide to show us the way to the town by a road cut through the wood. We partook of the welcome refreshment of tea, and, having gained a little strength by a short rest, we once more commenced our journey, guided by a ragged, but polite, Irish boy, whose frankness and good humour quite won our regards. He informed us he was one of seven orphans, who had lost father and mother in the cholera. It was a sad thing, he said, to be left fatherless and motherless, in a strange land; and he swept away the tears that gathered in his eyes as he told the simple, but sad tale of his early bereavement; but added, cheerfully, he had met with a kind master, who had taken some of his brothers and sisters into his service as well as himself.

Just as we were emerging from the gloom of the wood we found our progress impeded by a *creek*, as the boy called it, over which he told us we must pass by a log-bridge before we could get to the town. Now, the log-bridge was composed of one log, or rather a fallen tree, thrown across the stream, rendered very slippery by the heavy dew that had risen from the swamp. As the log admitted of only one person at a time, I could receive no assistance from my companions; and, though our little guide, with a natural politeness arising from the benevolence of his disposition, did me all the service in his power by holding the lantern close to the surface to throw all the light he could on the subject, I had the ill luck to fall in up to my knees in the water, my head turning quite giddy just as I came to the last step or two; thus was I wet as well as weary. To add to our misfortune we saw the lights disappear, one by one, in the village, till a solitary candle, glimmering from the upper chambers of one or two houses, were our only beacons. We had yet a lodging to seek, and it was near midnight before we reached the door of the principal inn; there, at least, thought I, our troubles for to-night will end; but great was our mortification on being told there was not a spare bed to be had in the house, every one being occupied by emigrants going up to one of the back townships.

I could go no further, and we petitioned for a place by the kitchen fire, where we might rest, at least, if not sleep, and I might dry my wet garments. On seeing my condition the landlady took compassion on me, led me to a blazing fire, which her damsels quickly roused up; one brought a warm bath for my feet, while another provided a warm potation, which, I really believe, strange and unusual to my lips as it was, did me good: in short, we received every kindness and attention that we required from mine host and hostess, who relinquished their own bed for our accommodation, contenting themselves with a shakedown before the kitchen fire.

I can now smile at the disasters of *that* day, but at the time they appeared no trifles, as you may well suppose.

Farewell, my dearest Mother.

LETTER VI.

Peterborough.—Manners and Language of the Americans.—Scotch Engineman.—Description of Peterborough and its Environs.—Canadian Flowers.—Shanties.—Hardships suffered by first Settlers.—Process of establishing a Farm.

Peterborough, Sept. 11, 1832.

IT is now settled that we abide here till after the government sale has taken place. We are, then, to remain with S—— and his family till we have got a few acres chopped, and a log-house put up on our own land. Having determined to go at once into the bush, on account of our military grant, which we have been so fortunate as to draw in the neighbourhood of S——, we have fully made up our minds to enter at once, and cheerfully, on the privations and inconveniences attending such a situation; as there is no choice between relinquishing that great advantage and doing our settlement duties. We shall not be worse off than others who have gone before us to the unsettled townships, many of whom, naval and military officers, with their families, have had to struggle with considerable difficulties, but who are now beginning to feel the advantages arising from their exertions.

In addition to the land he is entitled to as an officer in the British service, my husband is in treaty for the purchase of an eligible lot by small lakes. This will give us a water frontage, and a further inducement to bring us within a little distance of S——; so that we shall not be quite so lonely as if we had gone on to our government lot at once.

We have experienced some attention and hospitality from several of the residents of Peterborough. There is a very genteel society, chiefly composed of officers and their families, besides the professional men and storekeepers. Many of the latter are persons of respectable family and good education. Though a store is, in fact, nothing better than what we should call in the country towns at home a "*general shop*," yet the storekeeper in Canada holds a very different rank from the shopkeeper of the English village. The storekeepers are the merchants and bankers of the places in which they reside. Almost all money matters are transacted by them, and they are often men of landed property and consequence, not unfrequently filling the situations of magistrates, commissioners, and even members of the provincial parliament.

As they maintain a rank in society which entitles them to equality with the aristocracy of the country, you must not be surprised when I tell you that it is no uncommon circumstance to see the sons of naval and military officers and clergymen standing behind a counter, or wielding an axe in the woods with their fathers' choppers; nor do they lose their grade in society by such employment. After all, it is education and manners that must distinguish the gentleman in this country, seeing that the labouring man, if he is diligent and industrious, may soon become his equal in point of worldly possessions. The ignorant man, let him be ever so wealthy, can never be equal to the man of education. It is the mind that forms the distinction between the classes in this country—"Knowledge is power!"

We had heard so much of the odious manners of the Yankees in this country that I was rather agreeably surprised by the few specimens of native Americans that I have seen. They were, for the most part, polite, well-behaved people. The only peculiarities I observed in them were a certain nasal twang in speaking, and some few odd phrases; but these were only used by the lower class, who "*guess*" and "*calculate*" a little more than we do. One of their most remarkable terms is to "*Fix.*" Whatever work requires to be done it must be *fixed.* "Fix the room" is, set it in order. "Fix the table"—"Fix the fire," says the mistress to her servants, and the things are fixed accordingly.

I was amused one day by hearing a woman tell her husband the chimney wanted fixing. I thought it seemed secure enough, and was a little surprised when the man got a rope and a few cedar boughs, with which he dislodged an accumulation of soot that caused the fire to smoke. The chimney being *fixed*, all went right again. This odd term is not confined to the lower orders alone, and, from hearing it so often, it becomes a standard word even among the later emigrants from our own country.

With the exception of some few remarkable expressions, and an attempt at introducing fine words in their every-day conversation, the lower order of Yankees have a decided advantage over our English peasantry in the use of grammatical language: they speak better English than you will hear from persons of the same class in any part of England, Ireland, or Scotland; a fact that we should be unwilling, I suppose, to allow at home.

If I were asked what appeared to me the most striking feature in the manners of the Americans that I had met with, I should say it was coldness approaching to apathy. I do not at all imagine them to be deficient in feeling or real sensibility, but they do not suffer their emotion to be seen. They are less profuse in their expressions of welcome and kindness than we are, though probably quite as sincere. No one doubts their hospitality; but, after all, one likes to see the hearty shake of the hand, and hear the cordial word that makes one feel oneself welcome.

Persons who come to this country are very apt to confound the old settlers from Britain with the native Americans; and when they meet with people of rude, offensive manners, using certain Yankee words in their conversation, and making a display of independence not exactly suitable to their own aristocratical notions, they immediately suppose they must be genuine Yankees, while they are, in fact, only imitators; and you well know the fact that a bad imitation is always worse than the original.

You would be surprised to see how soon the new comers fall into this disagreeable manner and affectation of equality, especially the inferior class of Irish and Scotch; the English less so. We were rather entertained by the behaviour of a young Scotchman, the engineer of the steamer, on my husband addressing him with reference to the management of the engine. His manners were surly, and almost insolent. He scrupulously avoided the least approach to courtesy or outward respect; nay, he even went so far as to seat himself on the bench close beside me, and observed that "among the many advantages this country offered to settlers like him, he did not reckon it the least of them that he was not obliged to take off his hat when he spoke to people (meaning persons of our degree), or address them by any other title than their name; besides, he could go and take his seat beside any gentleman or lady either, and think himself to the full as good as them.

"Very likely," I replied, hardly able to refrain from laughing at this sally; "but I doubt you greatly overrate the advantage of such privileges, for you cannot oblige the lady or gentleman to entertain the same opinion of your qualifications, or to remain seated beside you unless it pleases them to do so." With these words I rose up and left the independent gentleman evidently a little confounded at the manœuvre: however, he soon recovered his self-possession, and continued swinging the axe he held in his hand, and said, "It is no crime, I guess, being born a poor man."

"None in the world," replied my husband; "a man's birth is not of his own choosing. A man can no more help being born poor than rich; neither is it the fault of a gentleman being born of parents who occupy a higher station in society than his neighbour. I hope you will allow this?"

The Scotchman was obliged to yield a reluctant affirmative to the latter position; but concluded with again repeating his satisfaction at not being obliged in this country to take off his hat, or speak with respect to gentlemen, as they styled themselves.

"No one, my friend, could have obliged you to be well mannered at home any more than in Canada. Surely you could have kept your hat on your head if you had been so disposed; no gentleman would have knocked it off, I am sure.

"As to the boasted advantage of rude manners in Canada, I should think something of it if it benefited you the least, or put one extra dollar in your pocket; but I have my doubts if it has that profitable effect."

"There is a comfort, I guess, in considering oneself equal to a gentleman."

"Particularly if you could induce the gentleman to think the same." This was a point that seemed rather to disconcert our candidate for equality, who commenced whistling and kicking his heels with redoubled energy.

"Now," said his tormentor, "you have explained your notions of Canadian independence; be so good as to explain the machinery of your engine, with which you seem very well acquainted."

The man eyed my husband for a minute, half sulking, half pleased at the implied compliment on his skill, and, walking off to the engine, discussed the management of it with considerable fluency, and from that time treated us with perfect respect. He was evidently struck with my husband's reply to his question, put in a most discourteous tone, "Pray, what makes a gentleman: I'll thank you to answer me that?" "Good manners and good education," was the reply. "A rich man or a high-born man, if he is rude, ill-mannered, and ignorant, is no more a gentleman than yourself."

This put the matter on a different footing, and the engineer had the good sense to perceive that rude familiarity did not constitute a gentleman.

But it is now time I should give you some account of Peterborough, which, in point of situation, is superior to any place I have yet seen in the Upper Province. It occupies a central point between the townships of Monaghan, Smith, Cavan, Otanabee, and Douro, and may with propriety be considered as the capital of the Newcastle district.

It is situated on a fine elevated plain, just above the small lake, where the river is divided by two low wooded islets. The original or government part of the town is laid out in half-acre lots; the streets, which are now fast filling up, are nearly at right angles with the river, and extend towards the plains to the north-east. These plains form a beautiful natural park, finely diversified with hill and dale, covered with a lovely green sward, enamelled with a variety of the most exquisite flowers, and planted, as if by Nature's own hand, with groups of feathery pines, oaks, balsam, poplar, and silver birch. The views from these plains are delightful; whichever way you turn your eyes they are gratified by a diversity of hill and dale, wood and water, with the town spreading over a considerable tract of ground.

The plains descend with a steep declivity towards the river, which rushes with considerable impetuosity between its banks. Fancy a long, narrow valley,

Spruce.

and separating the east and west portions of the town into two distinct villages.

The Otanabee bank rises to a loftier elevation than the Monaghan side, and commands an extensive view over the intervening valley, the opposite town, and the boundary forest and hills behind it: this is called Peterborough East, and is in the hands of two or three individuals of large capital, from whom the town lots are purchased.

Peterborough thus divided covers a great extent of ground, more than sufficient for the formation of a large city. The number of inhabitants are now reckoned at seven hundred and upwards, and if it continues to increase as rapidly in the next few years as it has done lately, it will soon be a very populous town *.

There is great water-power, both as regards the river and the fine broad creek which winds its way through the town, and falls into the small lake below. There are several saw and grist-mills, a distillery, fulling-mill, two principal inns, besides smaller ones, a number of good stores, a government school-house, which also serves for a church, till one more suitable should be built. The plains are sold off in park lots, and some pretty little dwellings are being built, but I much fear the natural beauties of this lovely spot will be soon spoiled.

I am never weary with strolling about, climbing the hills in every direction, to catch some new pros-

* Since this account of Peterborough was written, the town has increased at least a third in buildings and population.

pect, or gather some new flowers, which, though getting late in the summer, are still abundant.

Among the plants with whose names I am acquainted are a variety of shrubby asters, of every tint of blue, purple, and pearly white; a lilac *monarda*, most delightfully aromatic, even to the dry stalks and seed-vessels; the white *gnaphalium* or everlasting flower; roses of several kinds, a few late buds of which I found in a valley, near the church. I also noticed among the shrubs a very pretty little plant, resembling our box; it trails along the ground, sending up branches and shoots; the leaves turn of a deep copper red*; yet, in spite of this contradiction, it is an evergreen. I also noticed some beautiful lichens, with coral caps surmounting the grey hollow footstalks, which grow in irregular tufts among the dry mosses, or more frequently I found them covering the roots of the trees or half-decayed timbers. Among a variety of fungi I gathered a hollow cup of the most splendid scarlet within, and a pale fawn colour without; another very beautiful fungi consisted of small branches like clusters of white coral, but of so delicate a texture that the slightest touch caused them to break.

The ground in many places was covered with a thick carpet of strawberries of many varieties, which afford a constant dessert during the season to those who choose to pick them, a privilege of which I am sure I should gladly avail myself were I near them in the summer. Beside the plants I have myself observed in blossom, I am told the spring and summer

* Probably a *Gaultheria*.—Ed.

produce many others;—the orange lily; the phlox, or purple *lichnidea;* the mocassin flower, or ladies' slipper; lilies of the valley in abundance; and, towards the banks of the creek and the Otanabee, the splendid cardinal flower (*lobelia cardinalis*) waves its scarlet spikes of blossoms.

I am half inclined to be angry when I admire the beauty of the Canadian flowers, to be constantly reminded that they are scentless, and therefore scarcely worthy of attention; as if the eye could not be charmed by beauty of form and harmony of colours, independent of the sense of smelling being gratified.

To redeem this country from the censure cast on it by a very clever gentleman I once met in London, who said, "the flowers were without perfume, and the birds without song," I have already discovered several highly aromatic plants and flowers. The milkweed must not be omitted among these; a beautiful shrubby plant with purple flowers, which are alike remarkable for beauty of colour and richness of scent.

I shall very soon begin to collect a hortus siccus for Eliza, with a description of the plants, growth, and qualities. Any striking particulars respecting them I shall make notes of; and tell her she may depend on my sending my specimens, with seeds of such as I can collect, at some fitting opportunity.

I consider this country opens a wide and fruitful field to the inquiries of the botanist. I now deeply regret I did not benefit by the frequent offers Eliza made me of prosecuting a study which I once thought dry, but now regard as highly interesting, and the fertile source of mental enjoyment, especially to those who, living in the bush, must necessarily be shut out from the pleasures of a large circle of friends, and the varieties that a town or village offer.

On Sunday I went to church; the first opportunity I had had of attending public worship since I was in the Highlands of Scotland; and surely I had reason to bow my knees in thankfulness to that merciful God who had brought us through the perils of the great deep and the horrors of the pestilence.

Never did our beautiful Liturgy seem so touching and impressive as it did that day,—offered up in our lowly log-built church in the wilderness.

This simple edifice is situated at the foot of a gentle slope on the plains, surrounded by groups of oak and feathery pines, which, though inferior in point of size to the huge pines and oaks of the forest, are far more agreeable to the eye, branching out in a variety of fantastic forms. The turf here is of an emerald greenness: in short, it is a sweet spot, retired from the noise and bustle of the town, a fitting place in which to worship God in spirit and in truth.

There are many beautiful walks towards the Smith town hills, and along the banks that overlook the river. The summit of this ridge is sterile, and is thickly set with loose blocks of red and grey granite, interspersed with large masses of limestone scattered in every direction; they are mostly smooth and rounded, as if by the action of water. As they are detached, and merely occupy the surface of the ground, it seemed strange to me how they came at that elevation. A geologist would doubtless be able to solve the mystery in a few minutes. The oaks that grow on this high bank are rather larger and more flourishing than those in the valleys and more fertile portions of the soil.

Behind the town, in the direction of the Cavan and Emily roads, is a wide space which I call the "squatter's ground," it being entirely covered with shanties, in which the poor emigrants, commuted pensioners, and the like, have located themselves and families. Some remain here under the ostensible reason of providing a shelter for their wives and children till they have prepared a home for their reception on their respective grants; but not unfrequently it happens that they are too indolent, or really unable to work on their lots, often situated many miles in the backwoods, and in distant and unsettled townships, presenting great obstacles to the poor emigrant, which it requires more energy and courage to encounter than is possessed by a vast number of them. Others, of idle and profligate habits, spend the money they received, and sell the land, for which they gave away their pensions, after which they remain miserable squatters on the shanty ground.

The shanty is a sort of primitive hut in Canadian architecture, and is nothing more than a shed built of logs, the chinks between the round edges of the timbers being filled with mud, moss, and bits of wood; the roof is frequently composed of logs split and hollowed with the axe, and placed side by side, so that the edges rest on each other; the concave and convex surfaces being alternately uppermost, every other log forms a channel to carry off the rain and melting snow. The eaves of this building resemble the scolloped edges of a clamp shell; but rude as this covering is, it effectually answers the purpose of keeping the interior dry; far more so than the roofs formed of bark or boards, through which the rain will find entrance. Sometimes the shanty has a window, sometimes only an open doorway, which admits the light and lets out the smoke*. A rude chimney, which is often nothing better than an opening cut in one of the top logs above the hearth, a few boards fastened in a square form, serves as the vent for the smoke; the only precaution against the fire catching the log walls behind the hearth being a few large stones placed in a half circular form, or more commonly a bank of dry earth raised against the wall.

Nothing can be more comfortless than some of these shanties, reeking with smoke and dirt, the common receptacle for children, pigs, and fowls. But I have given you the dark side of the picture; I am happy to say all the shanties on the squatters' ground were not like these: on the contrary, by far the larger proportion were inhabited by tidy folks, and had one, or

* I was greatly amused by the remark made by a little Irish boy, that we hired to be our hewer of wood and drawer of water, who had been an inhabitant of one of these shanties. "Ma'am," said he, "when the weather was stinging cold, we did not know how to keep ourselves warm; for while we roasted our eyes out before the fire our backs were just freezing; so first we turned one side and then the other, just as you would roast a *guse* on a spit. Mother spent half the money father earned at his straw work (he was a straw chair-maker,) in whiskey to keep us warm; but I do think a larger mess of good hot *praters* (potatoes,) would have kept us warmer than the whiskey did."

Log-house

even two small windows, and a clay chimney regularly built up through the roof; some were even roughly floored, and possessed similar comforts with the small log-houses.

You will, perhaps, think it strange when I assure you that many respectable settlers, with their wives and families, persons delicately nurtured, and accustomed to every comfort before they came hither, have been contented to inhabit a hut of this kind during the first or second year of their settlement in the woods.

I have listened with feelings of great interest to the history of the hardships endured by some of the first settlers in the neighbourhood, when Peterborough contained but two dwelling-houses. Then there were neither roads cut nor boats built for communicating with the distant and settled parts of the district; consequently the difficulties of procuring supplies of provisions was very great, beyond what any one that has lately come hither can form any notion of.

When I heard of a whole family having had no better supply of flour than what could be daily ground by a small hand-mill, and for weeks being destitute of every necessary, not even excepting bread, I could not help expressing some surprise, never having met with any account in the works I had read concerning emigration that at all prepared one for such evils.

"These particular trials," observed my intelligent friend, "are confined principally to the first breakers of the soil in the unsettled parts of the country, as was our case. If you diligently question some of the families of the lower class that are located far from the towns, and who had little or no means to support them during the first twelve months, till they could take a crop off the land, you will hear many sad tales of distress."

Writers on emigration do not take the trouble of searching out these things, nor does it answer their purpose to state disagreeable facts. Few have written exclusively on the "Bush." Travellers generally make a hasty journey through the long settled and prosperous portions of the country; they see a tract of fertile, well-cultivated land, the result of many years of labour; they see comfortable dwellings, abounding with all the substantial necessaries of life; the farmer's wife makes her own soap, candles, and sugar; the family are clothed in cloth of their own spinning, and hose of their own knitting. The bread, the beer, butter, cheese, meat, poultry, &c. are all the produce of the farm. He concludes, therefore, that Canada is a land of Canaan, and writes a book setting forth these advantages, with the addition of obtaining land for a mere song; and advises all persons who would be independent and secure from want to emigrate.

He forgets that these advantages are the result of long years of unremitting and patient labour; that these things are the *crown*, not the *first-fruits* of the settler's toil; and that during the interval many and great privations must be submitted to by almost every class of emigrants.

Many persons, on first coming out, especially if they go back into any of the unsettled townships, are dispirited by the unpromising appearance of things

Log-Village—Arrival of a Stage-coach.

about them. They find none of the advantages and comforts of which they had heard and read, and they are unprepared for the present difficulties; some give way to despondency, and others quit the place in disgust.

A little reflection would have shown them that every rood of land must be cleared of the thick forest of timber that encumbers it before an ear of wheat can be grown; that, after the trees have been chopped, cut into lengths, drawn together, or *logged*, as we call it, and burned, the field must be fenced, the seed sown, harvested, and thrashed before any returns can be obtained; that this requires time and much labour, and, if hired labour, considerable outlay of ready money; and in the mean time a family must eat. If at a distance from a store, every article must be brought through bad roads either by hand or with a team, the hire of which is generally costly in proportion to the distance and difficulty to be encountered in the conveyance. Now these things are better known beforehand, and then people are aware what they have to encounter.

Even a labouring man, though he have land of his own, is often, I may say generally, obliged to *hire out* to work for the first year or two, to earn sufficient for the maintenance of his family; and even so many of them suffer much privation before they reap the benefit of their independence. Were it not for the hope and the certain prospect of bettering their condition ultimately, they would sink under what they have to endure; but this thought buoys them up. They do not fear an old age of want and pauperism;

the present evils must yield to industry and perseverance; they think also for their children; and the trials of the present time are lost in pleasing anticipations for the future.

"Surely," said I, "cows and pigs and poultry might be kept; and you know where there is plenty of milk, butter, cheese, and eggs, with pork and fowls, persons cannot be very badly off for food."

"Very true," replied my friend; "but I must tell you it is easier to talk of these things at first than to keep them, unless on cleared or partially cleared farms; but we are speaking of a *first* settlement in the backwoods. Cows, pigs, and fowls must eat, and if you have nothing to give them unless you purchase it, and perhaps have to bring it from some distance, you had better not be troubled with them, as the trouble is certain and the profit doubtful. A cow, it is true, will get her living during the open months of the year in the bush, but sometimes she will ramble away for days together, and then you lose the use of her, and possibly much time in seeking her; then in the winter she requires some additional food to the *browse* * that she gets during the chopping season, or ten to one but she dies before spring; and as cows generally lose their milk during the cold weather, if not very well kept, it is best to part with them in the fall and buy again in the spring, unless you have plenty of

* The cattle are supported in a great measure during the fall and winter by eating the tender shoots of the maple, beech, and bass, which they seek in the newly-chopped fallow; but they should likewise be allowed straw or other food, or they will die in the very hard weather.

food for them, which is not often the case the first winter. As to pigs they are great plagues on a newly cleared farm if you cannot fat them off-hand; and that you cannot do without you buy food for them, which does not answer to do at first. If they run loose they are a terrible annoyance both to your own crops and your neighbours if you happen to be within half a mile of one; for though you may fence out cattle you cannot pigs: even poultry require something more than they pick up about the dwelling to be of any service to you, and are often taken off by hawks, eagles, foxes, and pole-cats, till you have proper securities for them."

"Then how are we to spin our own wool and make our own soap and candles?" said I. "When you are able to kill your own sheep, and hogs, and oxen, unless you buy wool and tallow"—then, seeing me begin to look somewhat disappointed, he said, "Be not cast down, you will have all these things in time, and more than these, never fear, if you have patience, and use the means of obtaining them. In the mean while prepare your mind for many privations to which at present you are a stranger; and if you would desire to see your husband happy and prosperous, be content to use economy, and above all, be cheerful. In a few years the farm will supply you with all the necessaries of life, and by and by you may even enjoy many of the luxuries. Then it is that a settler begins to taste the real and solid advantages of his emigration; then he feels the blessings of a country where there are no taxes, tithes, nor poor-rates; then he truly feels the benefit of independence. It is looking forward to this happy fulfilment of his desires that makes the rough paths smooth, and lightens the burden of present ills. He looks round upon a numerous family without those anxious fears that beset a father in moderate circumstances at home; for he knows he does not leave them destitute of an honest means of support."

In spite of all the trials he had encountered, I found this gentleman was so much attached to a settler's life, that he declared he would not go back to his own country to reside for a permanence on any account; nor is he the only one that I have heard express the same opinion; and it likewise seems a universal one among the lower class of emigrants. They are encouraged by the example of others whom they see enjoying comforts that they could never have obtained had they laboured ever so hard at home; and they wisely reflect they must have had hardships to endure had they remained in their native land (many indeed had been driven out by want), without the most remote chance of bettering themselves or becoming the possessors of land free from all restrictions. "What to us are the sufferings of one, two, three, or even four years, compared with a whole life of labour and poverty," was the remark of a poor labourer, who was recounting to us the other day some of the hardships he had met with in this country. He said he "knew they were only for a short time, and that by industry he should soon get over them."

I have already seen two of our poor neighbours that left the parish a twelvemonth ago; they are settled in Canada Company lots, and are getting on well. They have some few acres cleared and cropped, but are obliged to "*hire out*", to enable their families to live, working on their own land when they can. The men are in good spirits, and say "they shall in a few years have many comforts about them that they never could have got at home, had they worked late and early; but they complain that their wives are always pining for home, and lamenting that ever they crossed the seas." This seems to be the general complaint with all classes; the women are discontented and unhappy. Few enter with their whole heart into a settler's life. They miss the little domestic comforts they had been used to enjoy; they regret the friends and relations they left in the old country; and they cannot endure the loneliness of the backwoods.

This prospect does not discourage me: I know I shall find plenty of occupation within-doors, and I have sources of enjoyment when I walk abroad that will keep me from being dull. Besides, have I not a right to be cheerful and contented for the sake of my beloved partner? The change is not greater for me than him; and if for his sake I have voluntarily left home, and friends, and country, shall I therefore sadden him by useless regrets? I am always inclined to subscribe to that sentiment of my favourite poet, Goldsmith,—

> "Still to ourselves in every place consign'd,
> Our own felicity we make or find."

But I shall very soon be put to the test, as we leave this town to-morrow by ten o'clock. The purchase of the Lake lot is concluded. There are three acres chopped and a shanty up; but the shanty is not a habitable dwelling, being merely an open shed that was put up by the choppers as a temporary shelter; so we shall have to build a house. Late enough we are; too late to get in a full crop, as the land is merely chopped, not cleared, and it is too late now to log and burn the fallow, and get the seed-wheat in: but it will be ready for spring crops. We paid five dollars and a half per acre for the lot; this was rather high for wild land, so far from a town, and in a scantily-settled part of the township; but the situation is good, and has a water frontage, for which my husband was willing to pay something more than if the lot had been further inland.

In all probability it will be some time before I find leisure again to take up my pen. We shall remain guests with —— till our house is in a habitable condition, which I suppose will be about Christmas.

Letter VII.

Journey from Peterborough.—Canadian Woods.—Waggon and Team.—Arrival at a Log-house on the Banks of a Lake.—Settlement, and first Occupations.

October 25, 1832.

I SHALL begin my letter with a description of our journey through the bush, and so go on, giving an account of our proceedings both within-doors and without. I know my little domestic details will not prove wholly uninteresting to you; for well I am assured that a mother's eye is never weary with reading lines traced by the hand of an absent and beloved child.

After some difficulty we succeeded in hiring a waggon and span (*i. e.* pair abreast) of stout horses to convey us and our luggage through the woods to the banks of one of the lakes, where S —— had appointed to ferry us across. There was no palpable road, only a blaze on the other side, encumbered by fallen trees, and interrupted by a great cedar swamp, into which one might sink up to one's knees, unless we took the precaution to step along the trunks of the mossy, decaying timbers, or make our footing sure on some friendly block of granite or limestone. What is termed in bush language a *blaze*, is nothing more than notches or slices cut off the bark of the trees, to mark out the line of road. The boundaries of the different lots are often marked by a blazed tree, also the concession-lines*. These blazes are of as much use as finger-posts of a dark night.

The road we were compelled to take lay over the Peterborough plains, in the direction of the river; the scenery of which pleased me much, though it presents little appearance of fertility, with the exception of two or three extensive clearings.

About three miles above Peterborough the road winds along the brow of a steep ridge, the bottom of which has every appearance of having been formerly the bed of a lateral branch of the present river, or perhaps some small lake, which has been diverted from its channel, and merged in the Otanabee.

On either side of this ridge there is a steep descent; on the right the Otanabee breaks upon you, rushing with great velocity over its rocky bed, forming rapids in miniature resembling those of the St. Laurence; its dark, frowning woods of sombre pine give a grandeur to the scenery that is very impressive. On the left lies below you a sweet secluded dell of evergreens, cedar, hemlock, and pine, enlivened by a few deciduous trees. Through this dell there is a road-track leading to a fine cleared farm, the green pas-

* These concession-lines are certain divisions of the townships; these are again divided into so many lots of 200 acres. The concession-lines used to be marked by a wide avenue being chopped, so as to form a road of communication between them; but this plan was found too troublesome; and in a few years the young growth of timber so choked the opening, that it was of little use. The lately-surveyed townships, I believe, are only divided by blazed lines.

Road through a Pine Forest.

tures of which were rendered more pleasing by the absence of the odious stumps that disfigure the clearings in this part of the country. A pretty bright stream flows through the low meadow that lies at the foot of the hill, which you descend suddenly close by a small grist-mill that is worked by the waters, just where they meet the rapids of the river.

I called this place "Glen Morrison," partly from the remembrance of the lovely Glen Morrison of the Highlands, and partly because it was the name of the settler that owned the spot.

Our progress was but slow on account of the roughness of the road, which is beset with innumerable obstacles in the shape of loose blocks of granite and limestone, with which the lands on the banks of the river and lakes abound; to say nothing of fallen trees, big roots, mud-holes, and corduroy bridges, over which you go jolt, jolt, jolt, till every bone in your body feels as if it were going to be dislocated. An experienced bush-traveller avoids many hard thumps by rising up or clinging to the sides of his rough vehicle.

As the day was particularly fine, I often quitted the waggon and walked on with my husband for a mile or so.

We soon lost sight entirely of the river, and struck into the deep solitude of the forest, where not a sound disturbed the almost awful stillness that reigned around us. Scarcely a leaf or bough was in motion, excepting at intervals we caught the sound of the breeze stirring the lofty heads of the pine-trees, and wakening a hoarse and mournful cadence. This, with the tapping of the red-headed and grey woodpeckers on the trunk of the decaying trees, or the shrill whistling cry of the little striped squirrel, called by the natives "chitmunk," was every sound that broke the stillness of the wild. Nor was I less surprised at the absence of animal life. With the exception of the aforesaid chitmunk, no living thing crossed our path during our long day's journey in the woods.

In these vast solitudes one would naturally be led to imagine that the absence of man would have allowed Nature's wild denizens to have abounded free and unmolested; but the contrary seems to be the case. Almost all wild animals are more abundant in the cleared districts than in the bush. Man's industry supplies their wants at an easier rate than seeking a scanty subsistence in the forest.

You hear continually of depredations committed by wolves, bears, racoons, lynxes, and foxes, in the long-settled parts of the province. In the backwoods the appearance of wild beasts is a matter of much rarer occurrence.

I was disappointed in the forest trees, having pictured to myself hoary giants almost primeval with the country itself, as greatly exceeding in majesty of form the trees of my native isles, as the vast lakes and mighty rivers of Canada exceed the locks and streams of Britain.

There is a want of picturesque beauty in the woods. The young growth of timber alone has any pretension to elegance of form, unless I except the hemlocks, which are extremely light and graceful, and of a lovely refreshing tint of green. Even when winter has stripped the forest it is still beautiful and verdant. The young beeches too are pretty enough, but you miss that fantastic bowery shade that is so delightful in our parks and woodlands at home.

There is no appearance of venerable antiquity in the Canadian woods. There are no ancient spreading oaks that might be called the patriarchs of the forest. A premature decay seems to be their doom. They are uprooted by the storm, and sink in their first maturity, to give place to a new generation that is ready to fill their places.

The pines are certainly the finest trees. In point of size there are none to surpass them. They tower above all the others, forming a dark line that may be distinguished for many miles. The pines being so much loftier than the other trees, are sooner uprooted, as they receive the full and unbroken force of the wind in their tops; thus it is that the ground is continually strewn with the decaying trunks of huge pines. They also seem more liable to inward decay, and blasting from lightning, and fire. Dead pines are more frequently met with than any other tree.

Much as I had seen and heard of the badness of the roads in Canada, I was not prepared for such a one as we travelled along this day: indeed, it hardly deserved the name of a road, being little more than an opening hewed out through the woods, the trees being felled and drawn aside, so as to admit a wheeled carriage passing along.

The swamps and little forest streams, that occasionally gush across the path, are rendered passable by logs placed side by side. From the ridgy and striped appearance of these bridges they are aptly enough termed corduroy.

Over these abominable corduroys the vehicle jolts, jumping from log to log, with a shock that must be endured with as good a grace as possible. If you could bear these knocks, and pitiless thumpings and bumpings, without wry faces, your patience and philosophy would far exceed mine;—sometimes I laughed because I would not cry.

Imagine you see me perched up on a seat composed of carpet-bags, trunks, and sundry packages, in a vehicle little better than a great rough deal box set on wheels, the sides being merely pegged in so that more than once I found myself in rather an awkward predicament, owing to the said sides jumping out. In the very midst of a deep mud-hole out went the front board, and with the shock went the teamster (driver), who looked rather confounded at finding himself lodged just in the middle of a slough as bad as the "Slough of Despond." For my part, as I could do no good, I kept my seat, and patiently awaited the restoration to order. This was soon effected, and all went on well again till a jolt against a huge pine-tree gave such a jar to the ill-set vehicle, that one of the boards danced out that composed the bottom, and a sack of flour and bag of salted pork, which was on its way to a settler's, whose clearing we had to pass in the way, were ejected. A good teamster is seldom taken aback by such trifles as these.

He is, or should be, provided with an axe. No waggon, team, or any other travelling equipage should be unprovided with an instrument of this kind; as no one can answer for the obstacles that may impede his progress in the bush. The disasters we met fortunately required but little skill in remedying. The sides need only a stout peg, and the loosened planks that form the bottom being quickly replaced, away you go again over root, stump, and stone, mud-hole, and corduroy; now against the trunk of some standing tree, now mounting over some fallen one, with an impulse that would annihilate any lighter equipage than a Canadian waggon, which is admirably fitted by its very roughness for such roads as we have in the bush.

The sagacity of the horses of this country is truly admirable. Their patience in surmounting the difficulties they have to encounter, their skill in avoiding the holes and stones, and in making their footing sure over the round and slippery timbers of the log-bridges, renders them very valuable. If they want the spirit and fleetness of some of our high-bred blood-horses, they make up in gentleness, strength, and patience. This renders them most truly valuable, as they will travel in such places that no British horse would, with equal safety to their drivers. Nor are the Canadian horses, when well fed and groomed, at all deficient in beauty of colour, size, or form. They are not very often used in logging; the ox is preferred in all rough and heavy labour of this kind.

Just as the increasing gloom of the forest began to warn us of the approach of evening, and I was getting weary and hungry, our driver, in some confusion, avowed his belief that, somehow or other, he had missed the track, though how, he could not tell, seeing there was but one road. We were nearly two miles from the last settlement, and he said we ought to be within sight of the lake if we were on the right road. The only plan, we agreed, was for him to go forward and leave the team, and endeavour to ascertain if he were near the water, and if otherwise, to return to the house we had passed and inquire the way.

After running full half a mile ahead he returned with a dejected countenance, saying we must be wrong, for he saw no appearance of water, and the road we were on appeared to end in a cedar swamp, as the further he went the thicker the hemlocks and cedars became; so, as we had no desire to commence our settlement by a night's lodging in a swamp—where, to use the expression of our driver, the cedars grew as thick as hairs on a cat's back,—we agreed to retrace our steps.

After some difficulty the lumbering machine was turned, and slowly we began our backward march. We had not gone more than a mile when a boy came along, who told us we might just go back again, as there was no other road to the lake; and added, with a knowing nod of his head, "Master, I guess if you had known the bush as well as I, you would never have been *fule* enough to turn when you were going just right. Why, any body knows that *them* cedars and himlocks grow thickest near the water; so you may just go back for your pains."

It was dark, save that the stars came forth with more than usual brilliancy, when we suddenly emerged from the depth of the gloomy forest to the shores of a beautiful little lake, that gleamed the more brightly from the contrast of the dark masses of foliage that hung over it, and the towering pine-woods that girt its banks.

Here, seated on a huge block of limestone, which was covered with a soft cushion of moss, beneath the shade of the cedars that skirt the lake, surrounded with trunks, boxes, and packages of various descriptions, which the driver had hastily thrown from the waggon, sat your child, in anxious expectation of some answering voice to my husband's long and repeated halloo.

But when the echo of his voice had died away we heard only the gurgling of the waters at the head of the rapids, and the distant and hoarse murmur of a waterfall some half mile below them.

We could see no sign of any habitation, no gleam of light from the shore to cheer us. In vain we strained our ears for the plash of the oar, or welcome sound of the human voice, or bark of some household dog, that might assure us we were not doomed to pass the night in the lone wood.

We began now to apprehend we had really lost the way. To attempt returning through the deepening darkness of the forest in search of any one to guide us was quite out of the question, the road being so ill defined that we should soon have been lost in the mazes of the woods. The last sound of the waggon-wheels had died away in the distance; to have overtaken it would have been impossible. Bidding me remain quietly where I was, my husband forced his way through the tangled underwood along the bank, in hope of discovering some sign of the house we sought, which we had every reason to suppose must be near, though probably hidden by the dense mass of trees from our sight.

As I sat in the wood in silence and in darkness, my thoughts gradually wandered back across the Atlantic to my dear mother and to my old home; and I thought what would have been your feelings could you at that moment have beheld me as I sat on the cold mossy stone in the profound stillness of that vast leafy wilderness, thousands of miles from all those holy ties of kindred and early associations that make home in all countries a hallowed spot. It was a moment to press upon my mind the importance of the step I had taken, in voluntarily sharing the lot of the emigrant—in leaving the land of my birth, to which, in all probability, I might never again return. Great as was the sacrifice, even at that moment, strange as was my situation, I felt no painful regret or fearful misgiving depress my mind. A holy and tranquil peace came down upon me, soothing and softening my spirits into a calmness that seemed as unruffled as was the bosom of the water that lay stretched out before my feet.

My reverie was broken by the light plash of a paddle, and a bright line of light showed a canoe dancing over the lake: in a few minutes a well-known and friendly voice greeted me as the little bark was moored among the cedars at my feet. My husband having gained a projecting angle of the shore, had discovered the welcome blaze of the wood fire in the log-house, and, after some difficulty, had succeeded in rousing the attention of its inhabitants. Our coming that day had long been given up, and our first call had been mistaken for the sound of the ox-bells in the wood: this had caused the delay that had so embarrassed us.

We soon forgot our weary wanderings beside the bright fire that blazed on the hearth of the log-house, in which we found S——— comfortably domiciled with his wife. To the lady I was duly introduced; and, in spite of all remonstrances from the affectionate and careful mother, three fair sleeping children were successively handed out of their cribs to be shown me by the proud and delighted father.

Our welcome was given with that unaffected cordiality that is so grateful to the heart: it was as sincere as it was kind. All means were adopted to soften the roughness of our accommodation, which, if they lacked that elegance and convenience to which we had been accustomed in England, were not devoid of rustic comfort; at all events they were such as many settlers of the first respectability have been glad to content themselves with, and many have not been half so well lodged as we now are.

We may indeed consider ourselves fortunate in not being obliged to go at once into the rude shanty that I described to you as the only habitation on our land. This test of our fortitude was kindly spared us by S———, who insisted on our remaining beneath his hospitable roof till such time as we should have put up a house on our own lot. Here then we are for the present *fixed*, as the Canadians say; and if I miss many of the little comforts and luxuries of life, I enjoy excellent health and spirits, and am very happy in the society of those around me.

The children are already very fond of me. They have discovered my passion for flowers, which they diligently search for among the stumps and along the lake shore. I have begun collecting, and though the season is far advanced, my hortus siccus boasts of several elegant specimens of fern; the yellow Canadian violet, which blooms twice in the year, in the spring and fall, as the autumnal season is expressively termed; two sorts of Michaelmas daisies, as we call the shrubby asters, of which the varieties here are truly elegant; and a wreath of the festoon pine, a pretty evergreen with creeping stalks, that run along the ground three or four yards in length, sending up, at the distance of five or six inches, erect, stiff, green stems, resembling some of our heaths in the dark, shining, green, chaffy leaves. The Americans ornament their chimney-glasses with garlands of this plant, mixed with the dried blossoms of the life-everlasting (the pretty white and yellow flowers we call love-everlasting): this plant is also called festoon-pine. In my rambles in the wood near the house I have discovered a trailing plant bearing a near resemblance to the cedar, which I consider has, with equal propriety, a claim to the name of ground or creeping cedar.

As much of the botany of these unsettled portions of the country are unknown to the naturalist, and the plants are quite nameless, I take the liberty of bestowing names upon them according to inclination or fancy. But while I am writing about flowers I am forgetting that you will be more interested in hearing what steps we are taking on our land.

My husband has hired people to log up (that is, to draw the chopped timbers into heaps for burning) and clear a space for building our house upon. He has also entered into an agreement with a young settler in our vicinity to complete it for a certain sum within and without, according to a given plan. We are, however, to call the "bee," and provide every thing necessary for the entertainment of our worthy *hive*. Now you know that a "bee," in American language, or rather phraseology, signifies those friendly meetings of neighbours who assemble at your summons to raise the walls of your house, shanty, barn, or any other building: this is termed a "raising bee." Then there are logging-bees, husking-bees, chopping-bees, and quilting-bees. The nature of the work to be done gives the name to the bee. In the more populous and long-settled districts this practice is much discontinued, but it is highly useful, and almost indispensable to new settlers in the remote townships, where the price of labour is proportionably high, and workmen difficult to be procured.

Imagine the situation of an emigrant with a wife and young family, the latter possibly too young and helpless to render him the least assistance in the important business of chopping, logging, and building, on their first coming out to take possession of a lot of wild land; how deplorable would their situation be, unless they could receive quick and ready help from those around them.

This laudable practice has grown out of necessity,

and if it has its disadvantages, such for instance as being called upon at an inconvenient season for a return of help, by those who have formerly assisted you, yet it is so indispensable to you that the debt of gratitude ought to be cheerfully repaid. It is, in fact, regarded in the light of a debt of honour; you cannot be forced to attend a bee in return, but no one that can does refuse, unless from urgent reasons; and if you do not find it possible to attend in person you may send a substitute in a servant or in cattle, if you have a yoke.

In no situation, and under no other circumstance, does the equalizing system of America appear to such advantage as in meetings of this sort. All distinctions of rank, education, and wealth are for the time voluntarily laid aside. You will see the son of the educated gentleman and that of the poor artisan, the officer and the private soldier, the independent settler and the labourer who works out for hire, cheerfully uniting in one common cause. Each individual is actuated by the benevolent desire of affording help to the helpless, and exerting himself to raise a home for the homeless.

At present so small a portion of the forest is cleared on our lot, that I can give you little or no description of the spot on which we are located, otherwise than that it borders on a fine expanse of water, which forms one of the Otanabee chain of Small Lake. I hope, however, to give you a more minute description of our situation in my next letter.

For the present, then, I bid you adieu.

LETTER VIII.

Inconveniences of first Settlement.—Difficulty of obtaining Provisions and other necessaries.—Snow-storm and Hurricane.—Indian Summer, and setting-in of Winter.—Process of clearing the Land.

November the 20th, 1832.

OUR log-house is not yet finished, though it is in a state of forwardness. We are still indebted to the hospitable kindness of S——— and his wife for a home. This being their first settlement on their land they have as yet many difficulties, in common with all residents in the backwoods, to put up with this year. They have a fine block of land, well situated; and S——— laughs at the present privations, to which he opposes a spirit of cheerfulness and energy that is admirably calculated to effect their conquest. They are now about to remove to a larger and more commodious house that has been put up this fall, leaving us the use of the old one till our own is ready.

We begin to get reconciled to our Robinson Crusoe sort of life, and the consideration that the present evils are but temporary, goes a great way towards reconciling us to them.

One of our greatest inconveniences arises from the badness of our roads, and the distance at which we are placed from any village or town where provisions are to be procured.

Till we raise our own grain and fatten our own hogs, sheep, and poultry, we must be dependent upon the stores for food of every kind. These supplies have to be brought up at considerable expense and loss of time, through our beautiful bush roads; which, to use the words of a poor Irish woman, "can't be no worser." "Och, darlint," she said, "but they are just bad enough, and can't be no worser. Och, but they arn't like to our iligant roads in Ireland."

You may send down a list of groceries to be forwarded when a team comes up, and when we examine our stores, behold rice, sugar, currants, pepper, and mustard all jumbled into one mess. What think you of a rice-pudding seasoned plentifully with pepper, mustard, and, may be, a little rappee or prince's mixture added by way of sauce. I think the recipe would cut quite a figure in the Cook's Oracle or Mrs. Dalgairn's Practice of Cookery, under the original title of a "bush pudding."

And then woe and destruction to the brittle ware that may chance to travel through our roads. Lucky, indeed, are we if, through the superior carefulness of the person who packs them, more than one-half happens to arrive in safety. For such mishaps we have no redress. The storekeeper lays the accident upon the teamster, and the teamster upon the bad roads, wondering that he himself escapes with whole bones after a journey through the bush.

This is now the worst season of the year;—this, and just after the breaking up of the snow. Nothing hardly but an ox-cart can travel along the roads, and even that with difficulty, occupying two days to perform the journey; and the worst of the matter is, that there are times when the most necessary articles of provisions are not to be procured at any price. You see, then, that a settler in the bush requires to hold himself pretty independent, not only of the luxuries and delicacies of the table, but not unfrequently even of the very necessaries.

One time no pork is to be procured; another time there is a scarcity of flour, owing to some accident that has happened to the mill, or for the want of proper supplies of wheat for grinding; or perhaps the weather and bad roads at the same time prevent a team coming up, or people from going down. Then you must have recourse to a neighbour, if you have the good fortune to be near one, or fare the best you can on potatoes. The potatoe is indeed a great blessing here; new settlers would otherwise be often greatly distressed, and the poor man and his family who are without resources, without the potatoe must starve.

Once our stock of tea was exhausted, and we were unable to procure more. In this dilemma milk would have been an excellent substitute, or coffee, if we had possessed it; but we had neither the one nor the other, so we agreed to try the Yankee tea—hemlock sprigs boiled. This proved, to my taste, a vile decoction; though I recognized some herb in the tea that was sold in London at five shillings a pound, which I am certain was nothing better than dried hemlock leaves reduced to a coarse powder.

S——— laughed at our wry faces, declaring the potation was excellent; and he set us all an example by drinking six cups of this truly sylvan beverage. His eloquence failed in gaining a single convert; we could not believe it was only second to young hyson. To his assurance that to its other good qualities it united medicinal virtues, we replied that, like all other physic, it was very unpalatable.

"After all," said S———, with a thoughtful air, "the blessings and the evils of this life owe their chief effect to the force of contrast, and are to be estimated by that principally. We should not appreciate the comforts we enjoy half so much did we not occasionally feel the want of them. How we shall value the conveniences of a cleared farm after a few years, when we can realize all the necessaries and many of the luxuries of life."

"And how we shall enjoy green tea after this odious decoction of hemlock," said I.

"Very true; and a comfortable frame-house, and nice garden, and pleasant pastures, after these dark forests, log-houses, and no garden at all."

"And the absence of horrid black stumps," rejoined I. "Yes, and the absence of horrid stumps. Depend upon it, my dear, your Canadian farm will seem to you a perfect paradise by the time it is all under cultivation; and you will look upon it with the more pleasure and pride from the consciousness that it was once a forest wild, which, by the effects of industry and well-applied means, has changed to fruitful fields. Every fresh comfort you realize around you will add to your happiness; every improvement within-doors or without will raise a sensation of gratitude and delight in your mind, to which those that revel in the habitual enjoyment of luxury, and even of the commonest advantages of civilization, must in a great degree be strangers. My pass-words are, 'Hope! Resolution! and Perseverance!'"

"This," said my husband, "is true philosophy; and the more forcible, because you not only recommend the maxim but practise it also."

I had reckoned much on the Indian summer, of which I had read such delightful descriptions, but I must say it has fallen far below my expectations. Just at the commencement of this month (November) we experienced three or four warm hazy days, that proved rather close and oppressive. The sun looked red through the misty atmosphere, tinging the fantastic clouds that hung in smoky volumes, with saffron and pale crimson light, much as I have seen the clouds above London look on a warm, sultry spring morning.

Not a breeze ruffled the waters, not a leaf (for the leaves had not entirely fallen) moved. This perfect stagnation of the air was suddenly changed by a hurricane of wind and snow that came on without any previous warning. I was standing near a group of tall pines that had been left in the middle of the clearing, collecting some beautiful crimson lichens, S—— not being many paces distant, with his oxen drawing fire-wood. Suddenly we heard a distant hollow rushing sound that momentarily increased, the air around us being yet perfectly calm. I looked up, and beheld the clouds, hitherto so motionless, moving with amazing rapidity in several different directions. A dense gloom overspread the heavens. S——, who had been busily engaged with the cattle, had not noticed my being so near, and now called to me to use all the speed I could to gain the house, or an open part ot the clearing, distant from the pine-trees. Instinctively I turned towards the house, while the thundering shock of trees falling in all directions at the edge of the forest, the rending of the branches from the pines I had just quitted, and the rush of the whirlwind sweeping down the lake, made me sensible of the danger with which I had been threatened.

The scattered boughs of the pines darkened the air as they whirled above me; then came the blinding snow-storm: but I could behold the progress of the tempest in safety, having gained the threshold of our house. The driver of the oxen had thrown himself on the ground, while the poor beasts held down their meek heads, patiently abiding "the pelting of the pitiless storm." S———, my husband, and the rest of the household, collected in a group, watched with anxiety the wild havoc of the warring elements. Not a leaf remained on the trees when the hurricane was over; they were bare and desolate. Thus ended the short reign of the Indian summer.

I think the notion entertained by some travellers, that the Indian summer is caused by the annual conflagration of forests by those Indians inhabiting the unexplored regions beyond the larger lakes is absurd. Imagine for an instant what immense tracts of woods must be yearly consumed to affect nearly the whole of the continent of North America: besides, it takes place at that season of the year when the fire is least likely to run freely, owing to the humidity of the ground from the autumnal rains. I should rather attribute the peculiar warmth and hazy appearance of

Newley cleard Land

the air that marks this season, to the fermentation going on of so great a mass of vegetable matter that is undergoing a state of decomposition during the latter part of October and beginning of November. It has been supposed by some persons that a great alteration will be effected in this season, as the process of clearing the land continues to decrease the quantity of decaying vegetation. Nay, I have heard the difference is already observable by those long acquainted with the American continent.

Hitherto my experience of the climate is favourable. The autumn has been very fine, though the frosts are felt early in the month of September; at first slightly, of a morning, but towards October more severely. Still, though the first part of the day is cold, the middle of it is warm and cheerful.

We already see the stern advances of winter. It commenced very decidedly from the breaking up of the Indian summer. November is not at all like the same month at home. The early part was soft and warm, the latter cold, with keen frosts and occasional falls of snow; but it does not seem to possess the dark, gloomy, damp character of our British Novembers. However, it is not one season's acquaintance with the climate that enables a person to form any correct judgment of its general character, but a close observance of its peculiarities and vicissitudes during many years' residence in the country.

I must now tell you what my husband is doing on our land. He has let out ten acres to some Irish choppers who have established themselves in the shanty for the winter. They are to receive fourteen dollars per acre for chopping, burning, and fencing in that quantity. The ground is to be perfectly cleared of every thing but the stumps: these will take from seven to nine or ten years to decay; the pine, hemlock, and fir remain much longer. The process of clearing away the stumps is too expensive for new beginners to venture upon, labour being so high that it cannot be appropriated to any but indispensable work. The working season is very short on account of the length of time the frost remains on the ground. With the exception of chopping trees, very little can be done. Those that understand the proper management of uncleared land, usually underbrush (that is, cut down all the small timbers and brushwood), while the leaf is yet on them; this is piled in heaps, and the windfallen trees are chopped through in lengths, to be logged up in the spring with the winter's chopping. The latter end of the summer and the autumn are the best seasons for this work. The leaves then become quite dry and sear, and greatly assist in the important business of burning off the heavy timbers. Another reason is, that when the snow has fallen to some depth, the light timbers cannot be cut close to the ground, or the dead branches and other incumbrances collected and thrown in heaps.

We shall have about three acres ready for spring-crops, provided we get a good burning of that which is already chopped near the site of the house,—this will be sown with oats, pumpkins, Indian corn, and potatoes: the other ten acres will be ready for putting in a crop of wheat. So you see it will be a long time before we reap a harvest. We could not even get in spring-wheat early enough to come to perfection this year.

We shall try to get two cows in the spring, as they are little expense during the spring, summer, and autumn ; and by the winter we shall have pumpkins and oat-straw for them.

Letter IX.

Loss of a yoke of Oxen.—Construction of a Log-house.—Glaziers' and Carpenters' work.—Description of new Log-house.—Wild Fruits of the Country.—Walks on the Ice.—Situation of the House.—Lake, and surrounding Scenery.

Lake House,
April 18, 1833.

But it is time that I should give you some account of our log-house, into which we moved a few days before Christmas. Many unlooked-for delays having hindered its completion before that time, I began to think it would never be habitable.

The first misfortune that happened was the loss of a fine yoke of oxen that were purchased to draw in the house-logs, that is, the logs for raising the walls of the house. Not regarding the bush as pleasant as their former master's cleared pastures, or perhaps foreseeing some hard work to come, early one morning they took into their heads to ford the lake at the head of the rapids, and march off, leaving no trace of their route excepting their footing at the water's edge. After many days spent in vain search for them, the work was at a stand, and for one month they were gone, and we began to give up all expectation of hearing any news of them. At last we learned they were some twenty miles off, in a distant township, having made their way through bush and swamp, creek and lake, back to their former owner, with an instinct that supplied to them the want of roads and compass.

Oxen have been known to traverse a tract of wild country to a distance of thirty or forty miles going in a direct line for their former haunts by unknown paths, where memory could not avail them. In the dog we consider it is scent as well as memory that guides him to his far-off home;—but how is this conduct of the oxen to be accounted for? They returned home through the mazes of interminable forests, where man, with all his reason and knowledge, would have been bewildered and lost.

It was the latter end of October before even the walls of our house were up. To effect this we called "a bee." Sixteen of our neighbours cheerfully obeyed our summons; and though the day was far from favourable, so faithfully did our hive perform their tasks, that by night the outer walls were raised.

The work went merrily on with the help of plenty of Canadian nectar (whiskey), the honey that our *bees* are solaced with. Some huge joints of salt pork, a peck of potatoes, with a rice-pudding, and a loaf as big as an enormous Cheshire cheese, formed the feast that was to regale them during the raising. This was spread out in the shanty, in a *very rural style*. In short, we laughed, and called it a *pic-nic in the backwoods;* and rude as was the fare, I can assure you, great was the satisfaction expressed by all the guests of every degree, our "bee" being considered as very well conducted. In spite of the difference of rank among those that assisted at the bee, the greatest possible harmony prevailed, and the party separated well pleased with the day's work and entertainment.

The following day I went to survey the newly-raised edifice, but was sorely puzzled, as it presented very little appearance of a house. It was merely an oblong square of logs raised one above the other, with open spaces between every row of logs. The spaces for the doors and windows were not then chopped out, and the rafters were not up. In short, it looked a very queer sort of a place, and I returned home a little disappointed, and wondering that my husband should be so well pleased with the progress that had been made. A day or two after this I again visited it. The *sleepers* were laid to support the floors, and the places for the doors and windows cut out of the solid timbers, so that it had not quite so much the look of a bird-cage as before.

After the roof was shingled, we were again at a stand, as no boards could be procured nearer than Peterborough, a long day's journey through horrible roads. At that time no saw-mill was in progress; now there is a fine one building within a little distance of us. Our flooring-boards were all to be sawn by hand, and it was some time before any one could be found to perform this necessary work, and that at high wages—six-and-sixpence per day. Well, the boards were at length down, but of course of unseasoned timber: this was unavoidable; so as they could not be planed we were obliged to put up with their rough unsightly appearance, for no better were to be had. I began to recall to mind the observation of the old gentleman with whom we travelled from

Cobourg to Rice Lake. We console ourselves with the prospect that by next summer the boards will all be seasoned, and then the house is to be turned topsy-turvy, by having the floors all relaid, jointed, and smoothed.

The next misfortune that happened, was, that the mixture of clay and lime that was to plaster the inside and outside of the house between the chinks of the logs was one night frozen to stone. Just as the work was about half completed, the frost suddenly setting in, put a stop to our proceeding for some time, as the frozen plaster yielded neither to fire nor to hot water, the latter freezing before it had any effect on the mass, and rather making bad worse. Then the workman that was hewing the inside walls to make them smooth, wounded himself with the broad axe, and was unable to resume his work for some time.

I state these things merely to show the difficulties that attend us in the fulfilment of our plans, and this accounts in a great measure for the humble dwellings that settlers of the most respectable description are obliged to content themselves with at first coming to this country,—not, you may be assured, from inclination, but necessity: I could give you such narratives of this kind as would astonish you. After all, it serves to make us more satisfied than we should be on casting our eyes around to see few better off than we are, and many not half so comfortable, yet of equal, and, in some instances, superior pretensions as to station and fortune.

Every man in this country is his own glazier; this you will laugh at: but if he does not wish to see and feel the discomfort of broken panes, he must learn to put them in his windows with his own hands. Workmen are not easily to be had in the backwoods when you want them, and it would be preposterous to hire a man at high wages to make two days' journey to and from the nearest town to mend your windows. Boxes of glass of several different sizes are to be bought at a very cheap rate in the stores. My husband amused himself by glazing the windows of the house preparatory to their being fixed in.

To understand the use of carpenter's tools, I assure you, is no despicable or useless kind of knowledge here. I would strongly recommend all young men coming to Canada to acquire a little acquaintance with this valuable art, as they will often be put to great inconvenience for the want of it.

I was once much amused with hearing the remarks made by a very fine lady, the reluctant sharer of her husband's emigration, on seeing the son of a naval officer of some rank in the service busily employed in making an axe-handle out of a piece of rock-elm.

"I wonder that you allow George to degrade himself so," she said, addressing his father.

The captain looked up with surprise. "Degrade himself! In what manner, madam? My boy neither swears, drinks whiskey, steals, nor tells lies."

"But you allow him to perform tasks of the most menial kind. What is he now better than a hedge carpenter; and I suppose you allow him to chop, too?"

"Most assuredly I do. That pile of logs in the

cart there was all cut by him after he had left study yesterday," was the reply,

"I would see my boys dead before they should use an axe like common labourers."

"Idleness is the root of all evil," said the captain. "How much worse might my son be employed if he were running wild about streets with bad companions."

"You will allow this is not a country for gentlemen or ladies to live in," said the lady.

"It is the country for gentlemen that will not work and cannot live without, to starve in," replied the captain bluntly; "and for that reason I make my boys early accustom themselves to be usefully and actively employed."

"My boys shall never work like common mechanics," said the lady, indignantly.

"Then, madam, they will be good for nothing as settlers; and it is a pity you dragged them across the Atlantic."

"We were forced to come. We could not live as we had been used to do at home, or I never would have come to this horrid country."

"Having come hither you would be wise to conform to circumstances. Canada is not the place for idle folks to retrench a lost fortune in. In some parts of the country you will find most articles of provision as dear as in London, clothing much dearer, and not so good, and a bad market to choose in."

"I should like to know, then, who Canada is good for?" said she, angrily.

"It is a good country for the honest, industrious

artisan. It is a fine country for the poor labourer, who, after a few years of hard toil, can sit down in his own log-house, and look abroad on his own land, and see his children well settled in life as independent freeholders. It is a grand country for the rich speculator, who can afford to lay out a large sum in purchasing land in eligible situations; for if he have any judgment, he will make a hundred per cent. as interest for his money after waiting a few years. But it is a hard country for the poor gentleman, whose habits have rendered him unfit for manual labour. He brings with him a mind unfitted to his situation; and even if necessity compels him to exertion, his labour is of little value. He has a hard struggle to live. The certain expenses of wages and living are great, and he is obliged to endure many privations if he would keep within compass, and be free of debt. If he have a large family, and brings them up wisely, so as to adapt themselves early to a settler's life, why he does well for them, and soon feels the benefit on his own land; but if he is idle himself, his wife extravagant and discontented, and the children taught to despise labour, why, madam, they will soon be brought down to ruin. In short, the country is a good country for those to whom it is adapted; but if people will not conform to the doctrine of necessity and expediency, they have no business in it. It is plain Canada is not adapted to every class of people."

"It was never adapted for me or my family," said the lady, disdainfully.

"Very true," was the laconic reply; and so ended the dialogue.

But while I have been recounting these remarks, I have wandered far from my original subject, and left my poor log-house quite in an unfinished state. At last I was told it was in a habitable condition, and I was soon engaged in all the bustle and fatigue attendant on removing our household goods. We received all the assistance we required from ——, who is ever ready and willing to help us. He laughed, and called it a "*moving* bee;" I said it was a "fixing bee;" and my husband said it was a "settling bee;" I know we were unsettled enough till it was over. What a din of desolation is a small house, or any house under such circumstances. The idea of chaos must have been taken from a removal or a setting to rights, for I suppose the ancients had their *flitting*, as the Scotch call it, as well as the moderns.

Various were the valuable articles of crockery-ware that perished in their short but rough journey through the woods. Peace to their manes. I had a good helper in my Irish maid, who soon roused up famous fires, and set the house in order.

We have now got quite comfortably settled, and I shall give you a description of our little dwelling. What is finished is only a part of the original plan; the rest must be added next spring, or fall, as circumstances may suit.

A nice small sitting-room with a store closet, a kitchen, pantry, and bed-chamber form the ground floor; there is a good upper floor that will make three sleeping-rooms.

"What a nut-shell!" I think I hear you exclaim. So it is at present; but we purpose adding a handsome frame front as soon as we can get boards from the mill, which will give us another parlour, long hall, and good spare bed-room. The windows and glass door of our present sitting-room command pleasant lake-views to the west and south. When the house is completed, we shall have a verandah in front; and at the south side, which forms an agreeable addition in the summer, being used as a sort of outer room, in which we can dine, and have the advantage of cool air, protected from the glare of the sunbeams. The Canadians call these verandahs "stoups." Few houses, either log or frame, are without them. The pillars look extremely pretty, wreathed with the luxuriant hop-vine, mixed with the scarlet creeper and "morning glory," the American name for the most splendid of major convolvuluses. These stoups are really a considerable ornament, as they conceal in a great measure the rough logs, and break the barn-like form of the building.

Our parlour is warmed by a handsome Franklin stove with brass gallery, and fender. Our furniture consists of a brass-railed sofa, which serves upon occasion for a bed, Canadian painted chairs, a stained pine table, green and white curtains, and a handsome Indian mat that covers the floor. One side of the room is filled up with our books. Some large maps and a few good prints nearly conceal the rough walls, and form the decoration of our little dwelling. Our bed-chamber is furnished with equal simplicity. We do not, however, lack comfort in our humble home; and though it is not exactly such as we could wish, it is as good as, under existing circumstances, we could have.

I am anxiously looking forward to the spring, that I may get a garden laid out in front of the house; as I mean to cultivate some of the native fruits and flowers, which, I am sure, will improve greatly by culture. The strawberries that grow wild in our pastures, woods, and clearings, are several varieties, and bear abundantly. They make excellent preserves, and I mean to introduce beds of them into my garden. There is a pretty little wooded islet on our lake, that is called Strawberry island, another Raspberry island; they abound in a variety of fruits—wild grapes, raspberries, strawberries, black and red currants, a wild gooseberry, and a beautiful little trailing plant that bears white flowers like the raspberry, and a darkish purple fruit consisting of a few grains of a pleasant brisk acid, somewhat like in flavour to our dewberry, only not quite so sweet. The leaves of this plant are of a bright light green, in shape like the raspberry, to which it bears in some respects so great a resemblance (though it is not shrubby or thorny) that I have called it the "trailing raspberry."

I suppose our scientific botanists in Britain would consider me very impertinent in bestowing names on the flowers and plants I meet with in these wild woods: I can only say, I am glad to discover the Canadian or even the Indian names if I can, and where they fail I consider myself free to become their floral godmother, and give them names of my own choosing.

Among our wild fruits we have plums, which, in some townships, are very fine and abundant; these make admirable preserves, especially when boiled in maple molasses, as is done by the American housewives. Wild cherries, also a sort called choke cherries, from their peculiar astringent qualities, high and low-bush cranberries, blackberries, which are brought by the Squaws in birch baskets,—all these are found on the plains and beaver meadows. The low-bush cranberries are brought in great quantities by the Indians to the towns and villages. They form a standing preserve on the tea-tables in most of the settlers' houses; but for richness of flavour, and for beauty of appearance, I admire the high-bush cranberries; these are little sought after, on account of the large flat seeds, which prevent them from being used as a jam: the jelly, however, is delightful, both in colour and flavour.

The bush on which this cranberry grows resembles the guelder rose. The blossoms are pure white, and grow in loose umbels; they are very ornamental, when in bloom, to the woods and swamps, skirting the lakes. The berries are rather of a long oval, and of a brilliant scarlet, and when just touched by the frosts are semi-transparent, and look like pendent bunches of scarlet grapes.

I was tempted one fine frosty afternoon to take a walk with my husband on the ice, which I was assured was perfectly safe. I must confess for the first half-mile I felt very timid, especially when the ice is so transparent that you may see every little pebble or weed at the bottom of the water. Sometimes the ice was thick and white, and quite opaque. As we kept within a little distance of the shore, I was struck by the appearance of some splendid red berries on the leafless bushes that hung over the margin of the lake, and soon recognized them to be the aforesaid high-bush cranberries. My husband soon stripped the boughs of their tempting treasure, and I, delighted with my prize, hastened home, and boiled the fruit with some sugar, to eat at tea with our cakes. I never ate any thing more delicious than they proved; the more so perhaps from having been so long without tasting fruit of any kind, with the exception of preserves, during our journey, and at Peterborough.

Soon after this I made another excursion on the ice, but it was not in quite so sound a state. We nevertheless walked on for about three-quarters of a mile. We were overtaken on our return by S—— with a handsleigh, which is a sort of wheelbarrow, such as porters use, without sides, and instead of a wheel, is fixed on wooden runners, which you can drag over the snow and ice with the greatest ease, if ever so heavily laden. S—— insisted that he would draw me home over the ice like a Lapland lady on a sledge. I was soon seated in state, and in another minute felt myself impelled forward with a velocity that nearly took away my breath. By the time we reached the shore I was in a glow from head to foot.

You would be pleased with the situation of our house. The spot chosen is the summit of a fine sloping bank above the lake, distant from the water's edge some hundred or two yards: the lake is not quite a mile from shore to shore. To the south again we command a different view, which will be extremely pretty when fully opened—a fine smooth basin of water, diversified with beautiful islands, that rise like verdant groves from its bosom. Below these there is a fall of some feet, where the waters of the lakes, confined within a narrow channel between beds of limestone, rush along with great impetuosity, foaming and dashing up the spray in mimic clouds.

During the summer the waters are much lower, and we can walk for some way along the flat shores, which are composed of different strata of limestone, full of fossil remains, evidently of very recent formation. Those shells and river-insects that are scattered loose over the surface of the limestone, left by the recession of the waters, are similar to the shells and insects incrusted in the body of the limestone. I am told that the bed of one of the lakes above us (I forget which) is of limestone; that it abounds in a variety of beautiful river-shells, which are deposited in vast quantities in the different strata, and also in the blocks of limestone scattered along the shores. These shells are also found in great profusion in the soil of the Beaver meadows.

When I see these things, and hear of them, I regret I know nothing of geology or conchology; as I might then be able to account for many circumstances that at present only excite my curiosity.

Just below the waterfall I was mentioning there is a curious natural arch in the limestone rock, which

Chart shewing the Interior Navigation of the Districts of Newcastle and Upper Canada.

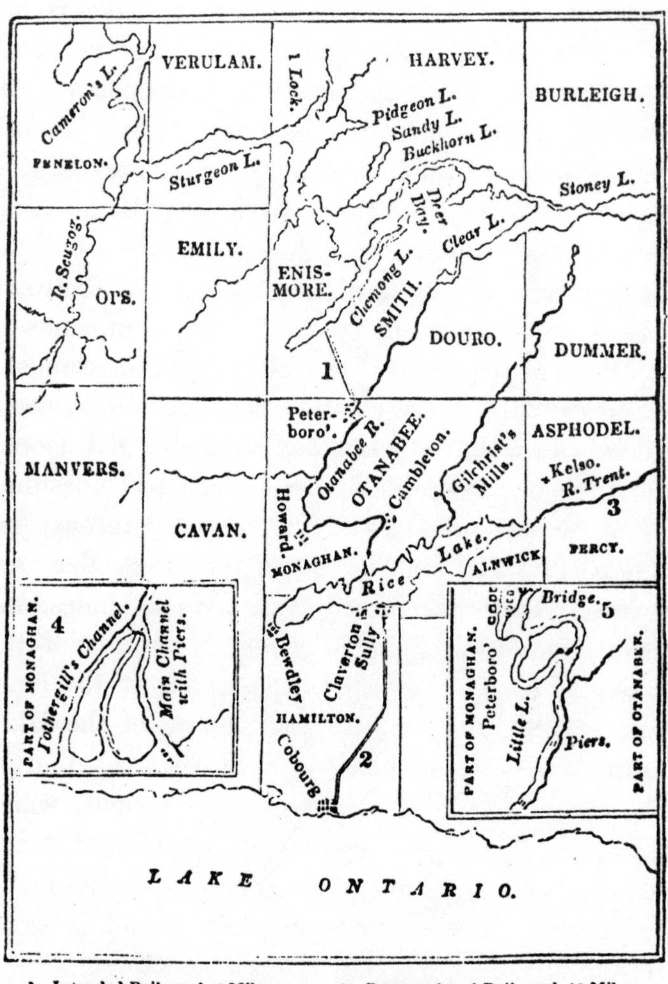

1 Intended Rail-road, 6 Miles. 2 Contemplated Rail-road, 13 Miles.
3 36 Miles of Steam Navigation to Heely's Falls.
4 Diagram of the Mouths of the River Otanabee, and part of the Rice Lake.
5 Diagram of the Little Lake, part of the River Otanabee, and the town of Peterborough.

at this place rises to a height of ten or fifteen feet like a wall; it is composed of large plates of grey limestone, lying one upon the other; the arch seems like a rent in the wall, but worn away, and hollowed, possibly, by the action of water rushing through it at some high flood. Trees grow on the top of this rock. Hemlock firs and cedars are waving on this elevated spot, above the turbulent waters, and clothing the stone barrier with a sad but never-fading verdure. Here, too, the wild vine, red creeper, and poison-elder, luxuriate, and wreathe fantastic bowers above the moss-covered masses of the stone. A sudden turn in this bank brought us to a broad, perfectly flat and smooth bed of the same stone, occupying a space of full fifty feet along the shore. Between the fissures of this bed I found some rose-bushes, and a variety of flowers that had sprung up during the spring and summer, when it was left dry, and free from the action of the water.

This place will shortly be appropriated for the building of a saw and grist-mill, which, I fear, will interfere with its natural beauty. I dare say, I shall be the only person in the neighbourhood who will regret the erection of so useful and valuable an acquisition to this portion of the township.

The first time you send a parcel or box, do not forget to enclose flower-seeds, and the stones of plums, damsons, bullace, pips of the best kinds of apples, in the orchard and garden, as apples may be raised here from seed, which will bear very good fruit without being grafted; the latter, however, are finer in size and flavour. I should be grateful for a few nuts from our beautiful old stock-nut trees. Dear old trees! how many gambols have we had in their branches when I was as light of spirit and as free from care as the squirrels that perched among the topmost boughs above us. —"Well," you will say, "the less that sage matrons talk of such wild tricks as climbing nut-trees, the better." Fortunately, young ladies are in no temptation here, seeing that nothing but a squirrel or a bear could climb our lofty forest-trees. Even a sailor must give it up in despair.

I am very desirous of having the seeds of our wild primrose and sweet violet preserved for me; I long to introduce them in our meadows and gardens. Pray let the cottage-children collect some.

My husband requests a small quantity of lucerne-seed, which he seems inclined to think may be cultivated to advantage.

LETTER X.

Variations in the Temperature of the Weather.—Electrical Phenomenon.—Canadian Winter.—Country deficient in Poetical Associations.—Sugar-making.—Fishing Season.—Mode of Fishing.—Duck-shooting.—Family of Indians.—*Papouses* and their Cradle-cases.—Indian Manufactures.—Frogs.

Lake House, May the 9th, 1833.

WHAT a different winter this has been to what I had anticipated. The snows of December were continually thawing; on the 1st of January not a flake was to be seen on our clearing, though it lingered in the bush. The warmth of the sun was so great on the first and second days of the new year that it was hardly possible to endure a cloak, or even shawl, out of doors; and within, the fire was quite too much for us. The weather remained pretty open till the latter part of the month, when the cold set in severely enough, and continued so during February. The 1st of March was the coldest day and night I ever experienced in my life; the mercury was down to twenty-five degrees in the house; abroad it was much lower. The sensation of cold early in the morning was very painful, producing an involuntary shuddering, and an almost convulsive feeling in the chest and stomach. Our breaths were congealed in hoar-frost on the sheets and blankets. Every thing we touched of metal seemed to freeze our fingers. This excessive degree of cold only lasted three days, and then a gradual amelioration of temperature was felt.

During this very cold weather I was surprised by the frequent recurrence of a phenomenon that I suppose was of an electrical nature. When the frosts were most intense I noticed that when I undressed, my clothes, which are at this cold season chiefly of woollen cloth, or lined with flannel, gave out when moved a succession of sounds, like the crackling and snapping of fire, and in the absence of a candle emitted sparks of a pale whitish blue light, similar to the flashes produced by cutting loaf-sugar in the dark, or stroking the back of a black cat: the same effect was also produced when I combed and brushed my hair*.

The snow lay very deep on the ground during February, and until the 19th of March, when a rapid thaw commenced, which continued without intermission till the ground was thoroughly freed from its hoary livery, which was effected in less than a fortnight's time. The air during the progress of the thaw was much warmer and more balmy than it usually is in England, when a disagreeable damp cold is felt during that process.

Though the Canadian winter has its disadvantages, it also has its charms. After a day or two of heavy snow the sky brightens, and the air becomes exquisitely clear and free from vapour; the smoke ascends in tall spiral columns till it is lost: seen against the saffron-tinted sky of an evening, or early of a clear

* This phenomenon is common enough everywhere when the air is very dry.—Ed.

morning, when the hoar-frost sparkles on the trees, the effect is singularly beautiful.

I enjoy a walk in the woods of a bright winter-day, when not a cloud, or the faint shadow of a cloud, obscures the soft azure of the heavens above; when but for the silver covering of the earth I might look upwards to the cloudless sky and say, "It is June, sweet June." The evergreens, as the pines, cedars, hemlock, and balsam firs, are bending their pendent branches, loaded with snow, which the least motion scatters in a mimic shower around, but so light and dry is it that it is shaken off without the slightest inconvenience.

The tops of the stumps look quite pretty, with their turbans of snow; a blackened pine-stump, with its white cap and mantle, will often startle you into the belief that some one is approaching you thus fancifully attired. As to ghosts or spirits they appear totally banished from Canada. This is too matter-of-fact country for such supernaturals to visit. Here there are no historical associations, no legendary tales of those that came before us. Fancy would starve for lack of marvellous food to keep her alive in the backwoods. We have neither fay nor fairy, ghost nor bogle, satyr nor wood-nymph; our very forests disdain to shelter dryad or hamadryad. No naiad haunts the rushy margin of our lakes, or hallows with her presence our forest-rills. No Druid claims our oaks; and instead of poring with mysterious awe among our curious limestone rocks, that are often singularly grouped together, we refer them to the geologist to exercise his skill in accounting for their appearance: instead of investing them with the solemn characters of ancient temples or heathen altars, we look upon them with the curious eye of natural philosophy alone.

Even the Irish and Highlanders of the humblest class seem to lay aside their ancient superstitions on becoming denizens of the woods of Canada. I heard a friend exclaim, when speaking of the want of interest this country possessed, "It is the most unpoetical of all lands; there is no scope for imagination; here all is new—the very soil seems newly formed; there is no hoary ancient grandeur in these woods; no recollections of former deeds connected with the country. The only beings in which I take any interest are the Indians, and they want the warlike character and intelligence that I had pictured to myself they would possess."

This was the lamentation of a poet. Now, the class of people to whom this country is so admirably adapted are formed of the unlettered and industrious labourers and artisans. They feel no regret that the land they labour on has not been celebrated by the pen of the historian or the lay of the poet. The earth yields her increase to them as freely as if it had been enriched by the blood of heroes. They would not spare the ancient oak from feelings of veneration, nor look upon it with regard for any thing but its use as timber. They have no time, even if they possessed the taste, to gaze abroad on the beauties of Nature, but their ignorance is bliss.

After all, these are imaginary evils, and can hardly be considered just causes for dislike to the country. They would excite little sympathy among every-day men and women, though doubtless they would have their weight with the more refined and intellectual members of society, who naturally would regret that taste, learning, and genius should be thrown out of its proper sphere.

For myself, though I can easily enter into the feelings of the poet and the enthusiastic lover of the wild and the wonderful of historic lore, I can yet make myself very happy and contented in this country. If its volume of history is yet a blank, that of Nature is open, and eloquently marked by the finger of God; and from its pages I can extract a thousand sources of amusement and interest whenever I take my walks in the forest or by the borders of the lakes.

But I must now tell you of our sugar-making, in which I take rather an active part. Our experiment was on a very limited scale, having but one kettle, besides two iron tripods; but it was sufficient to initiate us in the art and mystery of boiling the sap into molasses, and finally the molasses down to sugar.

The first thing to be done in tapping the maples, is to provide little rough troughs to catch the sap as it flows: these are merely pieces of pine-tree, hollowed with the axe. The tapping the tree is done by cutting a gash in the bark, or boring a hole with an auger. The former plan, as being most readily performed, is that most usually practised. A slightly-hollowed piece of cedar or elder is then inserted, so as to slant downwards and direct the sap into the trough; I have even seen a flat chip made the conductor. Ours were managed according to rule, you may be sure. The sap runs most freely after a frosty night, followed by a bright warm day; it should be collected during the day in a barrel or large trough, capable of holding all that can be boiled down the same evening; it should not stand more than twenty-four hours, as it is apt to ferment, and will not grain well unless fresh.

My husband, with an Irish lad, began collecting the sap the last week in March. A pole was fixed across two forked stakes, strong enough to bear the weight of the big kettle. Their employment during the day was emptying the troughs and chopping wood to supply the fires. In the evening they lit the fires and began boiling down the sap.

It was a pretty and picturesque sight to see the sugar-boilers, with their bright log-fire among the trees, now stirring up the blazing pile, now throwing in the liquid and stirring it down with a big ladle. When the fire grew fierce, it boiled and foamed up in the kettle, and they had to throw in fresh sap to keep it from running over.

When the sap begins to thicken into molasses, it is then brought to the sugar-boiler to be finished. The process is simple; it only requires attention in skimming and keeping the mass from boiling over, till it has arrived at the sugaring point, which is ascertained by dropping a little into cold water. When it is near the proper consistency, the kettle or pot becomes full of yellow froth, that dimples and rises in large bubbles from beneath. These throw out puffs of steam, and when the molasses is in this stage, it is nearly converted into sugar. Those who pay great attention to keeping the liquid free from scum, and understand the precise sugaring point, will produce an article little if at all inferior to muscovado *.

In general you see the maple-sugar in large cakes, like bees' wax, close and compact, without showing the crystallization; but it looks more beautiful when the grain is coarse and sparkling, and the sugar is broken in rough masses like sugar-candy.

The sugar is rolled or scraped down with a knife for use, as it takes long to dissolve in the tea without this preparation. I superintended the last part of the process, that of boiling the molasses down to sugar; and, considering it was a first attempt, and without any experienced person to direct me, otherwise than the information I obtained from ———. I succeeded tolerably well, and produced some sugar of a fine sparkling grain and good colour. Besides the sugar, I made about three gallons of molasses, which proved a great comfort to us, forming a nice ingredient in cakes and an excellent sauce for puddings.

The Yankees, I am told, make excellent preserves with molasses instead of sugar. The molasses boiled from maple-sap is very different from the molasses of the West Indies, both in flavour, colour, and consistency.

Beside the sugar and molasses, we manufactured a small cask of vinegar, which promises to be good. This was done by boiling five pails-full of sap down to two, and fermenting it after it was in the vessel with

* Good well-made maple-sugar bears a strong resemblance to that called powdered sugar-candy, sold by all grocers as a delicate article to sweeten coffee; it is more like maple-sugar in its regular crystallizations.

barm; it was then placed near the fire, and suffered to continue there in preference to being exposed to the sun's heat.

With regard to the expediency of making maple-sugar, it depends on circumstances whether it be profitable or not to the farmer. If he have to hire hands for the work, and pay high wages, it certainly does not answer to make it, unless on a large scale. One thing in its favour is, that the sugar season commences at a time when little else can be done on the farm, with the exception of chopping, the frost not being sufficiently out of the ground to admit of crops being sown; time is, therefore, less valuable than it is later in the spring.

Where there is a large family of children and a convenient sugar-bush on the lot, the making of sugar and molasses is decidedly a saving; as young children can be employed in emptying the troughs and collecting fire-wood, the bigger ones can tend the kettles and keep up the fire while the sap is boiling, and the wife and daughters can finish off the sugar within-doors.

Maple-sugar sells for four-pence and six-pence per pound, and sometimes for more. At first I did not particularly relish the flavour it gave to tea, but after awhile I liked it far better than muscovado, and as a sweetmeat it is to my taste delicious. I shall send you a specimen by the first opportunity, that you may judge for yourself of its excellence.

The weather is now very warm—oppressively so. We can scarcely endure the heat of the cooking-stove in the kitchen. As to a fire in the parlour there is not much need of it, as I am glad to sit at the open door and enjoy the lake-breeze. The insects are already beginning to be troublesome, particularly the black flies—a wicked-looking fly, with black body and white legs and wings; you do not feel their bite for a few minutes, but are made aware of it by a stream of blood flowing from the wound; after a few hours the part swells and becomes extremely painful.

These "*beasties*" chiefly delight in biting the sides of the throat, ears, and sides of the cheek, and with me the swelling continues for many days. The mosquitoes are also very annoying. I care more for the noise they make even than their sting. To keep them out of the house we light little heaps of damp chips, the smoke of which drives them away; but this remedy is not entirely effectual, and is of itself rather an annoyance.

This is the fishing season. Our lakes are famous for masquinongé, salmon-trout, white fish, black bass, and many others. We often see the lighted canoes of the fishermen pass and repass of a dark night before our door. S—— is considered very skilful as a spearsman, and enjoys the sport so much that he seldom misses a night favourable for it. The darker the night and the calmer the water the better it is for the fishing.

It is a very pretty sight to see these little barks slowly stealing from some cove of the dark pine-clad shores, and manœuvring among the islands on the lakes, rendered visible in the darkness by the blaze of light cast on the water from the jack—a sort of open grated iron basket, fixed to a long pole at the bows of the skiff or canoe. This is filled with a very combustible substance called fat-pine, which burns with a fierce and rapid flame, or else with rolls of birch-bark, which is also very easily ignited.

The light from above renders objects distinctly visible below the surface of the water. One person stands up in the middle of the boat with his fish-spear—a sort of iron trident, ready to strike at the fish that he may chance to see gliding in the still waters, while another with his paddle steers the canoe cautiously along. This sport requires a quick eye, a steady hand, and great caution in those that pursue it.

I delight in watching these torch-lighted canoes so quietly gliding over the calm waters, which are illuminated for yards with a bright track of light, by which we may distinctly perceive the figure of the spearsman standing in the centre of the boat, first glancing to one side, then the other, or poising his weapon ready for a blow. When four or five of these lighted vessels are seen at once on the fishing-ground, the effect is striking and splendid.

The Indians are very expert in this kind of fishing; the squaws paddling the canoes with admirable skill and dexterity. There is another mode of fishing in which these people also excel: this is fishing on the ice when the lakes are frozen over—a sport that requires the exercise of great patience. The Indian, provided with his tomahawk, with which he makes an opening in the ice, a spear, his blanket, and a decoy-fish of wood, proceeds to the place he has fixed upon. Having cut a hole in the ice he places himself on hands and knees, and casts his blanket over him, so as to darken the water and conceal himself from observation; in this position he will remain for hours, patiently watching the approach of his prey, which he strikes with admirable precision as soon as it appears within the reach of his spear.

The masquinongé thus caught are superior in flavour to those taken later in the season, and may be bought very reasonably from the Indians. I gave a small loaf of bread for a fish weighing from eighteen to twenty pounds. The masquinonjé is to all appearance a large species of the pike, and possesses the ravenous propensities of that fish.

One of the small lakes of the Otanabee is called Trout Lake, from the abundance of salmon-trout that occupy its waters. The white fish is also found in these lakes and is very delicious. The large sorts of fish are mostly taken with the spear, few persons having time for angling in this busy country.

As soon as the ice breaks up, our lakes are visited by innumerable flights of wild fowl: some of the ducks are extremely beautiful in their plumage, and are very fine-flavoured. I love to watch these pretty creatures, floating so tranquilly on the water, or suddenly rising and skimming along the edge of the pine-fringed shores, to drop again on the surface, and then remain stationary, like a little fleet at anchor. Sometimes we see an old duck lead out a brood of little ones from among the rushes; the innocent, soft things look very pretty, sailing round their mother, but at the least appearance of danger they disappear instantly by diving. The frogs are great enemies to the young broods; they are also the prey of the masquinongé, and, I believe, of other large fish that abound in these waters.

The ducks are in the finest order during the early part of the summer, when they resort to the rice-beds in vast numbers, getting very fat on the green rice, which they eagerly devour.

The Indians are very successful in their duck-shooting: they fill a canoe with green boughs, so that it resembles a sort of floating island; beneath the cover of these boughs they remain concealed, and are enabled by this device to approach much nearer than they otherwise could do to the wary birds. The same plan is often adopted by our own sportsmen with great success.

A family of Indians have pitched their tents very near us. On one of the islands in our lake we can distinguish the thin blue smoke of their wood fires, rising among the trees, from our front window, or curling over the bosom of the waters.

The squaws have been several times to see me; sometimes from curiosity, sometimes with the view of bartering their baskets, mats, ducks, or venison, for pork, flour, potatoes, or articles of wearing-apparel. Sometimes their object is to borrow "kettle to cook," which they are very punctual in returning.

Once a squaw came to borrow a washing-tub, but not understanding her language, I could not for some time discover the object of her solicitude; at last she took up a corner of her blanket, and, pointing to some soap, began rubbing it between her hands, imitated the action of washing, then laughed, and pointed to a tub; she then held up two fingers, to intimate it was for two days she needed the loan.

These people appear of gentle and amiable dispositions; and, as far as our experience goes, they are very honest. Once, indeed, the old hunter, Peter, obtained from me some bread, for which he promised to give a pair of ducks, but when the time came for payment, and I demanded my ducks, he looked gloomy, and replied with characteristic brevity, "No duck—Chippewa (meaning S——, this being the name they have affectionately given him) gone up lake with canoe—no canoe—duck by-and-by." By-and-by is a favourite expression of the Indians, signifying an indefinite point of time; may be it means to-morrow, or a week, or month, or it may be a year, or even more. They rarely give you a direct promise.

As it is not wise to let any one cheat you if you can prevent it, I coldly declined any further overtures to bartering with the Indians until my ducks made their appearance.

Some time afterwards I received one duck by the hands of Maquin, a sort of Indian Flibberty-gibbet: this lad is a hunchbacked dwarf, very shrewd, but a perfect imp; his delight seems to be tormenting the brown babies in the wigwam, or teazing the meek deer-hounds. He speaks English very fluently, and writes tolerably for an Indian boy; he usually accompanies the women in their visits, and acts as their interpreter, grinning with mischievous glee at his mother's bad English and my perplexity at not being able to understand her signs. In spite of his extreme deformity, he seemed to possess no inconsiderable share of vanity, gazing with great satisfaction at his face in the looking-glass. When I asked his name, he replied, "Indian name Maquin, but English name 'Mister Walker,' very good man;" this was the person he was called after.

These Indians are scrupulous in their observance of the Sabbath, and show great reluctance to having any dealings in the way of trading or pursuing their usual avocations of hunting or fishing on that day.

The young Indians are very expert in the use of a long bow, with wooden arrows, rather heavy and blunt at the end. Maquin said he could shoot ducks and small birds with his arrows; but I should think they were not calculated to reach objects at any great distance, as they appeared very heavy.

'Tis sweet to hear the Indians singing their hymns of a Sunday night; their rich soft voices rising in the still evening air. I have often listened to this little choir praising the Lord's name in the simplicity and fervour of their hearts, and have felt it was a reproach that these poor half-civilized wanderers should alone be found to gather together to give glory to God in the wilderness.

I was much pleased with the simple piety of our friend the hunter Peter's squaw, a stout, swarthy matron, of most amiable expression. We were taking our tea when she softly opened the door and looked in; an encouraging smile induced her to enter, and depositing a brown papouse (Indian for baby or little child) on the ground, she gazed round with curiosity and delight in her eyes. We offered her

Papouses.

some tea and bread, motioning to her to take a vacant seat beside the table. She seemed pleased by the invitation, and drawing her little one to her knee, poured some tea into the saucer, and gave it to the child to drink. She ate very moderately, and when she had finished, rose, and, wrapping her face in the folds of her blanket, bent down her head on her breast in the attitude of prayer. This little act of devotion was performed without the slightest appearance of pharisaical display, but in singleness and simplicity of heart. She then thanked us with a face beaming with smiles and good humour; and, taking little Rachel by the hands, threw her over her shoulder with a peculiar sleight that I feared would dislocate the tender thing's arms, but the papouse seemed well satisfied with this mode of treatment.

In long journeys the children are placed in upright baskets of a peculiar form, which are fastened round the necks of the mothers by straps of deer-skin; but the *young* infant is swathed to a sort of flat cradle, secured with flexible hoops, to prevent it from falling out. To these machines they are strapped, so as to be unable to move a limb. Much finery is often displayed in the outer covering and the bandages that confine the papouse.

There is a sling attached to this cradle that passes over the squaw's neck, the back of the babe being placed to the back of the mother, and its face outward. The first thing a squaw does on entering a house is to release herself from her burden, and stick it up against the wall or chair, chest, or any thing that will support it, where the passive prisoner stands, looking not unlike a mummy in its case. I have seen the picture of the Virgin and Child in some of the old illuminated missals, not unlike the figure of a papouse in its swaddling-clothes.

The squaws are most affectionate to their little ones. Gentleness and good humour appear distinguishing traits in the tempers of the female Indians; whether this be natural to their characters, the savage state, or the softening effects of Christianity, I cannot determine. Certainly in no instance does the Christian religion appear more lovely than when, untainted by the doubts and infidelity of modern sceptics, it is displayed in the conduct of the reclaimed Indian breaking down the strong-holds of idolatry and natural evil, and bringing forth the fruits of holiness and morality. They may be said to receive the truths of the Gospel as little children, with simplicity of heart and unclouded faith.

The squaws are very ingenious in many of their handiworks. We find their birch-bark baskets very convenient for a number of purposes. My bread-basket, knife-tray, sugar-basket, are all of this humble material. When ornamented and wrought in patterns with dyed quills, I can assure you, they are by no means inelegant. They manufacture vessels of birch-bark so well, that they will serve for many useful household purposes, such as holding water, milk, broth, or any other liquid; they are sewn or rather stitched together with the tough roots of the tamarack or larch, or else with strips of cedar-bark. They also weave very useful sorts of baskets from the inner rind of the bass-wood and white ash.

Some of these baskets, of a coarse kind, are made use of for gathering up potatoes, Indian corn, or turnips; the settlers finding them very good substitutes for the osier baskets used for such purposes in the old country.

The Indians are acquainted with a variety of dyes, with which they stain the more elegant fancy-baskets and porcupine-quills. Our parlour is ornamented with several very pretty specimens of their ingenuity in this way, which answer the purpose of note and letter-cases, flower-stands, and work-baskets.

They appear to value the useful rather more highly than the merely ornamental articles that you may exhibit to them. They are very shrewd and close in all their bargains, and exhibit a surprising degree of caution in their dealings. The men are much less difficult to trade with than the women: they display a singular pertinacity in some instances. If they have fixed their mind on any one article, they will come to you day after day, refusing any other you may offer to their notice. One of the squaws fell in love with a gay chintz dressing-gown belonging to my husband, and though I resolutely refused to part with it, all the squaws in the wigwam by turns came to look at "gown," which they pronounced with their peculiarly plaintive tone of voice; and when I said "no gown to sell," they uttered a melancholy exclamation of regret, and went away.

They will seldom make any article you want on purpose for you. If you express a desire to have baskets of a particular pattern that they do not happen to have ready made by them, they give you the usual vague reply of "by-and-by." If the goods you offer them in exchange for theirs do not answer their expectations, they give a sullen and dogged look or reply, "*Car-car*" (no, no), or "*Carwinni*," which is a still more forcible negative. But when the bargain pleases them, they signify their approbation by several affirmative nods of the head, and a note not much unlike a grunt; the ducks, fish, venison, or baskets, are placed beside you, and the articles of exchange transferred to the folds of their capacious blankets, or deposited in a sort of rushen wallets, not unlike those straw baskets in which English carpenters carry their tools.

The women imitate the dresses of the whites, and are rather skilful in converting their purchases. Many of the young girls can sew very neatly. I often give them bits of silk and velvet, and braid, for which they appear very thankful.

I am just now very busy with my garden. Some of our vegetable seeds are in the ground, though I am told we have been premature; there being ten chances to one but the young plants will be cut off by the late frosts, which are often felt through May, and even the beginning of June.

Our garden at present has nothing to boast of, being merely a spot of ground enclosed with a rough unsightly fence of split rails to keep the cattle from destroying the vegetables. Another spring, I hope to have a nice fence, and a portion of the ground devoted to flowers. This spring there is so much pressing work to be done on the land in clearing for the crops, that I do not like to urge my claims on behalf of a pretty garden.

Green Frogs.

The forest-trees are nearly all in leaf. Never did spring burst forth with greater rapidity than it has done this year. The verdure of the leaves is most vivid. A thousand lovely flowers are expanding in the woods and clearings. Nor are our Canadian songsters mute: the cheerful melody of the robin, the bugle-song of the blackbird and thrush, with the weak but not unpleasing call of the little bird called *Thitabebec*, and a wren, whose note is sweet and thrilling, fill our woods.

For my part, I see no reason or wisdom in carping at the good we do possess, because it lacks something of that which we formerly enjoyed. I am aware it is the fashion for travellers to assert that our feathered tribes are either mute or give utterance to discordant cries that pierce the ear, and disgust rather than please. It would be untrue were I to assert that our singing birds were as numerous or as melodious on the whole as those of Europe; but I must not suffer prejudice to rob my adopted country of her rights without one word being spoken in behalf of her feathered vocalists. Nay, I consider her very frogs have been belied: if it were not for the monotony of their notes, I really consider they are not quite unmusical. The green frogs are very handsome, being marked over with brown oval shields on the most vivid green coat: they are larger in size than the biggest of our English frogs, and certainly much handsomer in every respect. Their note resembles that of a bird, and has nothing of the creek in it.

The bull-frogs are very different from the green frogs. Instead of being angry with their comical

Bull-frog.

notes, I can hardly refrain from laughing when a great fellow pops up his broad brown head from the margin of the water, and says, "*Williroo, williroo, williroo,*" to which another bull-frog, from a distant part of the swamp, replies, in hoarser accents, "*Get out, get out, get out;*" and presently a sudden chorus is heard of old and young, as if each party was desirous of out-croaking the other.

In my next I shall give you an account of our logging-bee, which will take place the latter end of this month. I feel some anxiety respecting the burning of the log-heaps on the fallow round the house, as it appears to me rather a hazardous matter.

I shall write again very shortly. Farewell, dearest of friends.

LETTER XI.

Emigrants suitable for Canada.—Qualities requisite to ensure success.—Investment of Capital.—Useful Articles to be brought out.—Qualifications and Occupations of a Settler's Family.—Deficiency of Patience and Energy in some Females.—Management of the Dairy.—Cheese.—Indian Corn, and its Cultivation.—Potatoes.—Rates of Wages.

August 2, 1833.

WITH respect to the various questions, my dear friend, to which you request my particular attention, I can only promise that I will do my best to answer them as explicitly as possible, though at the same time I must remind you, that brevity in epistolary correspondence is not one of my excellencies. If I become too diffuse in describing mere matters of fact, you must bear with mine infirmity, and attribute it to my womanly propensity of over-much talking; so, for your comfort, if your eyes be wearied, your ears will at least escape.

I shall take your queries in due rotation; first, then, you ask, "Who are the persons best adapted for bush-settlers?"

To which I reply without hesitation—the poor hard-working sober labourers, who have industrious habits, a large family to provide for, and a laudable horror of the workhouse and parish-overseers: this will bear them through the hardships and privations of a first settlement in the backwoods; and in due time they will realize an honest independence, and be above want, though not work. Artisans of all crafts are bettter paid in village-towns, or long-cleared districts, than as mere bush-settlers.

"Who are the next best suited for emigration?"

Men of a moderate income or good capital may make money in Canada. If they have judgment, and can afford to purchase on a large scale, they will double or treble their capitals by judicious purchases and sales. But it would be easier for me to point out who are not fit for emigration than who are.

The poor gentleman of delicate and refined habits, who cannot afford to employ all the labour requisite to carry on the business of clearing on a tolerable large scale, and is unwilling or incapable of working himself, is not fitted for Canada, especially if his habits are expensive. Even the man of small income, unless he can condescend to take in hand the axe or the chopper, will find, even with prudent and economical habits, much difficulty in keeping free from debt for the first two or even three years. Many such have succeeded, but the struggle has been severe.

But there is another class of persons most unsuited to the woods: these are the wives and families of those who have once been opulent tradesmen, accustomed to the daily enjoyment of every luxury that money could procure or fashion invent; whose ideas of happiness are connected with a round of amusements, company, and all the novelties of dress and pleasure that the gay world can offer. Young ladies who have been brought up at fashionable boarding-schools, with a contempt of every thing useful or economical, make very indifferent settlers' wives. Nothing can be more unfortunate than the situations in the woods of Canada of persons so educated: disgusted with the unpleasant change in their mode of life, wearied and discontented with all the objects around them, they find every exertion a trouble, and every occupation a degradation.

For persons of this description (and there are such to be met with in the colonies), Canada is the worst country in the world. And I would urge any one, so unfitted by habit and inclination, under no consideration to cross the Atlantic; for miserable, and poor, and wretched they will become.

The emigrant, if he would succeed in this country, must possess the following qualities: perseverance, patience, industry, ingenuity, moderation, self-denial; and if he be a gentleman, a small income is almost indispensable; a good one is still more desirable.

The outlay for buying and clearing land, building, buying stock, and maintaining a family, paying servants' wages, with many other unavoidable expenses, cannot be done without some pecuniary means; and as the return from the land is but little for the first two or three years, it would be advisable for a settler to bring out some hundreds to enable him to carry on the farm and clear the above-mentioned expenses, or he will soon find himself involved in great difficulties.

Now, to your third query, "What will be the most profitable way of employing money, if a settler brought out capital more than was required for his own expenditure?"

On this head, I am not of course competent to give advice. My husband and friends, conversant with the affairs of the colonies, say, lend it on mortgage, on good landed securities, and at a high rate of interest. The purchase of land is often a good speculation, but not always so certain as mortgage, as it pays no interest; and though it may at some future time make great returns, it is not always so easy to dispose of it to an advantage when you happen to need it. A man possessing many thousand acres in different townships, may be distressed for twenty pounds if suddenly called upon for it when he is unprepared, if he invests all his capital in property of this kind.

It would be difficult for me to enumerate the many opportunities of turning ready money to account. There is so little money in circulation that those persons who are fortunate enough to have it at command can do almost any thing with it they please.

"What are the most useful articles for a settler to bring out?"

Tools, a good stock of wearing-apparel, and shoes, good bedding, especially warm blankets; as you pay high for them here, and they are not so good as you would supply yourself with at a much lower rate at home. A selection of good garden-seeds, as those you buy at the stores are sad trash; moreover, they are pasted up in packets not to be opened till paid for, and you may, as we have done, pay for little better than chaff, and empty husks, or old and worm-eaten seeds. This, I am sorry to say, is a Yankee trick; though I doubt not but John Bull would do the same if he had the opportunity, as there are rogues in all countries under the sun.

With respect to furniture and heavy goods of any kind, I would recommend little to be brought. Articles of hardware are not much more expensive here than at home, if at all, and often of a kind more suitable to the country than those you are at the trouble of bringing; besides, all land-carriage is dear.

We lost a large package of tools that have never been recovered from the forwarders, though their carriage was paid beforehand to Prescott. It is safest and best to ensure your goods, when the forwarders are accountable for them.

You ask, "If groceries and articles of household consumption are dear or cheap?"

They vary according to circumstances and situation. In towns situated in old cleared parts of the country, and near the rivers and navigable waters, they are cheaper than at home; but in newly-settled townships, where the water-communication is distant, and where the roads are bad, and the transport of goods difficult, they are nearly double the price. Where the supply of produce is inadequate to the demand, owing to the influx of emigrants in thinly-settled places, or other causes, then all articles of provisions are sold at a high price, and not to be procured without difficulty; but these are merely temporary evils, which soon cease.

Competition is lowering prices in Canadian towns, as it does in British ones, and you may now buy goods of all kinds nearly as cheap as in England.

Where prices depend on local circumstances, it is impossible to give any just standard; as what may do for one town would not for another, and a continual change is going on in all the unsettled or half-settled townships. In like manner the prices of cattle vary: they are cheaper in old settled townships, and still more so on the American side the river or lakes, than in the Canadas*.

"What are necessary qualifications of a settler's wife; and the usual occupations of the female part of a settler's family?" are your next questions.

To the first clause, I reply, a settler's wife should be active, industrious, ingenious, cheerful, not above putting her hand to whatever is necessary to be done in her household, nor too proud to profit by the advice and experience of older portions of the community, from whom she may learn many excellent lessons of practical wisdom.

Like that pattern of all good housewives described by the prudent mother of King Lemuel, it should be said of the emigrant's wife, "She layeth her hands to the spindle, and her hands hold the distaff." "She seeketh wool, and flax, and worketh willingly

* The duties on goods imported to the Canadas are exceedingly small, which will explain the circumstance of many articles of consumption being cheaper in places where there are facilities of transit than at home; while in the Backwoods, where roads are scarcely yet formed, there must be taken into the account the cost of carriage, and increased number of agents; the greater value of capital, and consequent increased rate of local profit, &c.—items which will diminish in amount as the country becomes settled and cleared.—Ed.

with her hands." "She looketh well to the ways of her household, and eateth not the bread of idleness."

Nothing argues a greater degree of good sense and good feeling than a cheerful conformity to circumstances, adverse though they be compared with a former lot; surely none that felt as they ought to feel, would ever despise a woman, however delicately brought up, for doing her duty in the state of life unto which it may have pleased God to call her. Since I came to this country, I have seen the accomplished daughters and wives of men holding no inconsiderable rank as officers, both naval and military, milking their own cows, making their own butter, and performing tasks of household work that few of our farmers' wives would now condescend to take part in. Instead of despising these useful arts, an emigrant's family rather pride themselves on their skill in these matters. The less silly pride and the more practical knowledge the female emigrant brings out with her, so much greater is the chance for domestic happiness and prosperity.

I am sorry to observe, that in many cases the women that come hither give way to melancholy regrets, and destroy the harmony of their fire-side, and deaden the energies of their husbands and brothers by constant and useless repining. Having once made up their minds to follow their husbands or friends to this country, it would be wiser and better to conform with a good grace, and do their part to make the burden of emigration more bearable.

One poor woman that was lamenting the miseries of this country was obliged to acknowledge that her prospects were far better than they ever had or could have been at home. What, then, was the cause of her continual regrets and discontent? I could hardly forbear smiling, when she replied, "She could not go to shop of a Saturday night to lay out her husband's earnings, and have a little chat with her *naibors*, while the shopman was serving the customers,—*for why?* there were no shops in the bush, and she was just dead-alive. If Mrs. Such-a-one (with whom, by the way, she was always quarrelling when they lived under the same roof) was near her she might not feel quite so lonesome." And so for the sake of a dish of gossip, while lolling her elbows on the counter of a village-shop, this foolish woman would have forgone the advantages, real solid advantages, of having land and cattle, and poultry and food, and firing and clothing, and all for a few years' hard work, which, her husband wisely observed, must have been exerted at home, with no other end in view than an old age of poverty or a refuge from starvation in a parish workhouse.

The female of the middling or better class, in her turn, pines for the society of the circle of friends she has quitted, probably for ever. She sighs for those little domestic comforts, that display of the refinements and elegancies of life, that she had been accustomed to see around her. She has little time now for those pursuits that were even her business as well as amusement. The accomplishments she has now to acquire are of a different order: she must become skilled in the arts of sugar-boiling, candle and soap-making, the making and baking of huge loaves, cooked in the bake-kettle, unless she be the fortunate mistress of a stone or clay oven. She must know how to manufacture *hop-rising* or *salt-rising* for leavening her bread; salting meat and fish, knitting stockings and mittens and comforters, spinning yarn in the big wheel (the French Canadian spinning-wheel), and dyeing the yarn when spun to have manufactured into cloth and coloured flannels, to clothe her husband and children, making clothes for herself, her husband and children;—for there are no tailors nor mantua-makers in the bush.

The management of poultry and the dairy must not be omitted; for in this country most persons adopt the Irish and Scotch method, that of churning the *milk*, a practice that in our part of England was not known. For my own part I am inclined to prefer the butter churned from cream, as being most economical, unless you chance to have Irish or Scotch servants who prefer buttermilk to new or sweet skimmed milk.

There is something to be said in favour of both plans, no doubt. The management of the calves differs here very much. Some persons wean the calf from the mother from its birth, never allowing it to suck at all: the little creature is kept fasting the first twenty-four hours; it is then fed with the finger with new milk, which it soon learns to take readily. I have seen fine cattle thus reared, and am disposed to adopt the plan as the least troublesome one.

The old settlers pursue an opposite mode of treatment, allowing the calf to suck till it is nearly half a year old, under the idea that it ensures the daily return of the cow; as, under ordinary circumstances, she is apt to ramble sometimes for days together, when the herbage grows scarce in the woods near the homesteads, and you not only lose the use of the milk, but often, from distention of the udder, the cow is materially injured, at least for the remainder of the milking season. I am disposed to think that were care taken to give the cattle regular supplies of salt, and a small portion of food, if ever so little, near the milking-place, they would seldom stay long away. A few refuse potatoes, the leaves of the garden vegetables daily in use, set aside for them, with the green shoots of the Indian corn that are stripped off to strengthen the plant, will ensure their attendance. In the fall and winter, pumpkins, corn, straw, and any other fodder you may have, with the browse they get during the chopping and underbrushing season, will keep them well.

The weanling calves should be given skimmed milk or buttermilk, with the leafy boughs of bass-wood and maple, of which they are extremely fond. A warm shed or fenced yard is very necessary for the cattle during the intense winter frosts: this is too often disregarded, especially in new settlements, which is the cause that many persons have the mortification of losing their stock, either with disease or cold. Naturally the Canadian cattle are very hardy, and when taken moderate care of, endure the severest winters well; but owing to the difficulties that attend a first settlement in the bush, they suffer every privation of cold and hunger, which brings on a complaint generally fatal, called the "*hollow horn*;" this originates in the spine, or extends to it, and is cured or palliated by boring the horn and inserting turpentine, pepper, or other heating substances.

When a new comer has not winter food for his cattle, it is wise to sell them in the fall and buy others in the spring: though at a seeming loss, it is perhaps less loss in reality than losing the cattle altogether. This was the plan my husband adopted, and we found it decidedly the better one, besides saving much care, trouble, and vexation.

I have seen some good specimens of native cheese, that I thought very respectable, considering that the grass is by no means equal to our British pastures. I purpose trying my skill next summer: who knows but that I may inspire some Canadian bard to celebrate the produce of my dairy as Bloomfield did the Suffolk cheese, yclept "Bang." You remember the passage, —for Bloomfield is your countryman as well as mine, —it begins:—

> "Unrivalled stands thy county cheese, O Giles," &c.

I have dwelt on the dairy information; as I know you were desirous of imparting all you could collect to your friends.

You wish to know something of the culture of Indian corn, and if it be a useful and profitable crop.

The cultivation of Indian corn on newly cleared lands is very easy, and attended with but little labour; on old farms it requires more. The earth is just raised with a broad hoe, and three or four corns dropped in with a pumpkin-seed, in about every third or fourth hole, and in every alternate row; the seed are set several feet apart. The pumpkins and the corn grow very amicably together, the broad leaves of the former shading the young plants and preventing the too great evaporation of the moisture from the ground; the roots strike little way, so that they rob the corn of a very small portion of nourishment. The one crop trails to an amazing length along the ground, while the other shoots up to the height of several feet above it. When the corn is beginning to branch, the ground should be hoed once over, to draw the earth a little to the roots, and cut down any weeds that might injure it. This is all that is done till the cob is beginning to form, when the blind and weak shoots are broken off, leaving four or five of the finest bearing shoots. The feather, when it begins to turn brown and dead, should also be taken off, that the plant may have all the nourishment to the corn.

We had a remarkable instance of smut in our corn last summer. The diseased cobs had large white bladders as big as a small puff-ball, or very large nuts, and these on being broken were full of an inky black liquid. On the same plants might be observed a sort of false fructification, the cob being deficient in kernels, which by some strange accident were transposed to the top feather or male blossoms. I leave botanists to explain the cause of this singular anomaly; I only state facts. I could not learn that the smut was a disease common to Indian corn, but last year smut or dust bran, as it is called by some, was very prevalent in the oat, barley, and wheat crops. In this country especially, new lands are very subject to the disease.

The ripe corn is either shocked as beans are at home, or the cobs pulled and braided on ropes after the manner of onions, and hung over poles or beams in the granaries or barns. The stripping of the corn gives rise among some people, to what they call a husking-bee, which, like all the other bees, is one of Yankee origin, and is not now so frequently adopted among the more independent or better class of settlers.

The Indian corn is a tender and somewhat precarious crop: it is liable to injury from the late frosts while young, for which reason it is never put in before the 20th of May, or beginning of June, and even then it will suffer; it has also many enemies, bears, racoons, squirrels, mice, and birds, and is a great temptation to *breachy* cattle, who, to come at it, will even toss down a fence with stakes and riders for protection, *i. e.* a pole or cross-bar, supported between crossed stakes, that surmounts the zig-zag rail fences, for better securing them from the incursions of cattle.

Even in Canada this crop requires a hot summer to ripen it perfectly; which makes me think Mr. Cobbett was deceiving the English farmer when he recommended it as a profitable crop in England. Profitable and highly useful it is under every disadvantage, as it makes the richest and sweetest food for all kinds of granivorous animals, even in its green state, and affords sound good food when ripe, or even partially ripe, for fattening beasts and working oxen.

Last summer was very favourable, and the crops

were abundant, but owing to the failure of the two preceding ones, fewer settlers grew it. Our small patch turned out very good. The flour makes a substantial sort of porridge, called by the Americans "*Supporne*;" this is made with water, and eaten with milk, or else mixed with milk; it requires long boiling. Bread is seldom if ever made without a large portion of wheaten flour, mixed with the corn meal.

With respect to the culture of other grain, I can tell you nothing but what every book that treats on emigration will give you. The potatoe instead of being sown in drills is planted in hills, which are raised over the sets: this crop requires hoeing.

With respect to the usual rate of wages, this also differs according to the populousness of the place: but the common wages now given to an active able man are from eight to eleven dollars per month; ten is perhaps the general average; from four to six for lads, and three and four for female servants. You may get a little girl, say from nine to twelve years, for her board and clothing; but this is far from a saving plan, as they soon wear out clothes and shoes thus bestowed. I have once tried this way, but found myself badly served, and a greater loser than if I had given wages. A big girl will go out to service for two and two and a half dollars per month, and will work in the fields also if required, binding after the reapers, planting and hoeing corn and potatoes. I have a very good girl, the daughter of a Wiltshire emigrant, who is neat and clever, and respectful and industrious, to whom I give three dollars only: she is a happy specimen of the lower order of English emigrants, and her family are quite acquisitions to the township in which they live.

I think I have now answered all your queries to the best of my ability; but I would have you bear in mind that my knowledge is confined to a small portion of the townships along the Otanabee lakes, therefore, my information after all, may be but local: things may differ, and do differ in other parts of the province, though possibly not very materially.

I must now say farewell. Should you ever feel tempted to try your fortune on this side the Atlantic, let me assure you of a warm welcome to our Canadian home, from your sincerely attached friend.

LETTER XII.

"A Logging Bee."—Burning of the Log-heaps.—Crops for the Season.—Farming Stock.—Comparative Value of Wheat and Labour.—Choice of Land, and relative Advantages.—Clearing Land.—Hurricane in the Woods.—Variable Weather.—Insects.

November the 2d, 1833.

MANY thanks, dearest mother, for the contents of the box which arrived in August. I was charmed with the pretty caps and worked frocks sent for my baby; the little fellow looks delightfully in his new robes, and I can almost fancy is conscious of the accession to his wardrobe, so proud he seems of his dress. He grows fat and lively, and, as you may easily suppose, is at once the pride and delight of his foolish mother's heart.

His father, who loves him as much as I do myself, often laughs at my fondness, and asks me if I do not think him the ninth wonder of the world. He has fitted up a sort of rude carriage on the hand-sleigh for the little fellow—nothing better than a tea-chest, lined with a black bear-skin, and in this humble equipage he enjoys many a pleasant ride over the frozen ground.

Nothing could have happened more opportunely for us than the acquisition of my uncle's legacy, as it has enabled us to make some useful additions to our farm, for which we must have waited a few years. We have laid out a part of the property in purchasing a fine lot of land adjoining our home lot. The quality of our new purchase is excellent, and, from its situation, greatly enhances the value of the whole property.

We had a glorious burning this summer after the ground was all logged up; that is, all the large timbers chopped into lengths, and drawn together in heaps with oxen. To effect this the more readily we called a logging-bee. We had a number of settlers attend, with yokes of oxen and men to assist us. After that was over, my husband, with the men-servants, set the heaps on fire; and a magnificent sight it was to see such a conflagration all round us. I was a little nervous at first on account of the nearness of some of the log-heaps to the house, but care is always taken to fire them with the wind blowing in a direction away from the building. Accidents have sometimes happened, but they are of rarer occurrence than might be expected, when we consider the subtlety and destructiveness of the element employed on the occasion.

If the weather be very dry, and a brisk wind blowing, the work of destruction proceeds with astonishing rapidity; sometimes the fire will communicate with the forest and run over many hundreds of acres. This is not considered favourable for clearing, as it destroys the underbush and light timbers, which are almost indispensable for ensuring a good burning. It is, however, a magnificent sight to see the blazing trees and watch the awful progress of the conflagration, as it hurries onward, consuming all before it, or leaving such scorching mementoes as have blasted the forest growth for years.

When the ground is very dry the fire will run all over the fallow, consuming the dried leaves, sticks, and roots. Of a night the effect is more evident; sometimes the wind blows particles of the burning fuel into the hollow pines and tall decaying stumps; these readily ignite, and after a time present an appearance that is exceedingly fine and fanciful. Fiery columns, the bases of which are hidden by the dense smoke wreaths, are to be seen in every direction, sending up showers of sparks that are whirled about like rockets and fire-wheels in the wind. Some of these tall stumps, when the fire has reached the summit, look like gas lamp-posts newly lit. The fire will sometimes continue unextinguished for days.

After the burning is over the brands are collected and drawn together again to be reburnt; and, strange as it may appear to you, there is no work that is more interesting and exciting than that of tending the log-heaps, rousing up the dying flames and closing them in, and supplying the fires with fresh fuel.

There are always two burnings: first, the brush heaps, which have lain during the winter till the drying winds and hot suns of April and May have rendered them sear, are set fire to; this is previous to forming the log-heaps.

If the season be dry, and a brisk wind abroad, much of the lighter timber is consumed, and the larger trees reduced during this first burning. After this is over, the rest is chopped and logged up for the second burning: and lastly, the remnants are collected and consumed till the ground be perfectly free from all encumbrances, excepting the standing stumps, which rarely burn out, and remain eye-sores for several years. The ashes are then scattered abroad, and the field fenced in with split timber; the great work of clearing is over.

Our crops this year are oats, corn, and pumpkins, and potatoes, with some turnips. We shall have wheat, rye, oats, potatoes, and corn next harvest, which will enable us to increase our stock. At present we have only a yoke of oxen (Buck and Bright, the names of three-fourths of all the working oxen in Canada), two cows, two calves, three small pigs, ten hens, and three ducks, and a pretty brown pony: but she is such a skilful clearer of seven-railed fences that we shall be obliged to part with her. *Breachy* cattle of any kind are great disturbers of public tranquillity and private friendship; for which reason any settler who values the good will of his neighbours would rather part with the best working yoke of oxen in the township, than keep them if they prove *breachy*.

A small farmer at home would think very poorly of our Canadian possessions, especially when I add that our whole stock of farming implements consists of two reaping-hooks, several axes, a spade, and a couple of hoes. Add to these a queer sort of harrow that is made in the shape of a triangle for the better passing between the stumps: this is a rude machine compared with the nicely painted instruments of the sort I have been accustomed to see used in Britain. It is roughly hewn, and put together without regard to neatness; strength for use is all that is looked to here. The plough is seldom put into the land before the third or fourth year, nor is it required; the general plan of cropping the first fallow with wheat or oats, and sowing grass-seeds with the grain to make pastures, renders the plough unnecessary till such time as the grass-lands require to be broken up. This method is pursued by most settlers while they are clearing bush-land; always chopping and burning enough to keep a regular succession of wheat and spring crops, while the former clearings are allowed to remain in grass.

The low price that is now given for grain of every kind, wheat having fetched only from two shillings and nine-pence to four shillings the bushel, makes the growing of it a matter of less importance than rearing and fatting of stock. Wages bear no proportion to the price of produce; a labourer receives ten and even eleven dollars and board a month, while wheat is selling at only three shillings, three shillings and sixpence or four shillings, and sometimes even still less. The returns are little compared with the outlay on the land; nor does the land produce that great abundance that men are apt to look for on newly cleared ground. The returns of produce, however, must vary with the situation and fertility of the soil, which is generally less productive in the immediate vicinity of the lakes and rivers than a little further back from them, the land being either swampy or ridgy, covered with pines and beset with blocks of limestone and granite, the sub-soil poor and sandy.

This is the case on the small lakes and on the banks of the Otanabee; the back lots are generally much finer in quality, producing hard wood, such as bass-wood, maple, hickory, butter-nut, oak, beach, and iron-wood; which trees always indicate a more productive soil than the pine tribe.

In spite of the indifference of the soil the advantage of a water frontage is considered a matter of great importance in the purchasing of land; and, lost with water privileges, usually fetch a much higher price than those further removed from it. These lands are in general in the possession of the higher class of settlers, who can afford to pay something extra for a pretty situation, and the prospect of future improvements when the country shall be under a higher state of cultivation and more thickly settled.

We cannot help regarding with infinite satisfaction the few acres that are cleared round the house and covered with crops. A space of this kind in the midst of the dense forest imparts a cheerfulness to the mind, of which those that live in an open country, or even a partially wooded one, can form no idea. The bright sunbeams and the blue and cloudless sky breaking in upon you, rejoices the eye and cheers the heart as much as the cool shade of a palm-grove would the weary traveller on the sandy wastes of Africa.

If we feel this so sensibly who enjoy the opening of a lake of full three-quarters of a mile in breadth directly in front of our windows, what must those do whose clearing is first opened in the depths of the forest, hemmed in on every side by a thick wall of trees, through the interminable shades of which the eye vainly endeavours to penetrate in search of other objects and other scenes; but so dense is the growth of timber, that all beyond the immediate clearing is wrapped in profound obscurity. A settler on first locating on his lot knows no more of its boundaries and its natural features than he does of the north-west passage.

Under such disadvantages it is ten chances to one if he chooses the best situation on the land for the site of his house. This is a very sufficient reason for not putting up an expensive building till the land is sufficiently cleared to allow its advantages and disadvantages to become evident. Many eligible spots often present themselves to the eye of the settler, in clearing his land, that cause him to regret having built before he could obtain a better choice of ground. But circumstances will seldom admit of delay in building in the bush; a dwelling must be raised speedily, and that generally on the first cleared acre. The emigrant, however, looks forward to some no very distant period when he shall be able to gratify both his taste and love of comfort in the erection of a handsomer and better habitation than his log-house or his shanty, which he regards only in the light of a temporary accommodation.

On first coming to this country nothing surprised me more than the total absence of trees about the dwelling-houses and cleared lands; the axe of the chopper relentlessly levels all before him. Man appears to contend with the trees of the forest as though they were his most obnoxious enemies; for he spares neither the young sapling in its greenness nor the ancient trunk in its lofty pride; he wages war against the forest with fire and steel.

There are several sufficient reasons to be given for this seeming want of taste. The forest-trees grow so thickly together that they have no room for expanding and putting forth lateral branches; on the contrary, they run up to an amazing height of stem, resembling seedlings on a hot-bed that have not duly been thinned out. Trees of this growth when unsupported by others are tall, weak, and entirely divested of those graces and charms of outline and foliage that would make them desirable as ornaments to our grounds; but this is not the most cogent reason for not leaving them, supposing some more sightly than others were to be found.

Instead of striking deep roots in the earth, the forest-trees, with the exception of the pines, have very superficial hold in the earth; the roots running along the surface have no power to resist the wind when it bends the tops, which thus act as a powerful lever in tearing them from their places.

The taller the tree the more liable it is to being uprooted by storms; and if those that are hemmed in, as in the thickly-planted forests, fall, you may suppose the certain fate of any isolated tree, deprived of its former protectors, when left to brave and battle with the storm. It is sure to fall, and may chance to injure any cattle that are within its reach. This is the great reason why trees are not left in the clearing. Indeed, it is a less easy matter to spare them when chopping than I at first imagined, but the fall of one tree frequently brings down two, three, or even more smaller ones that stand near it. A good chopper will endeavour to promote this as much as possible by partly chopping through smaller ones in the direction they purpose the larger one to fall.

I was so desirous of preserving a few pretty sapling beech-trees that pleased me, that I desired the choppers to spare them; but the only one that was saved from destruction in the chopping had to pass through a fiery ordeal, which quickly scorched and withered up its gay green leaves: it now stands a melancholy monument of the impossibility of preserving trees thus left. The only thing to be done if you desire trees, is to plant them while young in favourable situations, when they take deep root and spread forth branches the same as the trees in our parks and hedge-rows.

Another plan which we mean to adopt on our land is, to leave several acres of forest in a convenient situation, and chop and draw out the old timbers for fire-wood, leaving the younger growth for ornament. This method of preserving a grove of trees is not liable to the objections formerly stated, and combines the useful with the ornamental.

There is a strange excitement created in the mind whilst watching the felling of one of the gigantic pines or oaks of the forest. Proudly and immoveably it seems at first to resist the storm of blows that assail its massy trunk, from the united axes of three or even four choppers. As the work of destruction continues, a slight motion is perceived—an almost imperceptible quivering of the boughs. Slowly and slowly it inclines, while the loud rending of the trunk at length warns you that its last hold on earth is gone. The axe of the chopper has performed its duty; the motion of the falling tree becomes accelerated every instant, till it comes down in thunder on the plain, with a crash that makes the earth tremble, and the neighbouring trees reel and bow before it.

Though decidedly less windy than our British isles, Canada is subject at times to sudden storms, nearly approaching to what might be termed whirlwinds and hurricanes. A description of one of these tempests I gave you in an early letter. During the present summer I witnessed another hurricane, somewhat more violent and destructive in its effect.

The sky became suddenly overcast with clouds of a highly electric nature. The storm came from the north-west, and its fury appeared to be confined within the breadth of a few hundred yards. I was watching with some degree of interest the rapid movements in the lurid, black, and copper-coloured clouds that were careering above the lake, when I was surprised by the report of trees falling on the opposite shore, and yet more so by seeing the air filled with scattered remnants of the pines within less than a hundred yards of the house, while the wind was scarcely felt on the level ground on which I was standing.

In a few seconds the hurricane had swept over the water, and with irresistible power laid low not less than thirty or forty trees, bending others to the ground like reeds. It was an awful sight to see the tall forest rocking and bowing before the fury of the storm, and with the great trunks falling one after the other, as if they had been a pack of cards thrown down by a breath. Fortunately for us the current of the wind merely passed over our open clearing, doing us no further damage than uprooting three big pine-trees on the ridge above the lake. But in the direction of our neighbour ——— it did great mischief, destroying many rods of fencing, and crushing his crops with the prostrate trunks and scattered boughs, occasioning great loss and much labour to repair the mischief.

The upturned roots of trees thrown down by the wind are great nuisances and disfigurements in clearings, and cause much more trouble to remove than those that have been felled by the axe. Some of the stumps of these wind-fallen trees will right again if chopped from the trunk soon after they have been blown down, the weight of the roots and upturned soil being sufficient to bring them back into their former places; we have pursued this plan very frequently.

We have experienced one of the most changeable seasons this summer that was possible. The spring was warm and pleasant, but from the latter part of May till the middle of harvest we had heavy rains, cloudy skies, with moist hot days, and frequent tempests of thunder and lightning, most awfully grand, but seemingly less destructive than such storms are at home. Possibly the tall forest-trees divert the danger from the low dwellings, which are sufficiently sheltered from the effect of the lightning. The autumn has also proved wet and cold. I must say at present I do not think very favourably of the climate; however, it is not right to judge by so short an acquaintance with it, as every one says this summer has been unlike any of its predecessors.

The insects have been a sad annoyance to us, and I hailed the approach of the autumn as a respite from their attacks; for these pests are numerous and various, and no respecters of persons, as I have learned from sad experience.

I am longing for home-letters; let me hear from you soon.

Farewell, friends.

LETTER XIII.

Health enjoyed in the rigour of Winter.—Inconvenience suffered from the brightness of the Snow.—Sleighing.—Indian Orthography.—Visit to an Indian Encampment.—Story of an Indian.—An Indian Hunchback.—Canadian Ornithology.

Lake Cottage, March 14, 1834.

I RECEIVED your affectionate and interesting letter only last night. Owing to an error in the direction, it had made the round of two townships before it reached Peterborough, and though it bore as many new directions as the sailor's knife did new blades and handles, it did at last reach me, and was not less prized for its travelling dress, being somewhat the worse for wear.

I rejoiced to hear of your returning health and increased happiness;—may they long continue. Your expressions of regret for my exile, as you term my residence in this country, affected me greatly. Let the assurance that I am not less happy than when I left my native land, console you for my absence. If my situation be changed, my heart is not. My spirits are as light as ever, and at times I feel a gaiety that bids defiance to all care.

You say you fear the rigours of the Canadian winter will kill me. I never enjoyed better health, nor so good, as since it commenced. There is a degree of spirit and vigour infused into one's blood by the purity of the air that is quite exhilarating. The very snow seems whiter and more beautiful than it does in our damp vapoury climate. During a keen bright winter's day you will often perceive the air filled with minute frozen particles, which are quite dry, and slightly prick your face like needle-points, while the sky is blue and bright above you. There is a decided difference between the first snow-falls and those of mid-winter; the first are in large soft flakes, and seldom remain long without thawing, but those that fall after the cold has regularly set in are smaller, drier, and of the most beautiful forms, sometimes pointed like a cluster of rays, or else feathered in the most exquisite manner.

I find my eyes much inconvenienced by the dazzling glitter of the snow on bright sunny days, so as to render my sight extremely dull and indistinct for hours after exposure to its power. I would strongly advise any one coming out to this country to provide themselves with blue or green glasses; and by no means to omit green crape or green tissue veils. Poor Moses' gross of green spectacles would not have proved so bad a spec. in Canada*.

Some few nights ago as I was returning from visiting a sick friend, I was delighted by the effect produced by the frost. The earth, the trees, every stick, dried leaf, and stone in my path was glittering with mimic diamonds, as if touched by some magical power; objects the most rude and devoid of beauty had suddenly assumed a brilliancy that was dazzling beyond

* Oculists condemn coloured spectacles, as injuring weak eyes by the heat which they occasion. Coloured gauze or coloured shades are preferable.—Ed.

the most vivid fancy to conceive; every frozen particle sent forth rays of bright light. You might have imagined yourself in Sinbad's valley of gems; nor was the temperature of the air at all unpleasantly cold.

I have often felt the sensation of cold on a windy day in Britain far more severe than I have done in Canada, when the mercury indicated a much lower degree of temperature. There is almost a trance-like stillness in the air during our frosty nights that lessens the unpleasantness of the sensation.

There are certainly some days of intense cold during our winter, but this low temperature seldom continues more than three days together. The coldest part of the day is from an hour or two before sunrise to about nine o'clock in the morning; by that time our blazing log-fires or metal stoves have warmed the house, so that you really do not care for the cold without. When out of doors you suffer less inconvenience than you would imagine whilst you keep in motion, and are tolerably well clothed: the ears and nose are the most exposed to injury.

Gentlemen sometimes make a singular appearance coming in from a long journey, that if it were not for pity's sake would draw from you a smile;—hair, whiskers, eyebrows, eyelashes, beard, all incrusted with hoar-frost. I have seen young ladies going to evening parties with clustering ringlets, as jetty as your own, changed by the breath of Father Frost to silvery whiteness; so that you could almost fancy the fair damsels had been suddenly metamorphosed to their ancient grannies; fortunately for youth and beauty such change is but transitory.

In the towns and populous parts of the province the approach of winter is hailed with delight instead of dread; it is to all a season of leisure and enjoyment. Travelling is then expeditiously and pleasantly performed; even our vile bush-roads become positively very respectable; and if you should happen to be overturned once or twice during a journey of pleasure, very little danger attends such an event, and very little compassion is bestowed on you for your tumble in the snow; so it is wisest to shake off your light burden and enjoy the fun with a good grace if you can.

Sleighing is certainly a very agreeable mode of travelling; the more snow, the better the sleighing season is considered; and the harder it becomes, the easier the motion of the vehicle. The horses are all adorned with strings of little brass bells about their necks or middles. The merry jingle of these bells is far from disagreeable, producing a light lively sound.

The following lines I copied from the New York Albion for you; I think you will be pleased with them:—

SLEIGH BELLS.

'Tis merry to hear at evening time
By the blazing hearth the sleigh-bells chime;
To know each bound of the steed brings near
The form of him to our bosoms dear;
Lightly we spring the fire to raise,
Till the rafters glow with the ruddy blaze.

'Tis he—and blithely the gay bells sound,
As his steed skims over the frozen ground.
Hark! he has pass'd the gloomy wood;
He crosses now the ice-bound flood,

And sees the light from the open door,
To hail his toilsome journey o'er.

Our hut is small and rude our cheer,
But love has spread the banquet here;
And childhood springs to be caress'd
By our beloved and welcome guest;
With smiling brow his tale he tells,
They laughing ring the merry bells.

From the cedar swamp the wolf may howl,
From the blasted pine loud whoop the owl;
The sudden crash of the falling tree
Are sounds of terror no more to me;
No longer I list with boding fear,
The sleigh-bells' merry peal to hear*.

As soon as a sufficient quantity of snow has fallen all vehicles of every description, from the stage-coach to the wheelbarrow, are supplied with wooden runners, shod with iron, after the manner of skates. The usual equipages for travelling are the double sleigh, light waggon, and cutter; the two former are drawn by two horses abreast, but the latter, which is by far the most elegant-looking, has but one, and answers more to our gig or chaise.

Wrapped up in buffalo robes you feel no inconvenience from the cold, excepting to your face, which requires to be defended by a warm beaver or fur bonnet; the latter, I am surprised to find, is seldom if ever worn, from the nonsensical reason that it is not the fashion. The red, grey, and black squirrels are

* This little poem by Mrs. Moodie has since been printed in a volume of "Friendship's Offering," with some alterations by the editor that deprive it a good deal of the simplicity of the original.

abundant in our woods; the musk-rat inhabits little houses that he builds in the rushy parts of the lakes: these dwellings are formed of the roots of sedges, sticks, and other materials of a similar nature, and plastered with mud, over which a thick close thatch is raised to the height of a foot or more above the water; they are of a round or dome-shape, and are distinctly visible from the shore at some distance. The Indians set traps to ensnare these creatures in their houses, and sell their skins, which are very thick and glossy towards winter. The beaver, the bear, the black lynx, and foxes are also killed, and brought to the stores by the hunters, where the skins are exchanged for goods or money.

The Indians dress the deer-skins for making mocassins, which are greatly sought after by the settlers in these parts; they are very comfortable in snowy weather, and keep the feet very warm, but you require several wrappings of cloth round the feet before you put them on. I wore a beautiful pair all last winter, worked with porcupine-quills and bound with scarlet ribbon; these elegant mocassins were the handicraft of an old squaw, the wife of Peter the hunter: you have already heard of him in my former letters. I was delighted with a curious specimen of Indian orthography that accompanied the mocassins, in the form of a note, which I shall transcribe for your edification:—

Sir,

Pleas if you would give something; you must git in ordir in store is woyth (worth) them mocsin, porcupine quill on et. One dollers foure yard.

The Prairie.

This curious billet was the production of the hunter's eldest son, and is meant to intimate that if I would buy the mocassins the price was one dollar, or an order on one of the stores for four yards of calico; for so the squaw interpreted its meaning. The order for four yards of printed cotton was delivered over to Mrs. Peter, who carefully pinned it within the folds of her blanket, and departed well satisfied with the payment. And this reminds me of our visit to the Indian's camp last week. Feeling some desire to see these singular people in their winter encampment, I expressed my wish to S———, who happens to be a grand favourite with the old hunter and his family; as a mark of a distinction they have bestowed on him the title of Chippewa, the name of their tribe. He was delighted with the opportunity of doing the honours of the Indian wigwam, and it was agreed that he, with some of his brothers and sisters-in-law, who happened to be on a visit at his house, should come and drink tea with us and accompany us to the camp in the woods.

A merry party we were that sallied forth that evening into the glorious starlight; the snow sparkled with a thousand diamonds on its frozen surface, over which we bounded with hearts as light as hearts could be in this careful world. And truly never did I look upon a lovelier sight than the woods presented; there had been a heavy fall of snow the preceding day; owing to the extreme stillness of the air not a particle of it had been shaken from the trees. The evergreens were bending beneath their brilliant burden; every twig, every leaf, and spray was covered, and some of the weak saplings actually bowed down to the earth with the weight of snow, forming the most lovely and fanciful bowers and arcades across our path. As you looked up towards the tops of the trees the snowy branches seen against the deep blue sky formed a silvery veil, through which the bright stars were gleaming with a chastened brilliancy.

I was always an admirer of a snowy landscape, but neither in this country nor at home did I ever see any thing so surpassingly lovely as the forest appeared that night.

Leaving the broad road we struck into a bye-path, deep tracked by the Indians, and soon perceived the wigwam by the red smoke that issued from the open basket-work top of the little hut. This is first formed with light poles, planted round so as to enclose a circle of ten or twelve feet in diameter; between these poles are drawn large sheets of birch-bark both within and without, leaving an opening of the bare poles at the top so as to form an outlet for the smoke; the outer walls were also banked up with snow, so as to exclude the air entirely from beneath.

Some of our party, who were younger and lighter of foot than we sober married folks, ran on before; so that when the blanket, that served the purpose of a door, was unfastened, we found a motley group of the dark skins and the pale faces reposing on the blankets and skins that were spread round the walls of the wigwam.

The swarthy complexions, shaggy black hair, and singular costume of the Indians formed a striking contrast with the fair-faced Europeans that were mingled with them, seen as they were by the red and fitful glare of the wood-fire that occupied the centre of the circle. The deer-hounds lay stretched in indolent enjoyment, close to the embers, while three or four dark-skinned little urchins were playing with each other, or angrily screaming out their indignation against the apish tricks of the hunchback, my old acquaintance Maquin, that Indian Flibberty-gibbet, whose delight appeared to be in teazing and tormenting the little papouses, casting as he did so sidelong glances of impish glee at the guests, while as quick as thought his features assumed an impenetrable gravity when the eyes of his father or the squaws seemed directed towards his tricks.

There was a slight bustle among the party when we entered one by one through the low blanket-doorway. The merry laugh rang round among our friends, which was echoed by more than one of the Indian men, and joined by the peculiar half-laugh or chuckle of the squaws. "*Chippewa*" was directed to a post of honour beside the hunter Peter; and squaw Peter, with an air of great good humour, made room for me on a corner of her own blanket; to effect which two papouses and a hound were sent lamenting to the neighbourhood of the hunchback Maquin.

The most attractive persons in the wigwam were two Indian girls, one about eighteen,—Jane, the hunter's eldest daughter, and her cousin Margaret. I was greatly struck with the beauty of Jane; her features were positively fine, and though of gipsey darkness the tint of vermilion on her cheek and lip rendered it, if not beautiful, very attractive. Her hair, which was of jetty blackness, was soft and shining, and was neatly folded over her forehead, not hanging loose and disorderly in shaggy masses, as is generally the case with the squaws. Jane was evidently aware of her superior charms, and may be considered as an Indian belle, by the peculiar care she displayed in the arrangement of the black cloth mantle, bound with scarlet, that was gracefully wrapped over one shoulder, and fastened at her left side with a gilt brooch. Margaret was younger, of lower stature, and though lively and rather pretty, yet wanted the quiet dignity of her cousin; she had more of the squaw in face and figure. The two girls occupied a blanket by themselves, and were busily engaged in working some most elegant sheaths of deer-skin, richly wrought over with coloured quills and beads: they kept the beads and quills in a small tin baking-pan on their knees; but my old squaw (as I always call Mrs. Peter) held her porcupine-quills in her mouth, and the fine dried sinews of the deer, which they make use of instead of thread in work of this sort, in her bosom.

On my expressing a desire to have some of the porcupine-quills, she gave me a few of different colour that she was working a pair of mocassins with, but signified that she wanted "'*bead*' to work mocsin," by which I understood I was to give some in exchange for the quills. Indians never give since they have learned to trade with white men.

She was greatly delighted with the praises I bestowed on Jane. She told me Jane was soon to marry the young Indian who sat on one side of her in all the pride of a new blanket coat, red sash, embroidered powder-pouch, and great gilt clasps to the collar of his coat, which looked as warm and as white as a newly washed fleece. The old squaw evidently felt proud of the young couple as she gazed on them, and often repeated, with a good-tempered laugh, "Jane's husband—marry by and by."

We had so often listened with pleasure to the Indians singing their hymns of a Sunday night that I requested some of them to sing to us; the old hunter nodded assent; and, without removing his pipe, with the gravity and phlegm of a Dutchman, issued his commands, which were as instantly obeyed by the younger part of the community, and a chorus of rich voices filled the little hut with a melody that thrilled to our very hearts.

The hymn was sung in the Indian tongue, a language that is peculiarly sweet and soft in its cadences, and seems to be composed with many vowels. I could not but notice the modest air of the girls; as if anxious to avoid observation that they felt was attracted by their sweet voices, they turned away from the gaze of the strangers, facing each other and bending their heads down over the work they still held in their hands. The attitude, which is that of the Eastern nations; the dress, dark hair and eyes, the olive complexion, heightened colour, and meek expression of face, would have formed a study for a painter. I wish you could have witnessed the scene; I think you would not easily have forgotten it. I was pleased with the air of deep reverence that sat on the faces of the elders of the Indian family, as they listened to the voices of their children singing praise and glory to the God and Saviour they had learned to fear and love.

The Indians seem most tender parents; it is pleasing to see the affectionate manner in which they treat their young children, fondly and gently caressing them with eyes overflowing and looks of love. During the singing each papouse crept to the feet of its respective father and mother, and those that were too young to join their voices to the little choir, remained quite silent till the hymn was at an end. One little girl, a fat brown roly-poly, of three years old, beat time on her father's knee, and from time to time chimed in her infant voice; she evidently possessed a fine ear and natural taste for music.

I was at a loss to conceive where the Indians kept their stores, clothes, and other moveables, the wigwam being so small that there seemed no room for any thing besides themselves and their hounds. Their ingenuity, however, supplied the want of room, and I soon discovered a plan that answered all the purposes of closets, bags, boxes, &c., the inner lining of birch-bark being drawn between the poles so as to form hollow pouches all round; in these pouches were stowed their goods; one set held their stock of dried deer's flesh, another dried fish, a third contained some flat cakes, which I have been told they bake in a way peculiar to themselves, with hot ashes over and under; for my part I think they must be far from palatable so seasoned. Their dressed skins, clothes, materials for their various toys, such as beads, quills, bits of cloth, silk, with a thousand other miscellaneous articles, occupied the rest of these reservoirs.

Though open for a considerable space at the top, the interior of the wigwam was so hot, I could scarcely breathe, and was constrained to throw off all my wrappings during the time we staid. Before we went away the hunter insisted on showing us a game, which was something after the manner of our cup and ball, only more complicated, and requires more sleight of hand; the Indians seemed evidently well pleased at our want of adroitness. They also showed us another game, which was a little like nine-pins, only the number of sticks stuck in the ground was greater. I was unable to stay to see the little rows of sticks knocked out, as the heat of the wigwam oppressed me almost to suffocation, and I was glad to feel myself once more breathing the pure air.

In any other climate one would scarcely have undergone such sudden extremes of temperature without catching a severe cold; but fortunately that distressing complaint *catchée le cold*, as the Frenchman termed it, is not so prevalent in Canada as at home.

Some twenty years ago, while a feeling of dread still existed in the minds of the British settlers towards the Indians, from the remembrance of atrocities committed during the war of independence, a poor woman, the widow of a settler who occupied a farm in one of the then but thinly-settled townships back of the Ontario, was alarmed by the sudden appearance of an Indian within the walls of her log-hut. He had entered so silently that it was not till he planted himself before the blazing fire that he was perceived by the frightened widow and her little ones, who retreated, trembling with ill-concealed terror to the furthest corner of the room.

Without seeming to notice the dismay which his appearance had excited, the Indian proceeded to disencumber himself from his hunting accoutrements; he then unfastened his wet mocassins, which he hung up to dry, plainly intimating his design was to pass the night beneath their roof, it being nearly dark, and snowing heavily.

Scarcely daring to draw an audible breath, the little group watched the movements of their unwelcome guest. Imagine their horror when they beheld him take from his girdle a hunting-knife, and deliberately proceed to try its edge. After this his tomahawk and rifle underwent a similar examination.

The despair of the horror-stricken mother was now approaching a climax. She already beheld in idea the frightful mangled corpses of her murdered children upon that hearth which had so often been the scene of their innocent gambols. Instinctively she clasped the two youngest to her breast at a forward movement of the Indian. With streaming eyes she was about to throw herself at his feet, as he advanced towards her with the dreaded weapons in his hands, and implore his mercy for herself and her babes. What then was her surprise and joy when he gently laid the rifle, knife, and tomahawk beside her, signifying by this action that she had nothing to fear at his hands *.

* It is almost an invariable custom now for the Indians on entering a dwelling-house to leave all their weapons, as rifle, tomahawk, &c., outside the door, even if the weather be

A reprieve to a condemned criminal at the moment previous to his execution was not more welcome than this action of the Indian to the poor widow. Eager to prove her confidence and her gratitude at the same time, she hastened to prepare food for the refreshment of the now no longer dreaded guest; and, assisted by the eldest of her children, put clean sheets and the best blankets on her own bed, which she joyfully devoted to the accommodation of the stranger. An expressive "Hugh! hugh!" was the only reply to this act of hospitality; but when he went to take possession of his luxurious couch he seemed sorely puzzled. It was evident the Indian had never seen, and certainly never reposed on, an European bed. After a mute examination of the bed-clothes for some minutes, with a satisfied laugh, he sprang upon the bed, and, curling himself up like a dog, in a few minutes was sound asleep.

By dawn of day the Indian had departed; but whenever he came on the hunting-grounds in the neighbourhood of the widow, she was sure to see him. The children, no longer terrified at his swarthy countenance and warlike weapons, would gather round his knees, admire the feathered pouch that contained his shot, finger the beautiful embroidered sheath that held the hunting-knife, or the finely-worked mocassins and leggings; whilst he would pat their heads, and bestow upon them an equal share of caresses with his deer-hounds.

Such was the story related to me by a young mis-

ever so wet; as they consider it unpolite to enter a friendly dwelling armed.

sionary. I thought it might prove not uninteresting, as a trait of character of one of these singular people. *Chiboya* (for that was the name of the Indian) was one of the Chippewas of Rice Lake, most of whom are now converts to Christianity, and making considerable advancement in civilization and knowledge of agriculture. Hunting and fishing, however, appear to be their favourite pursuits: for these they leave the comfortable houses at the Indian villages, and return at stated times to their forest haunts. I believe it is generally considered that their numbers are diminishing, and some tribes have become nearly if not totally extinct in the Canadas *. The race is slowly passing away from the face of the earth, or mingling by degrees with the colonists, till, a few centuries hence, even the names of their tribes will scarcely remain to tell that they once existed.

When next you send a box or parcel, let me have a few good tracts and hymn-books; as they prize a gift of this sort extremely. I send you a hymn, the one they sang to us in the wigwam; it is the Indian translation, and written by the hunter, Peter's eldest son: he was delighted when I told him I wanted him to copy it for me, that I might send it across the seas to my own country, that English people might see how well Indians could write.

* It is stated that the North-West Company had a census of all the tribes, and that the whole Indian population of that immense continent did not now exceed 100,000 souls. In a Parliamentary document of 1834, the Indians of Lower Canada are estimated at 3,437, and those of Upper Canada at 13,700, which latter number is stated to include those on the shores of Lake Huron, and to the westward.—Ed.

The hunchback Maquin has made me a miniature canoe of birch-bark, which I send; you will prize it as a curiosity, and token of remembrance. The red and black squirrel-skins are for Jane; the feather fans, and papers of feathers, for Sarah. Tell the latter the next time I send a packet home, she shall have specimens fit for stuffing of our splendid red-

Red-bird.

bird, which, I am sure, is the Virginian nightingale; it comes in May or April, and leaves us late in the summer: it exactly corresponds to a stuffed Virginian nightingale that I saw in a fine collection of American birds. The blue-bird is equally lovely, and

Blue-bird.

migrates much about the same time; the plumage is of a celestial blue; but I have never seen one otherwise than upon the wing, so cannot describe it minutely. The cross-bills are very pretty; the male and female quite opposite in colour, one having a lovely mixture of scarlet and orange on the breast and back, shading into greenish olive and brown; the other more like our yellowhammer, only it is not quite so bright in colour, though much softer, and more innocent-looking: they come to our windows and doors in the winter as familiarly as your robins. During the winter most of our birds depart; even the hollow tapping of the red-headed and the small speckled grey and white woodpecker ceases to be heard; the sharp chittering of the squirrel, too, is seldomer distinguished; and silence, awful and unbroken silence, reigns in the forest during the season of midwinter.

I had well nigh forgotten my little favourites, a species of the titmouse, that does not entirely forsake us. Of a bright warm, sunny day we see flocks of these tiny birds swinging among the feathery sprigs of the hemlocks or shrubby pines on the plains or in the forest; and many a time have I stayed my steps to watch their playful frolics, and listen to their gay warbling. I am not quite certain, but I think this is the same little bird that is known among the natives by the name of Thit-a-be-bee; its note, though weak, and with few changes, is not unpleasing; and we prize it from its being almost the only bird that sings during the winter.

I had heard much of the snow-bunting, but never had seen it till the other day, and then not near enough to mark its form or colours. The day was one of uncommon brilliancy; the sky cloudless, and the air almost warm; when, looking towards the lake, I was surprised by the appearance of one of the pine-trees near the shore: it seemed as if covered with stars of silver that twinkled and sparkled against the blue sky. I was so charmed by the novelty, that I ran out to observe them nearer; when, to my surprise, my stars all took flight to another tree, where, by the constant waving and fluttering of their small white wings against the sunlight, they produced the beautiful effect that had at first attracted my observation: soon all the pines within sight of the window were illuminated by these lovely creatures. About mid-day they went away, and I have seen them but once since. They never lit on the ground, or any low tree or bough, for me to examine them nearer.

Of our singing-birds, the robin, the blackbird, and a tiny bird, like our common wren, are those I am most intimate with. The Canadian robin is much larger than our dear robin at home; he is too coarse and large a bird to realize the idea of our little favourite, "the household-bird with the red stomacher," as he is called by Bishop Carey, in a sonnet addressed to Elizabeth, the daughter of James I., on her marriage with the unfortunate Frederic Prince Palatine.

The song of the Canadian robin is by no means despicable; its notes are clear, sweet, and various; it possesses the same cheerful lively character that distinguishes the carol of its namesake; but the general habits of the bird are very dissimilar. The Canadian robin is less sociable with man, but more so with his own species: they assemble in flocks soon after the breeding season is over, and appear very amicable one to another; but seldom, if ever, approach very near to our dwelling. The breast is of a pinkish,

Snow-Bunting.

salmon colour; the head black; the back of a sort of bluish steel, or slate colour; in size they are as big as a thrush.

The blackbird is perhaps our best songster, according to my taste; full as fine as our English blackbird, and much handsomer in its plumage, which is a glossy, changeable, greenish black. The upper part of the wing of the male bird of full growth is of a lively orange; this is not apparent in the younger birds, nor in the female, which is slightly speckled.

Towards the middle of the summer, when the grain begins to ripen, these birds assemble in large flocks: the management of their marauding parties appears to be superintended by the elders of the family. When they are about to descend upon a field of oats or wheat, two or three mount guard as sentinels, and on the approach of danger, cry *Geck-geck-geck;* this precaution seems a work of supererogation, as they are so saucy that they will hardly be frightened away; and if they rise it is only to alight on the same field at a little distance, or fly up to the trees, where their look-out posts are.

They have a peculiarly melancholy call-note at times, which sounds exactly like the sudden twang of a harp-string, vibrating for a second or two on the ear. This, I am inclined to think, they use to collect their distant comrades, as I have never observed it when they were all in full assembly, but when a few were sitting in some tree near the lake's edge. I have called them the "*harpers*," from this peculiar note. I shall tire you with my ornithological sketches, but must enumerate two or three more birds.

The bald eagle frequently flies over our clearing; it has a dark body, and snow-white head. It is sometimes troublesome to the poultry-yards: those we have seen have disdained such low game, and soared majestically away across the lake.

The fish-hawk we occasionally see skimming the surface of the water, and it is regarded as an enemy by those who take delight in spearing fish upon the lakes.

Then we have the night or mosquito-hawk, which may be seen in the air pursuing the insect tribe in the higher regions, whilst hundreds of great dragon-flies pursue them below; notwithstanding their assistance, we are bitten mercilessly by those summer pests the mosquitoes and black flies.

The red-headed woodpecker is very splendid; the head and neck being of a rich crimson; the back, wings, and breast are divided between the most snowy white and jetty black. The incessant tapping of the woodpeckers, and the discordant shriek of the blue jay, are heard from sunrise to sunset, as soon as the spring is fairly set in.

I found a little family of woodpeckers last spring comfortably nested in an old pine, between the bark and the trunk of the tree, where the former had started away, and left a hollow space, in which the old birds had built a soft but careless sort of nest; the little creatures seemed very happy, poking their funny bare heads out to greet the old ones, who were knocking away at the old stumps in their neighbourhood to supply their cravings, as busy as so many carpenters at work.

Baltimore Oriole defending her Nest against the Black Snake.

A very curious bird's-nest was given me by one of our choppers; it was woven over a forked spray, so that it had all the appearance of having been sewn to the bough with grey thread. The nest was only secured at the two sides that formed the angle, but so strong was it fastened that it seemed to resist any weight or pressure of a moderate kind; it was composed of the fibres of the bass-wood bark, which are very thready, and may be drawn to great fineness: on the whole it was a curious specimen of the ingenuity of these admirable little architects. I could not discover the builder; but rather suspect the nest to have belonged to my protégé, the little winter titmouse that I told you of.

The nest of the Canadian robin, which I discovered while seeking for a hen's nest in a bush-heap, just at the further edge of the clearing, is very much like our home-robin's, allowing something for difference of size in the bird, and in the material; the eggs, five in number, were deep blue.

Before I quit the subject of birds, I must recall to your remembrance the little houses that the Americans build for the swallow; I have since found out one of their great reasons for cherishing this useful bird. It appears that a most rooted antipathy exists between this species and the hawk tribe, and no hawk will abide their neighbourhood; as they pursue them for miles, annoying them in every possible way, haunting the hawk like its evil genius: it is most singular that so small a creature should thus overcome one that is the formidable enemy of so many of the feathered race. I should have been somewhat sceptical on the subject, had I not myself been an eye-witness to the fact. I was looking out of my window one bright summer-day, when I noticed a hawk of a large description flying heavily along the lake, uttering cries of distress; within a yard or two of it was a small—in the distance it appeared to me a very small—bird pursuing it closely, and also screaming. I watched this strange pair till the pine-wood hid them from my sight; and I often marvelled at the circumstance, till a very intelligent French Canadian traveller happened to name the fact, and said so great was the value placed on these birds, that they had been sold at high prices to be sent to different parts of the province. They never forsake their old haunts when once naturalized, the same pairs constantly returning, year after year, to their old house.

The singular fact of these swallows driving the hawk from his haunts is worthy of attention; as it is well authenticated, and adds one more to the many interesting and surprising anecdotes recorded by naturalists of the sagacity and instinct of these birds.

I have, however, scribbled so many sheets, that I fear my long letter must weary you.

Adieu.

LETTER XIV.

Utility of Botanical Knowledge.—The Fire-Weed.—Sarsaparilla Plants.—Magnificent Water-Lily.—Rice-Beds.—Indian Strawberry.—Scarlet Columbine.—Ferns.—Grasses.

July 13, 1834.

OUR winter broke up unusually early this year: by the end of February the ground was quite free from snow, and the weather continued all through March mild and pleasant, though not so warm as the preceding year, and certainly more variable. By the last week in April and the beginning of May, the forest-trees had all burst into leaf, with a brilliancy of green that was exquisitely lovely.

On the 14th, 15th, and 16th of May, the air became suddenly cold, with sharp winds from the north-west, and heavy storms of snow that nipped the young buds, and destroyed many of the early-sown vegetable seeds; fortunately for us we were behind-hand with ours, which was very well, as it happened.

Our woods and clearings are now full of beautiful flowers. You will be able to form some idea of them from the dried specimens that I send you. You will recognize among them many of the cherished pets of our gardens and green-houses, which are here flung carelessly from Nature's lavish hand among our woods and wilds.

How often do I wish you were beside me in

my rambles among the woods and clearings: you would be so delighted in searching out the floral treasures of the place.

Deeply do I now regret having so idly neglected your kind offers while at home of instructing me in flower-painting; you often told me the time would come when I should have cause to regret neglecting the golden opportunity before me.

You proved a true prophetess; for I daily lament that I cannot make faithful representations of the flowers of my adopted country, or understand as you would do their botanical arrangement. With some few I have made myself acquainted, but have hardly confidence in my scanty stock of knowledge to venture on scientific descriptions, when I feel conscious that a blunder would be easily detected, and expose me to ridicule and contempt, for an assumption of knowledge that I did not possess. The only botanical work I have at my command is Pursh's North American Flora, from which I have obtained some information; but must confess it is tiresome blundering out Latin descriptions to one who knows nothing of Latin beyond what she derives through a knowledge of Italian.

I have made out a list of the plants most worthy of attention near us; there are many others in the township that I am a stranger to; some there are with whose names I am unacquainted. I subjoin a slight sketch, not with my pencil but my pen, of those flowers that pleased me particularly, or that possessed any remarkable qualities.

The same plants do not grow on cleared land that

formerly occupied the same spot when it was covered with forest-trees. A distinct class of vegetation makes its appearance as soon as the fire has passed over the ground.

The same thing may be remarked with regard to the change that takes place among our forests. As one generation falls and decays, new ones of a different character spring up in their places. This is illustrated in the circumstance of the resinous substance called fat-pine being usually found in places where the living pine is least abundant, and where the ground is occupied by oak, ash, buck, maple, and bass-wood.

The fire-weed, a species of tall thistle of rank and unpleasant scent, is the first plant that appears when the ground has been freed from timbers by fire: if a piece of land lies untilled the first summer after its being chopped, the following spring shows you a smothering crop of this vile weed. The next plant you notice is the sumach, with its downy stalks, and head of deep crimson velvety flowers, forming an upright obtuse bunch at the extremity of the branches: the leaves turn scarlet towards the latter end of the summer. This shrub, though really very ornamental, is regarded as a great pest in old clearings, where the roots run and send up suckers in abundance. The raspberry and wild gooseberry are next seen, and thousands of strawberry plants of different varieties carpet the ground, and mingle with the grasses of the pastures. I have been obliged this spring to root out with remorseless hand hundreds of sarsaparilla plants, and also the celebrated gingseng, which grows abundantly in our woods: it used formerly to be an article of export to China from the States, the root being held in high estimation by the Chinese.

Last week I noticed a succulent plant that made its appearance on a dry sandy path in my garden; it seems to me a variety of the hour-blowing mesembryanthium. It has increased so rapidly that it already covers a large space; the branches converging from the centre of the plant, and sending forth shoots from every joint. The leaves are rather small, three-sided and pointed, thick and juicy, yielding a green liquor when bruised like the common sedums. The stalks are thick and round, of a bright red, and trail along the ground; the leaves spring from each joint, and with them a constant succession of yellow starry flowers, that close in an hour or so from the time they first unfold. I shall send you some of the seed of this plant, as I perceived a number of little green pods that looked like the buds, but which, on opening, proved to be the seed-vessels. This plant covers the earth like a thick mat, and, I am told, is rather troublesome where it likes the soil.

I regret that among my dried plants I could not preserve some specimens of our superb water-lilies and irises; but they were too large and too juicy to dry well. As I cannot send you my favourites, I must describe them to you.

The first, then, is a magnificent water-lily, that I have called by way of distinction the "queen of the lakes," for she sits a crown upon the waters. This magnificent flower is about the size of a moderately large dahlia; it is double to the heart; every row of petals diminishing by degrees in size, and gradually deepening in tint from the purest white to the brightest lemon colour. The buds are very lovely, and may be seen below the surface of the water, in different stages of forwardness from the closely-folded bud, wrapped in its olive-green calix, to the half-blown flower, ready to emerge from its watery prison, and in all its virgin beauty expand its snowy bosom to the sun and genial air. Nor is the beauty of the flower its sole attraction: when unfolded it gives out a rich perfume not unlike the smell of fresh lemons. The leaves are also worthy of attention: at first they are of a fine dark green, but as the flower decays, the leaf changes its hue to a vivid crimson. Where a large bed of these lilies grow closely together, they give quite a sanguine appearance to the waters, that is distinguishable at some distance.

The yellow species of this plant is also very handsome, though it wants the silken texture and delicate colour of the former; I call this the "water-king." The flower presents a deep golden-coloured cup, the concave petals of which are clouded in the centre with a dark reddish-brown, that forms a striking contrast to the gay anthers, which are very numerous, and turn back from the centre of the flower, falling like fringes of gold one over the other, in successive rows, till they fill up the hollow flower-cup.

The shallows of our lakes abound with a variety of

elegant aquatic plants: I know not a more lovely sight than one of these floating gardens. Here you shall behold near the shore a bed of azure fleur-de-lis, from the palest pearl colour varying to the darkest purple. Nearer in shore, in the shallowest water, the rose-coloured persecaria sends up its beautiful spikes trailing below the surface; you see the red stalks and smooth dark green leaves veined underneath with rosy red: it is a very charming variety of this beautiful species of plants. Then a bed of my favourite white lilies, all in full bloom, floating on the water, with their double flowers expanding to the sun; near these, and rising in stately pride, a tall plant, with dark green spear-shaped leaves, and thick spike of bright blue flowers, is seen. I cannot discover the name of this very grand-looking flower, and I neglected to examine its botanical construction; so can give you no clue by which to discover its name or species.

Our rice-beds are far from being unworthy of admiration; seen from a distance they look like low green islands on the lakes: on passing through one of these rice-beds when the rice is in flower, it has a beautiful appearance with its broad grassy leaves and light waving spikes, garnished with pale yellow green blossoms, delicately shaded with reddish purple, from beneath which fall three elegant straw-coloured anthers, which move with every breath of air or slightest motion of the waters. I gathered several spikes when only just opened, but the tiresome things fell to pieces directly they became dry. Next summer I will make another attempt at preserving them, and it may be with better success.

The low shore of the lake is a complete shrubbery. We have a very pretty St. John's-wort, with handsome yellow flowers. The white and pink spiral frutex also abounds with some exquisite upright honeysuckles, shrubby plants about three feet in height; the blossoms grow in pairs or by fours, and hang beneath the light green leaves; elegant trumpet-shaped flowers of a delicate greenish white, which are succeeded by ruby-coloured berries. On gathering a branch of this plant, you cannot but be struck with the elegant arrangement of the flowers along the under part of the stalks. The two blossoms are connected at the nectary of each in a singular manner. The Americans call this honeysuckle "twinflower." I have seen some of the flowers of this plant pale pink: on the whole it is one of the most ornamental shrubs we have. I transplanted some young trees into my garden last spring; they promise to live and do well. I do not find any description of this shrub in Pursh's Flora, but know it to be a species of honeysuckle, from the class and order, the shape and colour of the leaves, the stalks, the trumpet-shaped blossom and the fruit; all bearing a resemblance to our honeysuckles in some degree. There is a tall upright bush, bearing large yellow trumpet-shaped flowers, springing from the extremities of the branches; the involucrum forms a boat-shaped cup that encircles the flowers from which they seem to spring, something after the manner of the scarlet trumpet-honeysuckle. The leaves and blossoms of this plant are coarse, and by no means to compare to the former.

We have a great variety of curious orchises, some brown and yellow, others pale flesh-coloured, striped with crimson. There is one species grows to the height of two feet, bearing long spikes of pale purple flowers; a white one with most fragrant smell, and a delicate pink one with round head of blossoms, finely fringed like the water-pinks that grow in our marshes; this is a very pretty flower, and grows in the beaver meadows.

Last autumn I observed in the pine-wood near us a very curious plant; it came up with naked brown stems, branching off like some miniature tree; the stalks of this plant were brown, slightly freckled and beset with little knobs. I watched the progress of maturity in this strange plant with some degree of interest, towards the latter end of October; the little knobs, which consisted of two angular hard cases, not unlike, when fully opened, to a boat in shape, burst asunder and displayed a pale straw-coloured chaffy substance that resembled fine saw-dust: these must have been the anthers, but they bore more resemblance to seeds; this singular flower would have borne examination with a microscope. One peculiarity that I observed, was, that on pulling up a plant with its roots, I found the blossoms open under ground, springing up from the lowest part of the flower-stems, and just as far advanced to maturity as those that grew on the upper stalks, excepting that they were somewhat blanched, from being covered up from the air. I can find no description of this plant, nor any person but myself seems to have taken notice of it. The specimen I had on being dried became so brittle that it fell to pieces.

I have promised to collect some of the most singular of our native flowers for one of the Professors of Botany in the Edinburgh University.

We have a very handsome plant that bears the closest affinity to our potatoe in its floral construction; it grows to the height of two or three feet in favourable situations, and sends up many branches; the blossoms are large, purely white, freckled near the bottom of the corolla with brownish yellow spots; the corolla is undivided: this is evidently the same plant as the cultivated potatoe, though it does not appear to form apples at the root. The fruit is very handsome, egg-shaped, of a beautiful apricot colour when ripe, and of a shining tempting appearance; the smell, however, betrays its poisonous nature: on opening one of the fruits you find it consists of a soft pulp filled with shining black seeds. The plant continues in blossom from June till the 'first frosts wither the leaves; it is far less coarse than the potatoe; the flower, when full blown, is about the size of a half-crown, and quite flat; I think it is what you call salver-shaped: it delights in light loamy soil, growing on the upturned roots of fallen trees, where the ground is inclined to be sandy. I have never seen this plant elsewhere than on our own fallow.

The hepatica is the first flower of the Canadian spring: it gladdens us with its tints of azure, pink, and white, early in April, soon after the snows have melted from the earth. The Canadians call it snowflower, from its coming so soon after the snow disappears. We see its gay tufts of flowers in the open clearings and the deep recesses of the forests; its leaves are also an enduring ornament through the open months of the year; you see them on every grassy mound and mossy root: the shades of blue are very various and delicate, the white anthers forming a lovely contrast with the blue petals.

The wood-cress, or as it is called by some, ginger-cress, is a pretty white cruciform flower; it is highly aromatic in flavour; the root is white and fleshy, having the pungency of horseradish. The leaves are of a sad green, sharply notched, and divided in three lobes; the leaves of some of them are slightly variegated; the plant delights in rich moist vegetable mould, especially on low and slightly swampy ground; the flower-stalk is sometimes naked, sometimes leafed, and is crowned with a loose spike of whitish cruciform flowers.

There is a cress that grows in pretty green tufts at the bottom of the waters in the creeks and small rivulets: it is more delicate and agreeable in flavour than any of the land-cresses; the leaves are of a pale tender green, winged and slender; the plant looks like a green cushion at the bottom of the water. The flowers are yellow, cruciform, and insignificant; it makes a very acceptable salad in the early spring, and at the fall of the year. There are also several species of land-cress, and plants resembling some of the cabbage tribes, that might be used as spring vegetables. There are several species of spinach, one known here by the name of lamb's quarter, that grows in great profusion about our garden, and in rich soil rises to two feet, and is very luxuriant in its foliage; the leaves are covered with a white rough powder. The top shoots and tender parts of this vegetable are boiled with pork, and, in place of a more delicate pot-herb, is very useful.

Then we have the Indian turnip; this is a very handsome arum, the root of which resembles the capava, I am told, when boiled: the leaves of this arum are handsome, slightly tinged with purple. The spathe is of a lively green, striped with purple: the Indians use the root as a medicine, and also as an esculent; it is often eaten by the settlers as a vegetable, but I never tasted it myself. Pursh calls this species *Arum atropurpureum.*

I must not pass over one of our greatest ornaments, the strawberry blite, strawberry-bearing spinach, or Indian strawberry, as it is variously named. This singular plant throws out many branches from one stem, these are garnished with handsome leaves, resembling in appearance our long-leaved garden spinach; the finest of this plant is of a bright crimson, pulpy like the strawberry, and containing a number of purple seeds, partially embedded in the surface, after the same manner as the strawberry. The fruit grows close to the stalk, completely surrounding it, and forming a long spike of the richest crimson berries. I have gathered branches a foot in length, closely covered with the beautiful looking fruit, and have regretted that it was so insipid in its flavour as to make it uneatable. On the banks of creeks and in rich ground, it grows most luxuriantly, one root sending up twenty or thirty branches, drooping with the weight of their magnificent burden. As the middle and superior stems ripen and decay, the lateral ones come on, presenting a constant succession of fruit from July till the frosts nip them off in September.

The Indians use the juice of this plant as a dye, and are said to eat the berries: it is often made use of as a substitute for red ink, but it is liable to fade unless mingled with alum. A friend of mine told me she had been induced to cross a letter she was sending to a relative in England with this strawberry ink, but not having taken the precaution to fix the colour, when the anxiously expected epistle arrived, one-half of it proved quite unintelligible, the colours having faded nearly to white; so that instead of affording satisfaction, it proved only a source of vexation and embarrassment to the reader, and of mortification to the writer.

The blood-root, sanguinaria, or puccoon, as it is termed by some of the native tribes, is worthy of attention from the root to the flower. As soon as the sun of April has warmed the earth and loosened it from its frozen bonds, you may distinguish a number of purely white buds, elevated on a naked footstalk, and partially enfolded in a handsome vine-shaped leaf, of a pale bluish green, curiously veined on the under side with pale orange. The leaf springs singly from a thick juicy fibrous root, which, on being broken, emits a quantity of liquor from its pores of a bright orange scarlet colour: this juice is used by the Indians as a dye, and also in the cure of rheumatic, and cutaneous complaints. The flowers of the sanguinaria resemble the white crocus very closely: when it first comes up the bud is supported by the leaf, and is folded together with it; the flower, however, soon elevates itself above its protector, while the leaf having performed its duty of guardian to the tender bud, expands to its full size. A rich black vegetable mould at the edges of the clearings seems the favourite soil for this plant.

The scarlet columbine is another of my favourite flowers; it is bright red, with yellow linings to the tubes. The nectaries are more elongated than the garden columbines, and form a sort of mural crown, surmounted with little balls at the tips. A tall graceful plant, with its brilliant waving blossoms, is this columbine; it grows both in the sunshine and the shade, not perhaps in deep shady woods, but where the under brush has been removed by the running of the fire or the axe of the chopper; it seems even to flourish in poor stony soils, and may be found near every dwelling. The feathered columbine delights in moist open swamps, and the banks of rivulets; it grows to the height of three, and even four and five feet, and is very ornamental.

Of Violets, we have every variety of colour, size and shape, looking only the delightful *viola odorata* of our home woodlands: yet I know not why we should quarrel with these meek daughters of the spring, because they want the fragrance of their more favoured sisters. Many of your wood-violets, though very beautiful, are also devoid of scent; here variety of colour ought to make some amends for want of perfume. We have violets of every shade of blue, some veined with purple, others shaded with darker blue. We have the delicate white, pencilled with purple: the bright brimstone coloured with black veinings: the pale primrose with dark blue veins; the two latter are remarkable for the luxuriance and size of the leaves: the flowers spring in bunches, several from each joint, and are succeeded by large capsules covered with thick white cottony down. There is a species of violet that grows in the woods, the leaves of which are exceedingly large; so are the seed-vessels, but the flower is so small and insignificant, that it is only to be observed by a close examination of the plant; this has given rise to the vulgar belief that it blooms under ground. The flowers are a pale greenish yellow. Bryant's beautiful poem of the Yellow Violet is descriptive of the first-mentioned violet.

There is an elegant *viola tricolor*, that blooms in the autumn; it is the size of a small heart's-ease, and is pure white, pale purple, and lilac; the upper petals are white, the lower lip purple, and the side wings a reddish lilac. I was struck with the elegance of this rare flower on a journey to Peterborough, on my way to Cobourg; I was unable to preserve the specimens, and have not travelled that road since. The flower grew among wild clover on the open side of the road; the leaves were small, roundish, and of a dark sad green.

Of the tall shrubby asters, we have several beautiful varieties, with large pale blue lilac, or white flowers; others with very small white flowers and crimson anthers, which look like tufts of red down, spangled with gold-dust; these anthers have a pretty effect, contrasted with the white starry petals. There is one variety of the tall asters that I have seen on the plains, it has flowers about the size of a sixpence, of a soft pearly tint of blue, with brown anthers; this plant grows very tall, and branches from the parent stem in many graceful flowery boughs; the leaves of this species are of a purple red on the under side, and inclining to heart-shape; the leaves and stalks are hairy.

I am not afraid of wearying you with my floral sketches, I have yet many to describe; among these are those elegant little evergreens, that abound in this country, under the name of winter-greens, of which there are three or four remarkable for beauty of foliage, flower, and fruit. One of these winter-greens that abounds in our pine-woods is extremely beautiful; it seldom exceeds six inches in height; the leaves are a bright shining green, of a long narrow oval, delicately notched like the edges of a rose-leaf; and the plant emerges from beneath the snow in the early part of the year, as soon as the first thaw takes place, as fresh and verdant as before they were covered up: it seems to be a shy blossomer. I have never seen specimens of the flowers in bloom but twice; these I carefully preserved for you, but the dried plant will afford but an imperfect idea of the original. You always called, you know, your dried specimens corpses of plants, and said, that when well painted, their representations were far more like themselves. The flower-stalk rises two or three inches from the centre of the plant, and is crowned with round crimson buds and blossoms, consisting of five petals, deepening from the palest pink to the brightest blush colour; the stigma is of an emerald greenness, forming a slightly ribbed turban in the centre, around which are disposed ten stamens of an amethyst colour: in short, this is one of the gems of the floral world, and might aptly be compared to an emerald ring, set round with amethysts. The contrast of colours in this flower is exceedingly pleasing, and the crimson buds and shining ever-green leaves are scarcely less to be admired than the flower; itself it would be considered a great acquisition to your collection of American shrubs, but I doubt if it would flourish when removed from the shade of the pine-woods. This plant appears to be the *Chimaphila corymbosa*, or winter-green, described by Pursh, with some trifling variation in the colour of the petals.

Another of our winter-greens grows in abundance on the Rice-Lake plains; the plant does not exceed four inches; the flowers are in little loose bunches, pale greenish white, in shape like the blossom of the arbutus; the berries are bright scarlet, and are known by the name of winter-berry, and partridge-berry; this must be *Gualtheria procumbens*. But a more beautiful little evergreen of the same species is to be found in our cedar swamps, under the name of pigeon-berry; it resembles the arbutus in leaf and flower more closely than the former plant; the scarlet berry is inserted in a scarlet cup or receptacle, divided at the edge in five points; it is fleshy, seeming to partake of the same nature as the fruit. The blossoms of this elegant little shrub, like the arbutus, of which it looks like the miniature, appear in drooping bunches at the same time the ripened berry of the former year is in perfection; this circumstance adds not a little to the charm of the plant. If I mistake not, this is the *Gualtheria Shallon*, which Pursh likens to the arbutus: this is also one of our winter-greens.

There is another pretty trailing plant, with delicate little funnel-shaped flowers, and a profusion of small dark green round buds, slightly variegated, and bright red berries, which are produced at the extremities of the branches. The blossoms of this plant grow in pairs, closely connected at the germen; so much so, that the scarlet fruit that supersedes the flowers appears like a double berry, each berry containing the seeds of both flowers and a double eye. The plant is also called winter-green, or twin-berry; it resembles none of the other winter-greens; it grows in mossy woods, trailing along the ground, appearing to delight in covering little hillocks and inequalities of the ground. In elegance of growth, delicacy of flower, and brightness of berry, this winter-green is little inferior to any of the former.

There is a plant in our woods, known by the names of man-drake, may-apple, and duck's-foot: the botanical name of the plant is Podophyllum; it belongs to the class and order *Polyandria monogynia*. The blossom is yellowish white, the corolla consisting of six petals; the fruit is oblong; when ripe, of a greenish yellow; in size that of an olive, or large damson; when fully ripe it has the flavour of preserved tamarind, a pleasant brisk acid; it appears to be a shy bearer, though it increases rapidly in rich moist woodlands. The leaves come up singly, are palmated and shade the ground very much when a number of them grow near each other; the stalk supports the leaf from the centre: when they first appear above the ground, they resemble a folded umbrella or parasol, all the edges of the leaves bending downward, by degrees expanding into a slightly convex canopy. The fruit would make a delicate preserve with sugar.

The lily tribe offer an extensive variety from the most minute to the very largest flowers. The red martagon grows abundantly on our plains; the dog's-tooth violet, *Erythronium*, with its spotted leaves and bending yellow blossom, delicately dashed with crimson spots within, and marked with fine purple lines on the outer part of the petal, proves a great attraction in our woods, where these plants increase: they form a beautiful bed; the leaves come up singly, one from each separate tuber. There are two varieties of this flower, the pale yellow, with neither spots nor lines, and the deep yellow with both; the anthers of this last are reddish-orange, and thickly covered with a fine powdery substance. The daffodil of our woods is a delicate bending flower, of a pale yellow; the leaves grow up the flower-stalk at intervals; three or more flowers usually succeed each other at the extremity of the stalk: its height is from six to eight inches; it delights in the deep shade of moist woods. This seems to unite the description of the jonquil and daffodil.

A very beautiful plant of the lily tribe abounds both in our woods and clearings; for want of a better name, I call it the douri-lily, though it is widely spread over a great portion of the continent. The

Americans term the white and red varieties of this species, the "white" and "red death." The flower is either deep red, or of a dazzling white, though the latter is often found stained with a delicate blush-pink, or a deep green; the latter appears to be caused by the calix running into the petal. Wherefore it bears so formidable a name has not yet transpired. The flower consists of three petals, the calix three; it belongs to the class and order *Hexandria monogynia;* style, three-cleft; seed-vessel of three valves; soil, dry woods and cleared lands; leaves growing in three, springing from the joints, large round, but a little pointed at the extremities.

We have lilies of the valley, and their cousins the Solomon's seals, a small flowered turk's-cap, of pale primrose colour, with an endless variety of small flowers of the lily tribe, remarkable for beauty of foliage or delicacy of form.

Our Ferns are very elegant and numerous; I have no less than eight different specimens, gathered from our immediate neighbourhood, some of which are extremely elegant, especially one that I call the "fairy fern," from its lightness. One elastic stem, of a purplish-red colour, supports several light branches, which are subdivided and furnished with innumerable leafets; each leafet has a footstalk, that attaches it to the branch, of so slight and hair-like a substance that the least breath of air sets the whole plant in motion.

Could we but imagine Canada to have been the scene of fairy revels, we should declare that these graceful ferns were well suited to shade the elfin court of Oberon and Titania.

When this fern first appears above the ground, it is scarcely to be distinguished from the decaying wood of the fallen pines; it is then of a light reddish brown, curiously curled up. In May and June, the leaves unfold, and soon assume the most delicate tint of green; they are almost transparent: the cattle are very fond of this fern.

The mocassin flower or lady's-slipper (mark the odd coincidence between the common name of the American and English species) is one of our most remarkable flowers; both on account of its beauty and its singularity of structure. Our plains and dry sunny pastures produce several varieties; among these, the *Cypripedium pubescens*, or yellow mocassin, and the *C. Arietinum* are the most beautiful of the species. The colour of the lip of the former is a lively canary yellow, dashed with deep crimson spots. The upper petals consist of two short and two long; in texture and colour resembling the sheath of some of the narcissus tribe; the short ones stand erect, like a pair of ears; the long or lateral pair are three times the length of the former, very narrow, and elegantly twisted, like the spiral horns of the Walachian ram: on raising a thick yellow fleshy sort of lid, in the middle of the flower, you perceive the exact face of an Indian hound, perfect in all its parts,—the eyes, nose, and mouth; below this depends an open sack, slightly gathered round at the opening, which gives it a hollow and prominent appearance; the inside of this bag is delicately dashed with deep crimson, or black spots: the stem of the flower is thick towards the upper part, and takes a direct bend; the leaves are large oval, a little pointed and ribbed; the plant scarcely exceeds six inches: the elegant colour and silken texture of the lower lip or bag renders this flower very much more beautiful to my taste than the purple and white variety, though the latter is much more striking on account of the size of the flower and leaves, besides the contrast between the white and red, or white and purple colours.

The formation of this species resembles the other, only with this difference, the horns are not twisted, and the face is that of a monkey; even the comical expression of the animal is preserved with such admirable fidelity, as to draw a smile from every one that sees the odd restless-looking visage, with its prominent round black eyes peering forth from under its covering.

These plants belong to class and order *Gynandria diàndria;* are described with some little variation by Pursh, who, however, likens the face of the latter to that of a sheep: if a sheep sat for the picture, methinks it must have been the most mischievous of the flock.

There is a curious aquatic plant that grows in shallow, stagnant, or slow-flowing waters; it will contain a full wine-glass of water. A poor soldier brought it to me, and told me it resembled a plant he used to see in Egypt, that the soldiers called the "Soldier's drinking-cup;" and many a good draught of pure water, he said, I have drank from them.

Another specimen was presented me by a gentleman, who knew my predilection for strange plants; he very aptly gave it the name of "Pitcher-plant;" it very probably belongs to the tribe that bear that name.

The flowers that afford the most decided perfumes are our wild roses, which possess a delicious scent: the milk-weed, which gives out a smell not unlike the night-blowing stock; the purple monarda, which is fragrance itself from the root to the flower, and even after months' exposure to the wintry atmosphere; its dried leaves and seed-vessels are so sweet as to impart perfume to your hands or clothes. All our Mints are strong scented: the lily of the valley is remarkable for its fine smell; then there is my queen of the lakes, and her consort, the water-king, with many other flowers I cannot now enumerate. Certain it is that among such a vast assemblage of flowers, there are, comparatively, very few that are gifted with fragrant scents. Some of our forest-trees give out a fine perfume. I have often paused in my walks to inhale the fragrance from a cedar swamp on some sunny day while the boughs were still wet with the dew-drops or recently fallen shower.

Nor is the balsam-poplar, or tacamahac, less delightfully fragrant, especially while the gummy buds are just beginning to unfold; this is an elegant growing tree, where it has room to expand into boughs. It grows chiefly on the shores of the lakes and in open swamps, but it also forms one of the attractions of our plains, with its silver bark and waving foliage; it emits a resinous clear gum in transparent globules on the bark, and the buds are covered with a highly aromatic gummy fluid.

Our Grasses are highly interesting; there are varieties that are wholly new to me, and when dried form the most elegant ornaments to our chimney-pieces, and would look very graceful on a lady's head; only fashionists always prefer the artificial to the natural.

One or two species of grass that I have gathered bear a close but of course minute resemblance to the Indian corn, having a top feather and eight-sided spike of little grains disposed at the side-joints. The *sisyrinchium*, or blue-eyed grass, is a pretty little flower of an azure blue, with golden spot at the base of each petal; the leaves are flat, stiff, and flag-like; this pretty flower grows in tufts on light sandy soils.

I have given you a description of the flowers most worthy of attention; and, though it is very probable some of my descriptions may not be exactly in the technical language of the correct botanist, I have at least described them as they appear.

My dear boy seems already to have a taste for flowers, which I shall encourage as much as possible. It is a study that tends to refine and purify the mind, and can be made, by simple steps, a ladder to heaven, as it were, by teaching a child to look with love and admiration to that bountiful God who created and made flowers so fair to adorn and fructify this earth.

Farewell, my dear sister.

LETTER XV.

Recapitulation of various Topics.—Progress of Settlement.—Canada, the Land of Hope.—Visit to the Family of a Naval Officer.—Squirrels.—Visit to, and Story of, an Emigrant Clergyman.—His early Difficulties.—The Temper, Disposition, and Habits of Emigrants essential Ingredients in Failure or Success.

September the 20th, 1834.

I PROMISED when I parted from you before I left England to write as soon as I could give you any satisfactory account of our settlement in this country. I shall do my best to redeem that promise, and forward you a slight sketch of our proceedings, with such remarks on the natural features of the place in which we have fixed our abode, as I think likely to afford you interest or amusement. Prepare your patience, then, my dear friend, for a long and rambling epistle, in which I may possibly prove somewhat of a Will-o'-the-wisp, and having made you follow me in my desultory wanderings,—

Over hill, over dale,
Through bush, through briar,
Over park, over pale,
Through flood, through fire,—

Possibly leave you in the midst of a big cedar swamp, or among the pathless mazes of our wild woods, without a clue to guide you, or even a *blaze* to light you on your way.

You will have heard, through my letters to my dear

mother, of our safe arrival at Quebec, of my illness at Montreal, of all our adventures and misadventures during our journey up the country, till after much weary wandering we finally found a home and resting-place with a kind relative, whom it was our happiness to meet after a separation of many years.

As my husband was anxious to settle in the neighbourhood of one so nearly connected with me, thinking it would rob the woods of some of the loneliness that most women complain so bitterly of, he purchased a lot of land on the shores of a beautiful lake, one of a chain of small lakes belonging to the Otanabee river.

Here, then, we are established, having now some five-and-twenty acres cleared, and a nice house built. Our situation is very agreeable, and each day increases its value. When we first came up to live in the bush, with the exception of S———, here were but two or three settlers near us, and no roads cut out. The only road that was available for bringing up goods from the nearest town was on the opposite side of the water, which was obliged to be crossed on a log, or birch-bark canoe; the former is nothing better than a large pine-log hollowed with the axe, so as to contain three or four persons; it is flat-bottomed, and very narrow, on which account it is much used on these shallow waters. The birch canoe is made of sheets of birch bark, ingeniously fashioned and sewn together by the Indians with the tough roots of the cedar, young pine, or larch (tamarack, as it is termed by the Indians); it is exceedingly light, so that it can be carried by two persons easily, or even by one. These, then, were our ferry-boats, and very frail they are, and require great nicety in their management; they are worked in the water with paddles, either kneeling or standing. The squaws are very expert in the management of the canoes, and preserve their balance with admirable skill, standing up while they impel the little bark with great velocity through the water.

Very great is the change that a few years have effected in our situation. A number of highly respectable settlers have purchased land along the shores of these lakes, so that we no longer want society. The roads are now cut several miles above us, and though far from good can be travelled by waggons and sleighs, and are, at all events, better than none.

A village has started up where formerly a thick pine-wood covered the ground; we have now within a short distance of us an excellent saw-mill, a grist-mill, and store, with a large tavern and many good dwellings. A fine timber bridge, on stone piers, was erected last year to connect the opposite townships and lessen the distance to and from Peterborough; and though it was unfortunately swept away early last spring by the unusual rising of the Otanabee lakes, a new and more substantial one has risen upon the ruins of the former, through the activity of an enterprising young Scotchman, the founder of the village.

But the grand work that is, sooner or later, to raise this portion of the district from its present obscurity, is the opening a line of navigation from Lake Huron through Lake Simcoe, and so through our chain of small lakes to Rice Lake, and finally through the Trent to the Bay of Quinte. This noble work would prove of incalculable advantage, by opening a direct communication between Lake Huron and the inland townships at the back of the Ontario with the St. Laurence. This project has already been under the consideration of the Governor, and is at present exciting great interest in the country: sooner or later there is little doubt but that it will be carried into effect. It presents some difficulties and expense, but it would be greatly to the advantage and prosperity of the country, and be the means of settling many of the back townships bordering upon these lakes.

I must leave it to abler persons than myself to discuss at large the policy and expediency of the measure; but as I suppose you have no intention of emigrating to our backwoods, you will be contented with my cursory view of the matter, and believe, as in friendship you are bound to do, that it is a desirable thing to open a market for inland produce.

Canada is the land of hope; here every thing is new; every thing going forward; it is scarcely possible for arts, sciences, agriculture, manufactures, to retrograde; they must keep advancing; though in some situations the progress may seem slow, in others they are proportionably rapid.

There is a constant excitement on the minds of emigrants, particularly in the partially settled townships, that greatly assists in keeping them from desponding. The arrival of some enterprising person gives a stimulus to those about him: a profitable speculation is started, and lo, the value of the land in the vicinity rises to double and treble what it was thought worth before; so that, without any design of befriending his neighbours, the schemes of one settler being carried into effect shall benefit a great number. We have already felt the beneficial effect of the access of respectable emigrants locating themselves in this township, as it has already increased the value of our own land in a three-fold degree.

All this, my dear friend, you will say is very well, and might afford subject for a wise discussion between grave men, but will hardly amuse us women; so pray turn to some other theme, and just tell me how you contrive to pass your time among the bears and wolves of Canada.

One lovely day last June I went by water to visit the bride of a young naval officer, who had purchased a very pretty lot of land some two miles higher up the lake; our party consisted of my husband, baby, and myself; we met a few pleasant friends, and enjoyed our excursion much. Dinner was laid out in the *stoup*, which, as you may not know what is meant by the word, I must tell you that it means a sort of wide verandah, supported on pillars, often of unbarked logs; the floor is either of earth beaten hard, or plank; the roof covered with sheets of bark or else shingled. These stoups are of Dutch origin, and were introduced, I have been told, by the first Dutch settlers in the states, since which they have found their way all over the colonies.

Wreathed with the scarlet creeper, a native plant of our woods and wilds, the wild vine, and also with the hop, which here grows luxuriantly, with no labour or attention to its culture, these stoups have a very rural appearance; in summer serving the purpose of an open ante-room, in which you can take your meals and enjoy the fanning breeze without being inconvenienced by the extreme heat of the noon-day sun.

The situation of the house was remarkably well chosen, just on the summit of a little elevated plain, the ground sloping with a steep descent to a little valley, at the bottom of which a bright rill of water divided the garden from the opposite corn-fields, which clothed a corresponding bank. In front of the stoup, where we dined, the garden was laid out with a smooth plot of grass, surrounded with borders of flowers, and separated from a ripening field of wheat by a light railed fence, over which the luxuriant hop-vine flung its tendrils and graceful blossoms. Now I must tell you the hop is cultivated for the purpose of making a barm for raising bread. As you take great interest in housewifery concerns, I shall send you a recipe for what we call hop-rising*.

The Yankees use a fermentation of salt, flour, and warm water or milk; but though the *salt-rising* makes beautiful bread to look at, being far whiter and firmer than the hop-yeast bread, there is a peculiar flavour imparted to the flour that does not please every one's taste, and it is very difficult to get your salt-rising to work in very cold weather.

And now, having digressed while I gave you my recipes, I shall step back to my party within the stoup, which, I can assure you, was very pleasant, and most cordially disposed to enjoy the meeting. We had books and drawings, and good store of pretty Indian toys, the collection of many long

* See Appendix.

voyages to distant shores, to look at and admire. Soon after sun-set we walked down through the woods to the landing at the lake shore, where we found our bark canoe ready to convey us home.

During our voyage, just at the head of the rapids, our attention was drawn to some small object in the water, moving very swiftly along; there were various opinions as to the swimmer, some thinking it to be a water-snake, others a squirrel, or a musk-rat; a few swift strokes of the paddles brought us up so as to intercept the passage of the little voyager; it proved to be a fine red squirrel, bound on a voyage of discovery from a neighbouring island. The little animal, with a courage and address that astonished his pursuers, instead of seeking safety in a different direction, sprung lightly on the point of the uplifted paddle, and from thence with a bound to the head of my astonished baby, and having gained my shoulder, leaped again into the water, and made direct for the shore, never having deviated a single point from the line he was swimming in when he first came in sight of our canoe. I was surprised and amused by the agility and courage displayed by this innocent creature; I could hardly have given credence to the circumstance, had I not been an eye-witness of its conduct, and moreover been wetted plentifully on my shoulder by the sprinkling of water from his coat.

Perhaps you may think my squirrel anecdote incredible; but I can vouch for the truth of it on my own personal experience, as I not only saw but also felt it: the black squirrels are most lovely and elegant animals, considerably larger than the red, the grey, and the striped: the latter are called by the Indians "chit-munks."

We were robbed greatly by these little depredators last summer; the red squirrels used to carry off great quantities of our Indian corn not only from the stalks, while the crop was ripening, but they even came into the house through some chinks in the log-walls, and carried off vast quantities of the grain, stripping it very adroitly from the cob, and conveying the grain away to their storehouses in some hollow log or subterranean granary.

These little animals are very fond of the seeds of the pumpkins, and you will see the soft creatures whisking about among the cattle, carrying away the seeds as they are scattered by the beasts in breaking the pumpkins: they also delight in the seeds of the sunflowers, which grow to a gigantic height in our gardens and clearings. The fowls are remarkably fond of the sunflower-seeds, and I saved the plants with the intention of laying up a good store of winter food for my poor chicks. One day I went to cut the ripe heads, the largest of which was the size of a large dessert-plate, but found two wicked red squirrels busily employed gathering in the seeds, not for me, be sure, but themselves. Not contented with picking out the seeds, these little thieves dexterously sawed through the stalks, and conveyed away whole heads at once: so bold were they that they would not desist when I approached till they had secured their object, and, encumbered with a load twice the weight of their own agile bodies, ran with a swiftness along the rails, and over root, stump, and log, till they eluded my pursuit.

Red Squirrels.

Great was the indignation expressed by this thrifty little pair on returning again for another load to find the plant divested of the heads. I had cut what remained and put them in a basket in the sun, on a small block in the garden, close to the open glass-door, on the steps of which I was sitting shelling some seed-beans, when the squirrels drew my attention to them by their sharp scolding notes, elevating their fine feathery tails and expressing the most lively indignation at the invasion: they were not long before they discovered the Indian basket with the ravished treasure; a few rapid movements brought the little pair to the rails within a few paces of me and the sunflower-heads; here, then, they paused, and sitting up looked in my face with the most imploring gestures. I was too much amused by their perplexity to help them, but turning away my head to speak to the child, they darted forward, and in another minute had taken possession of one of the largest of the heads, which they conveyed away, first one carrying it a few yards, then the other, it being too bulky for one alone to carry it far at a time. In short, I was so well amused by watching their manœuvres that I suffered them to rob me of all my store. I saw a little family of tiny squirrels at play in the spring on the top of a hollow log, and really I think they were, without exception, the liveliest, most graceful creatures I ever looked upon.

The flying-squirrel is a native of our woods, and exceeds in beauty, to my mind, any of the tribe. Its colour is the softest, most delicate tint of grey; the fur thick and short, and as silken as velvet; the eyes like all the squirrel kind, are large, full, and soft the whiskers and long hair about the nose black; the membrane that assists this little animal in its flight is white and delicately soft in texture, like the fur of the chinchilla; it forms a ridge of fur between the fore and hind legs; the tail is like an elegant broad grey feather. I was agreeably surprised by the appearance of this exquisite little creature; the pictures I had seen giving it a most inelegant and *bat-*

Flying Squirrel.

like look, almost disgusting. The young ones are easily tamed, and are very playful and affectionate when under confinement.

How my little friend Emily would delight in such a pet! Tell her if ever I should return to dear old England, I will try to procure one for her; but at present she must be contented with the stuffed specimens of the black, red, and striped squirrels which I enclose in my parcel. I wish I could offer you any present more valuable, but our arts and manufactures being entirely British, with the exception of the Indians' toys, I should find it a difficult matter to send you any thing worth your attention; therefore I am obliged to have recourse to the natural productions of our woods as tokens of remembrance to our friends *at home*, for it is ever thus we speak of the land of our birth.

You wish to know if I am happy and contented in my situation, or if my heart pines after my native land. I will answer you candidly, and say that, as far as regards matters of taste, early association, and all those holy ties of kindred, and old affections that make "home" in all countries, and among all nations in the world, a hallowed spot, I must ever give the preference to Britain.

On the other hand, a sense of the duties I have chosen, and a feeling of conformity to one's situation, lessen the regret I might be inclined to indulge in. Besides, there are new and delightful ties that bind me to Canada: I have enjoyed much domestic happiness since I came hither;—and is it not the birthplace of my dear child? Have I not here first tasted the rapturous delight arising from maternal feelings? When my eye rests on my smiling darling, or I feel his warm breath upon my cheek, I would not exchange the joy that fills my breast for any pleasure the world could offer me. "But this feeling is not confined to the solitude of your Canadian forests, my dear friend," you will say. I know it; but here there is nothing to interfere with your little nursling. You are not tempted by the pleasures of a gay world to forget your duties as a mother; there is nothing to supplant him in your heart; his presence endears every place; and you learn to love the spot that gave him birth, and to think with complacency upon the country, because it is *his* country; and in looking forward to his future welfare you naturally become doubly interested in the place that is one day to be his.

Perhaps I rather estimate the country by my own feelings; and when I find, by impartial survey of my present life, that I am to the full as happy, if not really happier, than I was in the old country, I cannot but value it.

Possibly, if I were to enter into a detail of the advantages I possess, they would appear of a very negative character in the eyes of persons revelling in all the splendour and luxury that wealth could procure, in a country in which nature and art are so eminently favourable towards what is usually termed the pleasures of life; but I never was a votary at the shrine of luxury or fashion. A round of company, a routine of pleasure, were to me sources of weariness, if not of disgust. "There's nothing in all this to satisfy the heart," says Schiller; and I admit the force of the sentiment.

I was too much inclined to spurn with impatience the fetters that etiquette and fashion are wont to impose on society, till they rob its followers of all freedom and independence of will; and they soon are obliged to live for a world that in secret they despise and loathe, for a world, too, that usually regards them with contempt, because they dare not act with an independence, which would be crushed directly it was displayed.

And I must freely confess to you that I do prize and enjoy my present liberty in this country exceedingly: in this we possess an advantage over you, and over those that inhabit the towns and villages in *this* country, where I see a ridiculous attempt to keep up an appearance that is quite foreign to the situation of those that practise it. Few, very few, are the emigrants that come to the colonies, unless it is with the view of realizing an independence for themselves or their children. Those that could afford to live in ease at home, believe me, would never expose themselves to the privations and disagreeable consequences of a settler's life in Canada: therefore, this is the natural inference we draw, that the emigrant has come hither under the desire and natural hope of bettering his condition, and benefiting a family that he had not the means of settling in life in the home country. It is foolish, then, to launch out in a style of life that every one knows cannot be maintained; rather ought such persons to rejoice in the consciousness that they can, if they please, live according to their circumstances, without being the less regarded for the practice of prudence, economy, and industry.

Now, we *bush-settlers* are more independent: we do what we like; we dress as we find most suitable, and most convenient; we are totally without the fear of any Mr. or Mrs. Grundy; and having shaken off the trammels of Grundyism, we laugh at the absurdity of those who voluntarily forge afresh and hug their chains.

If our friends come to visit us unexpectedly we make them welcome to our humble homes, and give them the best we have; but if our fare be indifferent, we offer it with good will, and no apologies are made or expected: they would be out of place; as every one is aware of the disadvantages of a new settlement; and any excuses for want of variety, or the delicacies of the table, would be considered rather in the light of a tacit reproof to your guest for having unseasonably put your hospitality to the test.

Our society is mostly military or naval; so that we meet on equal grounds, and are, of course, well acquainted with the rules of good breeding and polite life; too much so to allow any deviation from those laws that good taste, good sense, and good feeling have established among persons of our class.

Yet here it is considered by no means derogatory to the wife of an officer or gentleman to assist in the work of the house, or to perform its entire duties, if occasion requires it; to understand the mystery of soap, candle, and sugar-making; to make bread, butter, and cheese, or even to milk her own cows; to knit and spin, and prepare the wool for the loom. In these matters we bush-ladies have a wholesome disregard of what Mr. or Mrs. So-and-so thinks or says. We pride ourselves on conforming to circumstances; and as a British officer must needs be a gentleman and his wife a lady, perhaps we repose quietly on that incontestable proof of our gentility, and can afford to be useful without injuring it.

Our husbands adopt a similar line of conduct: the officer turns his sword into a ploughshare, and his lance into a sickle; and if he be seen ploughing among the stumps in his own field, or chopping trees on his own land, no one thinks less of his dignity, or considers him less of a gentleman, than when he appeared upon parade in all the pride of military etiquette, with sash, sword and epaulette. Surely this is as it should be in a country where independence is inseparable from industry; and for this I prize it.

Among many advantages we in this township possess, it is certainly no inconsiderable one that the lower or working class of settlers are well disposed, and quite free from the annoying Yankee manners that distinguish many of the earlier-settled townships. Our servants are as respectful, or nearly so, as those at home; nor are they admitted to our tables, or placed on an equality with us, excepting at "bees," and such kinds of public meetings; when they usually conduct themselves with a propriety that would afford an example to some that call themselves gentlemen, viz., young men who voluntarily throw aside those restraints that society expects from persons filling a respectable situation.

Intemperance is too prevailing a vice among all ranks of people in this country; but I blush to say it belongs most decidedly to those that consider themselves among the better class of emigrants. Let none such complain of the airs of equality displayed towards them by the labouring class, seeing that they degrade themselves below the honest, sober settler, however poor. If the sons of gentlemen lower themselves, no wonder if the sons of poor men endeavour to exalt themselves above him in a country where they all meet on equal ground; and good conduct is the distinguishing mark between the classes.

Some months ago, when visiting a friend in a distant part of the country, I accompanied her to stay a few days in the house of a resident clergyman, curate of a flourishing village in the township of ———. I was struck by the primitive simplicity of the mansion and its inhabitants. We were introduced into the little family sitting-room, the floor of which was painted after the Yankee fashion; instead of being carpeted, the walls were of unornamented deal, and the furniture of the room of corresponding plainness. A large spinning-wheel, as big as a cart-wheel, nearly occupied the centre of the room, at which a neatly-dressed matron, of mild and lady-like appearance, was engaged spinning yarn; her little daughters were knitting beside the fire, while their father was engaged in the instruction of two of his sons; a third was seated affectionately in a little straw chair between his feet, while a fourth was plying his axe with nervous strokes in the court-yard, casting from time to time wistful glances through the parlour-window at the party within.

The dresses of the children were of a coarse sort of stuff, a mixture of woollen and thread, the produce of the farm and their mother's praiseworthy industry. The stockings, socks, muffatees, and warm comforters were all of home manufacture. Both girls and boys wore mocassins, of their own making: good sense, industry, and order presided among the members of this little household.

Both girls and boys seemed to act upon the principle, that nothing is disgraceful but that which is immoral and improper.

Hospitality without extravagance, kindness without insincerity of speech, marked the manners of our worthy friends. Every thing in the house was conducted with attention to prudence and comfort. The living was but small (the income arising from it, I should have said), but there was glebe land, and a small dwelling attached to it, and, by dint of active exertion without-doors, and economy and good management within, the family were maintained with respectability: in short, we enjoyed during our sojourn many of the comforts of a cleared farm; poultry of every kind, beef of their own killing, excellent mutton and pork: we had a variety of preserves at our tea-table, with honey in the comb, delicious butter, and good cheese, with divers sorts of cakes; a kind of little pancake, made from the flour of buck-wheat, which are made in a batter, and raised with barm, afterwards dropped into boiling lard, and fried; also a preparation made of Indian corn-flour, called supporne-cake, which is fried in slices, and eaten with maple-syrup, were among the novelties of our breakfast-fare.

I was admiring a breed of very fine fowls in the poultry-yard one morning, when my friend smiled and said, "I do not know if you will think I came honestly by them."

"I am sure you did not acquire them by dishonest means," I replied, laughing; "I will vouch for your principles in that respect."

"Well," replied my hostess, "they were neither given me, nor sold to me, and I did not steal them. I found the original stock in the following manner. An old black hen most unexpectedly made her appearance one spring morning at our door; we hailed the stranger with surprise and delight; for we could not muster a single domestic fowl among our little colony at that time. We never rightly knew by what means the hen came into our possession, but suppose some emigrant's family going up the country must have lost or left her; she laid ten eggs, and hatched chickens from them; from this little brood we raised a stock, and soon supplied all our neighbours with fowls. We prize the breed, not only on account of its fine size, but from the singular, and, as we thought, providential, manner in which we obtained it."

I was much interested in the slight sketch given by the pastor one evening, as we all assembled round the blazing log-fire, that was piled half-way up the chimney, which reared its stone fabric so as to form deep recesses at either side of its abutments.

Alluding to his first settlement, he observed, "it was a desolate wilderness of gloomy and unbroken forest-trees when we first pitched our tent here: at that time an axe had not been laid to the root of a tree, nor a fire, save by the wandering Indians, kindled in these woods.

"I can now point out the identical spot where my wife and little ones ate their first meal, and raised their feeble voices in thankfulness to that Almighty and merciful Being who had preserved them through the perils of the deep, and brought them in safety to this vast solitude.

"We were a little flock wandering in a great wilderness, under the special protection of our mighty Shepherd.

"I have heard you, my dear young lady," he said, addressing the companion of my visit, "talk of the hardships of the bush; but, let me tell you, you know but little of its privations compared with those that came hither some years ago.

"Ask these, my elder children and my wife, what were the hardships of a bush-settler's life ten years ago, and they will tell you it was to endure cold, hunger, and all its accompanying evils; to know at times the want of every necessary article of food. As to the luxuries and delicacies of life, we saw them not;—how could we? we were far removed from the opportunity of obtaining these things: potatoes, pork, and flour were our only stores, and often we failed of the two latter before a fresh supply could be procured. We had not mills nearer than thirteen miles, through roads marked only by blazed lines;

nor were there at that time any settlers near us. Now you see us in a cleared country, surrounded with flourishing farms and rising villages; but at the time I speak of it was not so: there were no stores of groceries or goods, no butchers' shops, no cleared farms, dairies, nor orchards; for these things we had to wait with patience till industry should raise them.

"Our fare knew no other variety than salt pork, potatoes, and sometimes bread, for breakfast; pork and potatoes for dinner; pork and potatoes for supper; with a porridge of Indian corn-flour for the children. Sometimes we had the change of pork without potatoes, and potatoes without pork; this was the first year's fare: by degrees we got a supply of flour of our own growing, but bruised into a coarse meal with a hand-mill; for we had no water or windmills within many miles of our colony, and good bread was indeed a luxury we did not often have.

"We brought a cow with us, who gave us milk during the spring and summer; but owing to the wild garlic (a wild herb, common to our woods), on which she fed, her milk was scarcely palatable, and for want of shelter and food, she died the following winter, greatly to our sorrow: we learned experience in this and in many other matters at a hard cost; but now we can profit by it."

"Did not the difficulties of your first settlement incline you to despond, and regret that you had ever embarked on a life so different to that you had been used to?" I asked.

"They might have had that effect had not a higher motive than mere worldly advancement actuated me in leaving my native country to come hither. Look you, it was thus: I had for many years been the pastor of a small village in the mining districts of Cumberland. I was dear to the hearts of my people, and they were my joy and crown in the Lord. A number of my parishioners, pressed by poverty and the badness of the times, resolved on emigrating to Canada.

"Urged by a natural and not unlawful desire of bettering their condition, they determined on crossing the Atlantic, encouraged by the offer of considerable grants of wild land, which at that period were freely awarded by Government to persons desirous of becoming colonists.

"But previous to this undertaking, several of the most respectable came to me, and stated their views and reasons for the momentous step they were about to take; and at the same time besought me in the most moving terms, in the name of the rest of their emigrant friends, to accompany them into the Wilderness of the West, lest they should forget their Lord and Saviour when abandoned to their own spiritual guidance.

"At first I was startled at the proposition; it seemed a wild and visionary scheme: but by degrees I began to dwell with pleasure on the subject. I had few ties beyond my native village; the income arising from my curacy was too small to make it any great obstacle: like Goldsmith's curate, I was

'Passing rich with forty pounds a year.'

My heart yearned after my people; ten years I had been their guide and adviser. I was the friend of the old, and the teacher of the young. My Mary was chosen from among them; she had no foreign ties to make her look back with regret upon the dwellers of the land in distant places; her youth and maturity had been spent among these very people; so that when I named to her the desire of my parishioners, and she also perceived that my own wishes went with them, she stifled any regretful feeling that might have arisen in her breast, and replied to me in the words of Ruth:—

"'Thy country shall be my country; thy people shall be my people; where thou diest will I die, and there will I be buried: the Lord do so to me, and more also, if ought but death part thee and me.'

"A tender and affectionate partner hast thou been to me, Mary," he added, turning his eyes affectionately on the mild and dignified matron, whose expressive countenance bespoke with more eloquence than words the feelings passing in her mind. She replied not by words, but I saw the big bright tears fall on the work she held in her hand. They sprang from emotions too sacred to be profaned by intrusive eyes, and I hastily averted my glance from her face; while the pastor proceeded to narrate the particulars of their leaving England, their voyage, and finally, their arrival in the land that had been granted to the little colony in the then unbroken part of the township of ———.

"We had obtained a great deal of useful advice and assistance from the Government agents previous to our coming up hither, and also hired some choppers at high wages to initiate us in the art of felling, logging, burning, and clearing the ground; as it was our main object to get in crops of some kind, we turned to without any delay further than what was necessary for providing a temporary shelter for our wives and children, and prepared the ground for spring crops, helping each other as we could with the loan of oxen and labour. And here I must observe, that I experienced every attention and consideration from my friends. My means were small, and my family all too young to render me any service; however, I lacked not help, and had the satisfaction of seeing a little spot cleared for the growth of potatoes and corn, which I could not have effected by my single exertions.

"My biggest boy John was but nine years old, Willie seven, and the others still more helpless; the two little ones you see there," pointing to two young children, "have been born since we came hither. That yellow-haired lassie knitting beside you was a babe at the breast;—a helpless, wailing infant, so weak and sickly before we came here that she was scarcely ever out of her mother's arms; but she grew and throve rapidly under the rough treatment of a bush-settler's family.

"We had no house built, or dwelling of any kind to receive us when we arrived at our destination; and the first two nights were passed on the banks of the creek that flows at the foot of the hill, in a hut of cedar and hemlock boughs that I cut with my axe, and, with the help of some of my companions, raised to shelter my wife and the little ones.

"Though it was the middle of May the nights were chilly, and we were glad to burn a pile of wood in front of our hut to secure us from the effects of the cold and the stings of the mosquitoes, that came up in myriads from the stream, and which finally drove us higher up the bank.

"As soon as possible we raised a shanty, which now serves as a shed for my young cattle; I would not pull it down, though often urged to do so, as it stands in the way of a pleasant prospect from the window; but I like to look on it, and recall to mind the first years I passed beneath its lowly roof. We need such mementos to remind us of our former state; but we grow proud, and cease to appreciate our present comforts.

"Our first Sabbath was celebrated in the open air: my pulpit was a pile of rude logs; my church the deep shade of the forest, beneath which we assembled ourselves; but sincerer or more fervent devotion I never witnessed than that day. I well remember the text I chose, for my address to them was from the viiith chapter of Deuteronomy, the 6th, 7th, and 9th verses, which appeared to me applicable to our circumstances.

"The following year we raised a small block-house, which served as a school-house and church. At first our progress in clearing the land was slow, for we had to buy experience, and many and great were the disappointments and privations that befel us during the first few years. One time we were all ill with ague, and not one able to help the other; this was a sad time; but better things were in store for us. The tide of emigration increased, and the little settlement we had formed began to be well spoken of. One man came and built a saw mill; a grist-mill followed soon after; and then one store and then another, till we beheld a flourishing village spring up around us. Then the land began to increase in value, and many of the first settlers sold their lots to advantage, and retreated further up the woods. As the village increased, so, of course, did my professional duties, which had for the first few years been paid for in acts of kindness and voluntary labour by my little flock; now I have the satisfaction of reaping a reward without proving burdensome to my parishioners. My farm is increasing, and besides the salary arising from my curacy I have something additional for the school, which is paid by Government. We may now say it is good for us to be here, seeing that God has been pleased to send down a blessing upon us."

I have forgotten many very interesting particulars relating to the trials and shifts this family were put to in the first few years; but the pastor told us enough to make me quite contented with my lot, and I returned home, after some days' pleasant sojourn with this delightful family, with an additional stock of contentment, and some useful and practical knowledge, that I trust I shall be the better for all my life.

I am rather interested in a young lad that has come out from England to learn Canadian farming.

The poor boy had conceived the most romantic notions of a settler's life, partly from the favourable accounts he had read, and partly through the medium of a lively imagination, which had aided in the deception, and led him to suppose that his time would be chiefly spent in the fascinating amusements and adventures arising from hunting the forest in search of deer and other game, pigeon and duck-shooting, spearing fish by torchlight, and voyaging on the lakes in a birch-bark canoe in summer, skating in winter, or gliding over the frozen snow like a Laplander in his sledge, wrapped up to the eyes in furs, and travelling at the rate of twelve miles an hour to the sound of an harmonious peal of bells. What a felicitous life to captivate the mind of a boy of fourteen, just let loose from the irksome restraint of boarding-school!

How little did he dream of the drudgery inseparable from the duties of a lad of his age, in a country where the old and young, the master and the servant, are alike obliged to labour for a livelihood, without respect to former situation or rank!

Here the son of the gentleman becomes a hewer of wood and drawer of water; he learns to chop down trees, to pile brush-heaps, split rails for fences, attend the fires during the burning season, dressed in a coarse over-garment of hempen cloth, called a logging-shirt, with trousers to correspond, and a Yankee straw hat flapped over his eyes, and a handspike to assist him in rolling over the burning brands. To tend and drive oxen, plough, sow, plant Indian corn and pumpkins, and raise potatoe-hills, are among some of the young emigrant's accomplishments. His relaxations are but comparatively few, but they are seized with a relish and avidity that give them the greater charm.

You may imagine the disappointment felt by the poor lad on seeing his fair visions of amusement fade before the dull realities and distasteful details of a young settler's occupation in the backwoods.

Youth, however, is the best season for coming to this country; the mind soon bends itself to its situation, and becomes not only reconciled, but in time pleased with the change of life. There is a consolation, too, in seeing that he does no more than others of equal pretensions as to rank and education are obliged to submit to, if they would prosper; and perhaps he lives to bless the country which has robbed him of a portion of that absurd pride that made him look with contempt on those whose occupations were of a humble nature. It were a thousand pities wilfully to deceive persons desirous of emigrating with false and flattering pictures of the advantages to be met with in this country. Let the *pro* and *con* be fairly stated, and let the reader use his best judgment, unbiassed by prejudice or interest in a matter of such vital importance not only as regards himself, but the happiness and welfare of those over whose destinies Nature has made him the guardian. It is, however, far more difficult to write on the subject of emigration than most persons think: it embraces so wide a field that what would be perfectly correct as regards one part of the province would by no means prove so as regarded another. One district differs from another, and one township from another, according to its natural advantages; whether it be long settled or unsettled, possessing water privileges or not; the soil and even the climate will be different, according to situation and circumstances.

Much depends on the tempers, habits, and dispositions of the emigrants themselves. What suits one will not another; one family will flourish, and accumulate every comfort about their homesteads, while others languish in poverty and discontent. It would take volumes to discuss every argument for and against, and to point out exactly who are and who are not fit subjects for emigration.

Have you read Dr. Dunlop's spirited and witty "Backwoodsman?" If you have not, get it as soon as you can; it will amuse you. I think a Backwoodswoman might be written in the same spirit, setting forth a few pages, in the history of bush-ladies, as examples for our sex. Indeed, we need some wholesome admonitions on our duties and the folly of repining at following and sharing the fortunes of our spouses, whom we have vowed in happier hours to love "in riches and in poverty, in sickness and in health." Too many pronounce these words without heeding their importance, and without calculating the chances that may put their faithfulness to the severe test of quitting home, kindred, and country, to share the hard lot of a settler's life; for even this sacrifice renders it hard to be borne; but the truly attached wife will do this, and more also, if required by the husband of her choice.

But now it is time I say farewell: my dull letter, grown to a formidable packet, will tire you, and make you wish it at the bottom of the Atlantic.

Letter XVI.

Indian Hunters.—Sail in a Canoe.—Want of Libraries in the Backwoods.—New Village.—Progress of Improvement.—Fire-flies.

Having in a former letter given you some account of a winter visit to the Indians, I shall now give a short sketch of their summer encampment, which I went to see one beautiful afternoon in June, accompanied by my husband and some friends that had come in to spend the day with us.

The Indians were encamped on a little peninsula jutting out between two small lakes; our nearest path would have been through the bush, but the ground was so encumbered by fallen trees that we agreed to go in a canoe. The day was warm, without being oppressively hot, as it too often is during the summer months: and for a wonder the mosquitoes and black-flies were so civil as not to molest us. Our light bark skimmed gaily over the calm waters, beneath the overhanging shade of cedars, hemlock, and balsams, that emitted a delicious fragrance as the passing breeze swept through the boughs. I was in raptures with a bed of blue irises mixed with snow-white water-lilies that our canoe passed over. Turning the stony bank that formed the point, we saw the thin blue smoke of the camp curling above the trees, and soon our canoe was safely moored alongside of those belonging to the Indians, and by help of the straggling branches and underwood I contrived to scramble up a steep path, and soon found myself in front of the tent. It was a Sunday afternoon; all the men were at home; some of the younger branches of the families (for there were three that inhabited the wigwam) were amusing themselves with throwing the tomahawk at a notch cut in the bark of a distant tree, or shooting at a mark with their bows and arrows, while the elders reposed on their blankets within the shade, some reading, others smoking, and gravely eyeing the young rival marksmen at their feats of skill.

Only one of the squaws was at home; this was my old acquaintance the hunter's wife, who was sitting on a blanket; her youngest, little David, a papouse of three years, who was not yet weaned, was reposing between her feet; she often eyed him with looks of great affection, and patted his shaggy head from time to time. Peter, who is a sort of great man, though not a chief, sat beside his spouse, dressed in a handsome blue surtout-coat, with a red worsted sash about his waist. He was smoking a short pipe, and viewing the assembled party at the door of the tent with an expression of quiet interest; sometimes he lifted his pipe for an instant to give a sort of inward exclamation at the success or failure of his sons' attempts to hit the mark on the tree. The old squaw, as soon as she saw me, motioned me forward, and pointing to a vacant portion of her blanket, with a good-natured smile, signed for me to sit beside her, which I did, and amused myself with taking note of the interior of the wigwam and its inhabitants. The building was of an oblong form, open at both ends, but at night I was told the openings were closed by blankets; the upper part of the roof was also open; the sides were rudely fenced with large sheets of birch bark, drawn in and out between the sticks that made the frame-work of the tent; a long slender pole of iron-wood formed a low beam, from which depended sundry iron and brass pots and kettles, also some joints of fresh-killed venison and dried fish; the fires occupied the centre of the hut, around the embers of which reposed several meek deer-hounds; they evinced something of the quiet apathy of their masters, merely opening their eyes to look upon the intruders, and seeing all was well returned to their former slumbers, perfectly unconcerned by our entrance.

The hunter's family occupied one entire side of the building, while Joseph Muskrat with his family, and Joseph Bolans and his squaw shared the opposite one, their several apartments being distinguished by their blankets, fishing-spears, rifles, tomahawks, and other property; as to the cooking utensils they seemed from their scarcity to be held in common among them; perfect amity appeared among the three families; and, if one might judge from outward appearance, they seemed happy and contented. On examining the books that were in the hands of the young men, they proved to be hymns and tracts, one side printed in English, the other the Indian translation. In compliance with our wishes the men sang one of the hymns, which sounded very well, but we missed the sweet voices of the Indian girls, whom I had left in front of the house, sitting on a pine-log and amusing themselves with my baby, and seeming highly delighted with him and his nurse.

Outside the tent the squaw showed me a birch-bark canoe that was building; the shape of the canoe is marked out by sticks stuck in the ground at regular distances; the sheets of bark being wetted, and secured in their proper places by cedar laths, which are bent so as to serve the purpose of ribs or timbers; the sheets of bark are stitched together with the tough roots of the tamarack, and the edges of the canoe also sewed or laced over with the same material; the whole is then varnished over with a thick gum.

I had the honour of being paddled home by Mrs. Peter in a new canoe, just launched, and really the motion was delightful; seated at the bottom of the little bark, on a few light hemlock boughs, I enjoyed my voyage home exceedingly. The canoe, propelled by the Amazonian arm of the swarthy matron, flew swiftly over the waters, and I was soon landed in a little cove within a short distance from my own door. In return for the squaw's civility I delighted her by a present of a few beads for working mocassins and knife-sheaths, with which she seemed very well pleased, carefully securing her treasure by tying them in a corner of her blanket with a bit of thread.

With a peculiar reserve and gravity of temper, there is at the same time a degree of childishness about the Indians in some things. I gave the hunter and his son one day some coloured prints, which they seemed mightily taken with, laughing immoderately at some of the fashionably dressed figures. When they left the house they seated themselves on a fallen tree, and called their hounds round them, displaying to each severally the pictures.

The poor animals, instead of taking a survey of the gaily dressed ladies and gentlemen, held up their meek heads and licked their masters' hands and faces; but old Peter was resolved the dogs should share the amusement of looking at the pictures and turned their faces to them, holding them fast by their long ears when they endeavoured to escape. I could hardly have supposed the grave Indian capable of such childish behaviour.

These Indians appear less addicted to gay and tinselly adornments than formerly, and rather affect a European style in their dress; it is no unusual sight to see an Indian habited in a fine cloth coat and trousers, though I must say the blanket-coats provided for them by Government, and which form part of their annual presents, are far more suitable and becoming. The squaws, too, prefer cotton or stuff gowns, aprons and handkerchiefs, and such useful articles, to any sort of finery, though they like well enough to look at and admire them; they delight nevertheless in decking out the little ones, embroidering their cradle wrappings with silks and beads, and tacking the wings of birds to their shoulders. I was a little amused by the appearance of one of these Indian Cupids, adorned with the wings of the American war-bird; a very beautiful creature, something like our British bullfinch, only far more lively in plumage: the breast and under-feathers of the wings being a tint of the most brilliant carmine, shaded with black and white. This bird has been called the "war-bird," from its having first made its appearance in this province during the late American war; a fact that I believe is well authenticated, or at any rate has obtained general credence.

I could hardly help smiling at your notion that we in the backwoods can have easy access to a circulating library. In one sense, indeed, you are not so far from truth, for every settler's library may be called a circulating one, as their books are sure to pass from friend to friend in due rotation; and, fortunately for us, we happen to have several excellently furnished ones in our neighbourhood, which are always open to us. There is a public library at York, and a small circulating library at Cobourg, but they might just as well be on the other side of the Atlantic for any access we can have to them.

I know how it is; at home you have the same idea of the facility of travelling in this country as I once had: now I know what bush-roads are, a few miles' journey seems an awful undertaking. Do you remember my account of a day's travelling through the woods? I am sorry to say they are but little amended since that letter was written. I have only once ventured to perform a similar journey, which took several hours' *hard* travelling, and, more by good luck than any other thing, arrived with whole bones at my destination. I could not help laughing at the frequent exclamations of the teamster, a shrewd Yorkshire lad, "Oh, if I had but the driving of his excellency the governor along this road, how I would make the old horses trot over the stumps and stones, till he should cry out again; I warrant he'd do *summut* to mend them before he came along them again."

Unfortunately it is not a statute-road on this side the river, and has been cut by the settlers for their own convenience, so that I fear nothing will be done to improve it, unless it is by the inhabitants themselves.

We hope soon to have a market for our grain nearer at hand than Peterborough; a grist-mill has just been raised at the new village that is springing up. This will prove a great comfort to us; we have at present to fetch flour up at a great expense, through bad roads, and the loss of time to those that are obliged to send wheat to the town to be ground, is a serious evil; this will soon be remedied, to the joy of the whole neighbourhood.

You do not know how important these improvements are, and what effect they have in raising the spirits of the emigrant, besides enhancing the value of his property in no trifling degree. We have already experienced the benefit of being near the saw-mill, as it not only enables us to build at a smaller expense, but enables us to exchange logs for sawn lumber. The great pine-trees which, under other circumstances, would be an encumbrance and drawback to clearing the land, prove a most profitable crop when cleared off in the form of saw-logs, which is easily done where they are near the water; the logs are sawn to a certain length, and dragged by oxen, during the winter, when the ground is hard, to the lake's edge; when the ice breaks up, the logs float down with the current and enter the mill-race; I have seen the lake opposite to our windows covered with these floating timbers, voyaging down to the saw-mill.

How valuable would the great oaks and gigantic pines be on an estate in England; while here they are as little thought of as saplings would be at home. Some years hence the timbers that are now burned up will be regretted. Yet it is impossible to preserve them; they would prove a great encumbrance to the farmer. The oaks are desirable for splitting, as they make the most durable fences; pine, cedar, and white ash are also used for rail-cuts; maple and dry beech are the best sorts of wood for fires: white ash burns well. In making ley for soap, care is taken to use none but the ashes of hard wood, as oak, ash, maple, beech; any of the resinous trees are bad for the purpose, and the ley will not mingle with the fat In boiling, to the great mortification of the uninitiated soap-boiler, who, by being made acquainted with this simple fact, might have been spared much useless trouble and waste of material, after months of careful saving.

An American settler's wife told me this, and bade me be careful not to make use of any of the pine-wood ashes in running the ley. And here I must observe, that of all people the Yankees, as they are termed, are the most industrious and ingenious; they are never at a loss for an expedient: if one thing fails them they adopt another, with a quickness of thought that surprises me, while to them it seems only a matter of course. They seem to possess a sort of innate presence of mind, and instead of wasting their energies in words, they *act*. The old settlers that have been long among them seem to acquire the same sort of habits, insomuch that it is difficult to distinguish them. I have heard the Americans called a loquacious boasting people; now, as far as my limited acquaintance with them goes, I consider they are almost laconic, and if I dislike them it is for a certain cold brevity of manner that seems to place a barrier between you and them.

I was somewhat struck with a remark made by a travelling clock-maker, a native of the state of Ohio. After speaking of the superior climate of Ohio, in answer to some questions of my husband, he said, he was surprised that gentlemen should prefer the Canadas, especially the bush, where for many years they must want all the comforts and luxuries of life, to the rich, highly cultivated, and fruitful state of Ohio, where land was much cheaper, both cleared and wild.

To this we replied that, in the first place, British subjects preferred the British government; and, besides, they were averse to the manners of his countrymen. He candidly admitted the first objection; and in reply to the last observed, that the Americans at large ought not to be judged by the specimens to be found in the British colonies, as they were, for the most part, persons of no reputation, many of whom had fled to the Canadas to escape from debt, or other disgraceful conduct; and added, "It would be hard if the English were to be judged as a nation by the convicts of Botany Bay."

Now there was nothing unfair or rude in the manners of this stranger, and his defence of his nation was mild and reasonable, and such as any unprejudiced person must have respected him for.

I have just been interrupted by a friend, who has called to tell me he has an opportunity of sending safe and free of expense to London or Liverpool, and that he will enclose a packet for me in the box he is packing for England.

I am delighted by the intelligence, but regret that I have nothing but a few flower-seeds, a specimen of Indian workmanship, and a few butterflies to send you —the latter are for Jane. I hope all will not share the fate of the last I sent. Sarah wrote me word, when they came to look for the green moth I had enclosed in a little box, nothing of his earthly remains was visible beyond a little dust and some pink feet. I have, with some difficulty, been able to procure another and finer specimen; and, for fear it should meet with a similar annihilation, I will at least preserve the memory of its beauties, and give you a description of it.

It is just five inches from wing to wing; the body the thickness of my little finger, snow-white, covered with long silken hair; the legs bright red, so are the antennæ, which are toothed like a comb on either side, shorter than those of butterflies and elegantly curled; the wings, both upper and under, are of the most exquisite pale tint of green, fringed at the edges with golden colour; each wing has a small shaded crescent of pale blue, deep red, and orange; the blue forming the centre, like a half-closed eye; the lower wings elongated in deep scollop, so as to form two long tails, like those of the swallow-tail butterfly, only a full inch in length and deeply fringed; on the whole this moth is the most exquisite creature I have ever seen.

We have a variety of the peacock butterfly, that is very rich, with innumerable eyes on the wings. The yellow swallow-tail is also very common, and the black and blue admiral, and the red, white, and black admiral, with many other beautiful varieties that I cannot describe. The largest butterfly I have yet seen is a gay vermilion, marked with jet black lines that form an elegant black lace pattern over its wide wings.

Then for dragon-flies, we have them of every size, shape, and colour. I was particularly charmed by a pair of superb blue ones that I used to see this summer in my walk to visit my sister. They were as large as butterflies, with black gauze wings; on each pair was marked a crescent of the brightest azure blue, shaded with scarlet; the bodies of these beautiful creatures were also blue. I have seen them scarlet and black, yellow and black, copper-coloured, green, and brown; the latter are great enemies to the mosquitoes and other small insects, and may be seen in vast numbers flitting around in all directions of an evening in search of prey.

The fire-flies must not be forgotten, for of all others they are the most remarkable; their appearance generally precedes rain; they are often seen after dark, on mild damp evenings, sporting among the cedars at the edge of the wood, and especially near swamps, when the air is illuminated with their brilliant dancing light. Sometimes they may be seen in groups, glancing like falling stars in mid-air, or descending so low as to enter your dwelling and flit about among the draperies of your bed or window-curtains; the light they emit is more brilliant than that of the glowworm; but it is produced in the same manner from the under part of the body. The glow-worm is also frequently seen, even as late as September, on mild, warm, dewy nights.

We have abundance of large and small beetles, some most splendid: green and gold, rose-colour, red and black, yellow and black; some quite black, formidably large, with wide branching horns. Wasps are not so troublesome as in England, but I suppose it is because we cannot offer such temptations as our home gardens hold out to these ravenous insects.

One of our choppers brought me the other day what he called a hornet's nest; it was certainly too small and delicate a piece of workmanship for so large an insect; and I rather conjecture that it belonged to the beautiful black and gold insect called the wasp-fly, but of this I am not certain. The nest was about the size and shape of a turkey's egg, and was composed of six paper cups inserted one within the other, each lessening till the innermost of all appeared not larger than a pigeon's egg. On looking carefully within the orifice of the last cup, a small comb, containing twelve cells, of the most exquisite neatness, might be perceived, if anything, superior in regularity to the cells in the comb of the domestic bee, one of which was at least equal to three of these. The substance that composed the cups was of a fine silver grey silken texture, as fine as the finest India silk paper, and extremely brittle; when slightly wetted it became glutinous, and adhered a little to the finger; the whole was carefully fixed to a stick: I have seen one since fastened to a rough rail. I could not but admire the instinctive care displayed in the formation of this exquisite piece of insect architecture to guard the embryo animal from injury, either from the voracity of birds or the effect of rain, which could scarcely find entrance in the interior.

I had carefully, as I thought, preserved my treasure, by putting it in one of my drawers, but a wicked little thief of a mouse found it out and tore it to pieces for the sake of the drops of honey contained in one or two of the cells. I was much vexed, as I purposed sending it by some favourable opportunity to a dear friend living in Gloucester Place, who took great delight in natural curiosities, and once showed me a nest of similar form to this, that had been found in a bee-hive; the material was much coarser, and, if I remember right, had but two cases instead of six.

I have always felt a great desire to see the nest of a humming-bird, but hitherto have been disappointed. This summer I had some beds of mignionette and other flowers, with some most splendid major convolvuluses or "morning gloves," as the Americans call them; these lovely flowers tempted the humming-birds to visit my garden, and I had the pleasure of seeing a pair of those beautiful creatures, but their flight is so peculiar that it hardly gives you a perfect sight of their colours; their motion when on the wing resembles the whirl of a spinning-wheel, and the sound they make is like the hum of a wheel at work; I shall plant flowers to entice them to build near us.

I sometimes fear you will grow weary of my long dull letters; my only resources are domestic details and the natural history of the country, which I give whenever I think the subject has novelty to recommend it to your attention. Possibly I may sometimes disappoint you by details that appear to place the state of the emigrant in an unfavourable light; I merely give facts as I have seen, or heard them stated. I could give you many flourishing accounts of settlers in this country; I could also reverse the picture, and you would come to the conclusion that there are many arguments to be used both for and against emigration. Now, the greatest argument, and that which has the most weight, is NECESSITY, and this will always turn the scale in the favour of emigration; and that same imperative dame Necessity tells me it is *necessary* for me to draw my letter to a conclusion.

Farewell, ever faithfully and affectionately, your attached sister.

Letter XVII.

Ague.—Illness of the Family.—Probable Cause.—Root-house.—Setting-in of Winter.—Insect termed a "Sawyer."—Temporary Church.

November the 28th, 1834.

You will have been surprised, and possibly distressed, by my long silence of several months, but when I tell you it has been occasioned by sickness, you will cease to wonder that I did not write.

My dear husband, my servant, the poor babe, and myself, were all at one time confined to our beds with ague. You know how severe my sufferings always were at home with intermittents, and need not marvel if they were no less great in a country where lake-fevers and all kinds of intermittent fevers abound.

Few persons escape the second year without being afflicted with this weakening complaint; the mode of treatment is repeated doses of calomel, with castor-oil or salts, and is followed up by quinine. Those persons who do not choose to employ medical advice on the subject, dose themselves with ginger-tea, strong infusion of hyson, or any other powerful green tea, pepper, and whiskey, with many other remedies that have the sanction of custom or quackery.

I will not dwell on this uncomfortable period, further than to tell you that we considered the complaint to have had its origin in a malaria, arising from a cellar below the kitchen. When the snow melted, this cellar became half full of water, either from the moisture draining through the spongy earth, or from the rising of a spring beneath the house; be it as it may, the heat of the cooking and Franklin stoves in the kitchen and parlour, caused a fermentation to take place in the stagnant fluid before it could be emptied; the effluvia arising from this mass of putrifying water affected us all. The female servant, who was the most exposed to its baneful influence, was the first of our household that fell sick, after which, we each in turn became unable to assist each other. I think I suffer an additional portion of the malady from seeing the sufferings of my dear husband and my beloved child.

I lost the ague in a fortnight's time,—thanks to calomel and quinine; so did my babe and his nurse: it has, however, hung on my husband during the whole of the summer, and thrown a damp upon his exertions and gloom upon his spirits. This is the certain effect of ague, it causes the same sort of depression on the spirits as a nervous fever. My dear child has not been well ever since he had the ague, and looks very pale and spiritless.

We should have been in a most miserable condition, being unable to procure a female servant, a nurse, or any one to attend upon us, and totally unable to help ourselves; but for the prompt assistance of Mary on one side, and Susannah on the other, I know not what would have become of us in our sore trouble.

This summer has been excessively hot and dry; the waters in the lakes and rivers being lower than they had been known for many years; scarcely a drop of rain fell for several weeks. This extreme drought rendered the potatoe-crop a decided failure. Our Indian-corn was very fine; so were the pumpkins. We had some fine vegetables in the garden, especially the peas and melons; the latter were very large and fine. The cultivation of the melon is very simple: you first draw the surrounding earth together with a broad hoe into a heap; the middle of this heap is then slightly hollowed out, so as to form a basin, the mould being raised round the edges; into this hollow you insert several melon-seeds, and leave the rest to the summer heat; if you water the plants from time to time, it is well for them; the soil should be fine black mould; and if your hills are inclining to a hollow part of your ground, so as to retain the moisture, so much the finer will be your fruit. It is the opinion of practical persons who have bought wisdom by some years' experience of the country, that in laying out and planting a garden, the beds should not be raised, as is the usual custom; and give us a reason, that the sun having such great power draws the moisture more readily from the earth where the beds are elevated above the level, and, in consequence of the dryness of the ground, the plants wither away.

As there appears some truth in the remark, I am inclined to adopt the plan.

Vegetables are in general fine, and come quickly to maturity, considering the lateness of the season in which they are usually put into the ground. Peas are always fine, especially the marrowfats, which are sometimes grown in the fields, on cleared lands that are under the plough. We have a great variety of beans, all of the French or kidney kind; there is a very prolific white runner, of which I send you some of the seed: the method of planting them is to raise a small hillock of mould by drawing the earth up with the hoe; flatten this, or rather hollow it a little in the middle, and drop in four or five seeds round the edges; as soon as the bean puts forth its runners insert a pole of five or six feet in the centre of the hill; the plants will all meet and twine up it, bearing a profusion of pods, which are cut and foiled as the scarlet-runners, or else, in their dry or ripe state, stewed and eaten with salt meat; this, I believe, is the more usual way of cooking them. The early bush-bean is a dwarf, with bright yellow seed.

Lettuces are very fine, and may be cultivated easily, and very early, by transplanting the seedlings that appear as soon as the ground is free from snow. Cabbages and savoys, and all sorts of roots, keep during the winter in the cellars or root-houses; but to the vile custom of keeping green vegetables in the shallow, moist cellars below the kitchens, much of the sickness that attacks settlers under the various forms of agues, intermittent, remittent, and lake-fevers, may be traced.

Many, of the lower class especially, are not sufficiently careful in clearing these cellars from the decaying portions of vegetable matter, which are often suffered to accumulate from year to year to infect the air of the dwelling. Where the house is small, and the family numerous, and consequently exposed to its influence by night, the baneful consequences may be readily imagined. "Do not tell me of lakes and swamps as the cause of fevers and agues; look to your cellars," was the observation of a blunt but experienced Yankee doctor. I verily believe it was the cellar that was the cause of sickness in our house all the spring and summer.

A root-house is indispensably necessary for the comfort of a settler's family; if well constructed, with double log-walls, and the roof secured from the soaking in of the rain or melting snows, it preserves vegetables, meat, and milk excellently. You will ask if the use be so great, and the comfort so essential, why does not every settler build one?

Now, dear mamma, this is exactly what every new comer says; but he has to learn the difficulty there is at first of getting these matters accomplished, unless, indeed, he have (which is not often the case) the command of plenty of ready money, and can afford to employ extra workmen. Labour is so expensive, and the working seasons so short, that many useful and convenient buildings are left to a future time; and a cellar, which one man can excavate in two days, if he work well, is made to answer the purpose, till the season of leisure arrives, or necessity obliges the root-house to be made. We are ourselves proof of this very sort of unwilling procrastination; but the logs are now cut for the root-house, and we shall have one early in the spring. I would, however, recommend any one that could possibly do so at first, to build a root-house without delay, and also to have a well dug; the springs lying very few feet below the surface renders this neither laborious or very expensive. The creeks will often fail in very dry weather, and the lake and river-waters grow warm and distasteful during the spring and summer. The spring-waters are generally cold and pure, even in the hottest weather, and delightfully refreshing.

Our winter seems now fairly setting in: the snow has twice fallen, and as often disappeared, since the middle of October; but now the ground is again hardening into stone; the keen north-west wind is abroad; and every outward object looks cold and wintry. The dark line of pines that bound the opposite side of the lake is already hoary and heavy with snow, while the half-frozen lake has a deep leaden tint, which is only varied in shade by the masses of ice which shoot out in long points, forming mimic bays and peninsulas. The middle of the stream, where the current is strongest, is not yet frozen over, but runs darkly along like a river between its frozen banks. In some parts where the banks are steep and overhung with roots and shrubs, the fallen snow and water take the most fantastic forms.

I have stood of a bright winter day looking with infinite delight on the beautiful mimic waterfalls congealed into solid ice along the bank of the river; and by the mill-dam, from contemplating these petty frolics of Father Frost, I have been led to picture to myself the sublime scenery of the arctic regions.

In spite of its length and extreme severity, I do like the Canadian winter: it is decidedly the healthiest season of the year; and it is no small enjoyment to be exempted from the torments of the insect tribes, that are certainly great drawbacks to your comfort in the warmer months.

We have just received your last packet;—a thousand thanks for the contents. We are all delighted with your useful presents, especially the warm shawls and merinos. My little James looks extremely well in his new frock and cloak; they will keep him very warm this cold weather: he kissed the pretty fur-lined slippers you sent me, and said, "Pussy, pussy." By the way, we have a fine cat called Nora Crena, the parting gift of our friend ———, who left her as a keepsake for my boy. Jamie dotes upon her; and I do assure you I regard her almost as a second Whittington's cat: neither mouse nor chitmunk has dared intrude within our log-walls since she made her appearance; the very crickets, that used to distract us with their chirping from morning till night, have forsaken their old haunts. Besides the crickets, which often swarm so as to become intolerable nuisances, destroying your clothes and woollens, we are pestered by large black ants, that gallop about, eating up sugar preserves, cakes, anything nice they can gain access to; these insects are three times the size of the black ants of Britain, and have a most voracious appetite: when they find no better prey they kill each other, and that with the fierceness and subtilty of the spider. They appear less sociable in their habits than other ants; though, from the numbers that invade your dwellings, I should think they formed a community like the rest of their species.

The first year's residence in a new log-house you are disturbed by a continual creaking sound which grates upon the ears exceedingly, till you become accustomed to it: this is produced by an insect commonly called a "sawyer." This is the larvæ of some fly that deposits its eggs in the bark of the pine-trees. The animal in its immature state is of a whitish colour; the body composed of eleven rings; the head armed with a pair of short, hard pincers: the skin of this creature is so rough that on passing your finger over it, it reminds you of a rasp, yet to the eye it is perfectly smooth. You would be surprised at the heap of fine saw-dust that is to be seen below the hole they have been working in all night. These sawyers form a fine feast for the woodpeckers, and jointly they assist in promoting the rapid decomposition of the gigantic forest-trees, that would otherwise encumber the earth from age to age. How infinite is that Wisdom that rules the natural world! How often do we see great events brought about by seemingly insignificant agents! Yet are they all servants of the Most High, working his will, and fulfilling his behests. One great want which has been sensibly felt in this distant settlement, I mean the want of public worship on the Sabbath-day, promises to be speedily remedied. A subscription is about to be opened among the settlers of this and part of the adjacent township for the erection of a small building, which may answer the purpose of church and school-house; also for the means of paying a minister for stated seasons of attendance. ——— has allowed his parlour to be used as a temporary church, and service has been several times performed by a highly respectable young Scotch clergyman; and I can assure you we have a considerable congregation, considering how scattered the inhabitants are, and that the emigrants consist of catholics and dissenters, as well as episcopalians.

These distinctions, however, are not carried to such lengths in this country as at home; especially where the want of religious observances has been sensibly felt. The word of God appears to be listened to with gladness. May a blessing attend those that in spirit and in truth would restore again to us the public duties of the Sabbath, which, left to our own guidance, we are but too much inclined to neglect.

Farewell.

Letter XVIII.

Busy Spring.—Increase of Society and Comfort,—Recollections of Home —Aurora Borealis.

This has been a busy spring with us. First, sugar-making on a larger scale than our first attempt was, and since that we had workmen making considerable addition to our house; we have built a large and convenient kitchen, taking the former one for a bed-room; the root-house and dairy are nearly completed. We have a well of excellent water close beside the door, and a fine frame-barn was finished this week, which includes a good granary and stable, with a place for my poultry, in which I take great delight.

Besides a fine brood of fowls, the produce of two hens and a cock, or *rooster*, as the Yankees term that bird, I have some ducks, and am to have turkeys and geese this summer. I lost several of my best fowls, not by the hawk but a horrid beast of the same nature as our polecat, called here a scunck; it is far more destructive in its nature than either fox or the hawk, for he comes like a thief in the night and invades the perch, leaving headless mementos of his barbarity and blood-thirsty propensities.

We are having the garden, which hitherto has been nothing but a square enclosure for vegetables, laid out in a prettier form; two half circular wings sweep off from the entrance to each side of the house; the fence is a sort of rude basket or hurdle-work, such as you see at home, called by the country folk wattled fence: this forms a much more picturesque fence than those usually put up of split timber.

Along this little enclosure I have begun planting a sort of flowery hedge with some of the native shrubs that abound in our woods and lake-shores.

Among those already introduced are two species of shrubby honeysuckle, white and rose-blossomed: these are called by the American botanists *quilostium*.

Then I have the white *Spiræa frutex*, whieh grows profusely on the lake-shore; the Canadian wild rose; the red flowering raspberry (*rubus spectabilis*), leather-wood (*dircas*), called American mezereon, or moose-wood; this is a very pretty, and at the same time useful shrub, the bark being used by farmers as a substitute for cord in tying sacks, &c.; the Indians sew their birch-bark baskets with it occasionally.

Wild gooseberry, red and black currants, apple-trees, with here and there a standard hawthorn, the native tree bearing nice red fruit I named before, are all I have as yet been able to introduce.

The stoup is up, and I have just planted hops at the base of the pillars. I have got two bearing shoots of a purple wild grape from the island near us, which I long to see in fruit.

My husband is in good spirits; our darling boy is well, and runs about everywhere. We enjoy a pleasant and friendly society, which has increased so much within the last two years that we can hardly regret our absence from the more populous town.

My dear sister and her husband are comfortably

settled in their new abode, and have a fine spot cleared and cropped. We often see them, and enjoy a chat of home—sweet, never-to-be-forgotten home; and cheat ourselves into the fond belief that, at no very distant time we may again retrace its fertile fields and flowery dales.

With what delight we should introduce our young Canadians to their grandmother and aunts; my little bushman shall early be taught to lisp the names of those unknown but dear friends, and to love the lands that gave birth to his parents, the bonny hills of the north and my own beloved England.

Not to regret my absence from my native land, and one so fair and lovely withal, would argue a heart of insensibility; yet I must say, for all its roughness, I love Canada, and am as happy in my humble log-house as if it were courtly hall or bower; habit reconciles us to many things that at first were distasteful. It has ever been my way to extract the sweet rather than the bitter in the cup of life, and surely it is best and wisest so to do. In a country where constant exertion is called for from all ages and degrees of settlers, it would be foolish to a degree to damp our energies by complaints, and cast a gloom over our homes by sitting dejectedly down to lament for all that was so dear to us in the old country. Since we are here, let us make the best of it, and bear with cheerfulness the lot we have chosen. I believe that one of the chief ingredients in human happiness is a capacity for enjoying the blessings we possess.

Though at our first outset we experienced many disappointments, many unlooked-for expenses, and many annoying delays, with some wants that to us seemed great privations, on the whole we have been fortunate, especially in the situation of our land, which has increased in value very considerably; our chief difficulties are now over, at least we hope so, and we trust soon to enjoy the comforts of a cleared farm.

My husband is becoming more reconciled to the country, and I daily feel my attachment to it strengthening. The very stumps that appeared so odious, through long custom, seem to lose some of their hideousness; the eye becomes familiarized even with objects the most displeasing, till they cease to be observed. Some century hence how different will this spot appear! I can picture it to my imagination with fertile fields and groves of trees planted by the hand of taste;—all will be different; our present rude dwellings will have given place to others of a more elegant style of architecture, and comfort and grace will rule the scene which is now a forest wild.

You ask me if I like the climate of Upper Canada; to be candid I do not think it deserves all that travellers have said of it. The summer heat of last year was very oppressive; the drought was extreme, and in some respects proved rather injurious, especially to the potatoe crop. The frosts set in early, and so did the snows; as to the far-farmed Indian summer it seems to have taken its farewell of the land, for little of it have we seen during three years' residence. Last year there was not a semblance of it, and this year one horrible dark gloomy day, that reminded me most forcibly of a London fog, and which was to the full as dismal and depressing, was declared by the old inhabitants to be the commencement of the Indian summer; the sun looked dim and red, and a yellow lurid mist darkened the atmosphere, so that it became almost necessary to light candles at noonday. If this be Indian summer, then might a succession of London fogs be termed the "London summer," thought I, as I groped about in a sort of bewildering dusky light all that day; and glad was I when, after a day or two's heavy rain, the frost and snow set in.

Very variable, as far as our experience goes, this climate has been; no two seasons have been at all alike, and it is supposed it will be still more variable as the work of clearing the forest goes on from year to year. Near the rivers and great lakes the climate is much milder and more equable; more inland, the snow seldom falls so as to allow of sleighing for weeks after it has become general; this, considering the state of our bush-roads, is rather a point in our favour, as travelling becomes less laborious, though still somewhat rough.

I have seen the aurora borealis several times; also a splendid meteoric phenomenon that surpassed every thing I had ever seen or even heard of before. I was very much amused by overhearing a young lad giving a gentleman a description of the appearance made by a cluster of the shooting-stars as they followed each other in quick succession athwart the sky. "Sir," said the boy, "I never saw such a sight before, and I can only liken the chain of stars to a logging-chain." Certainly a most natural and unique simile, quite in character with the occupation of the lad, whose business was often with the oxen and their logging-chain, and after all not more rustic than the familiar names given to many of our most superb constellations, — Charles's wain, the plough, the sickle, &c.

Coming home one night last Christmas from the house of a friend, I was struck by a splendid pillar of pale greenish light in the west: it rose to some height above the dark line of pines that crowned the opposite shores of the Otanabee, and illumined the heavens on either side with a chaste pure light, such as the moon gives in her rise and setting; it was not quite pyramidical, though much broader at the base than at its highest point; it gradually faded, till a faint white glimmering light alone marked where its place had been, and even that disappeared after some half hour's time. It was so fair and lovely a vision I was grieved when it vanished into thin air, and could have cheated fancy into the belief that it was the robe of some bright visitor from another and a better world;—imagination apart, could it be a phosphoric exhalation from some of our many swamps or inland lakes, or was it at all connected with the aurora that is so frequently seen in our skies?

I must now close this epistle; I have many letters to prepare for friends, to whom I can only write when I have the opportunity of free conveyance, the inland postage being very high; and you must not only pay for all you receive but all you send to and from New York.

Adieu, my kindest and best of friends.

Douro, May 1st, 1835.

APPENDIX.

[The following Communications have been received from the Writer of this Work during its progress through the Press.]

Maple-Sugar.

This spring I have made maple-sugar of a much finer colour and grain than any I have yet seen; and have been assured by many old settlers it was the best, or nearly the best, they had ever met with: which commendation induces me to give the plan I pursued in manufacturing it. The sap having been boiled down in the sugar-bush from about sixteen pailsful to two, I first passed it through a thin flannel bag, after the manner of a jelly-bag, to strain it from the first impurities, which are great. I then passed the liquor through another thicker flannel into the iron pot, in which I purposed boiling down the sugar, and while yet cold, or at best but lukewarm, beat up the white of one egg to a froth, and spread it gently over the surface of the liquor, watching the pot carefully after the fire began to heat it, that I might not suffer the scum to boil into the sugar. A few minutes before it comes to a boil, the scum must be carefully removed with a skimmer, or ladle,—the former is best. I consider that on the care taken to remove every particle of scum depends, in a great measure, the brightness and clearness of the sugar. The best rule I can give as to the sugaring-off, as it is termed, is to let the liquid continue at a fast boil: only be careful to keep it from coming over by keeping a little of the liquid in your stirring-ladle, and when it boils up to the top, or you see it rising too fast, throw in a little from time to time to keep it down; or if you boil on a cooking-stove, throwing open one or all the doors will prevent boiling over. Those that sugar-off outside the house have a wooden crane fixed against a stump, the fire being lighted against the stump, and the kettle suspended on the crane: by this simple contrivance, (for any bush-boy can fix a crane of the kind,) the sugar need never rise over if common attention be paid to the boiling; but it does require constant watching: one idle glance may waste much of the precious fluid. I had only a small cooking-stove to boil my sugar on, the pots of which were thought too small, and not well shaped, so that at first my fears were that I must relinquish the trial; but I persevered, and experience convinces me a stove is an excellent furnace for the purpose; as you can regulate the heat as you like.

One of the most anxious periods in the boiling I found to be when the liquor began first to assume a yellowish frothy appearance, and cast up so great a volume of steam from its surface as to obscure the contents of the pot; as it may then rise over almost unperceived by the most vigilant eye. As the liquor thickens into molasses, it becomes a fine yellow, and seems nothing but thick froth. When it is getting pretty well boiled down, the drops begin to fall clear and ropy from the ladle; and if you see little bright grainy-looking bubbles in it, drop some on a cold plate, and continue to stir or rub it till it is quite cold: if it is ready to granulate, you will find it gritty, and turn whitish or pale straw colour, and stiff. The sugar may then safely be poured off into a tin dish, pail, basin, or any other utensil. I tried two different methods after taking the sugar from the fire, but could find little difference in the look of the sugar, except that in one the quantity was broken up more completely; in the other the sugar remained in large lumps, but equally pure and sparkling. In the first I kept stirring the sugar till it began to cool and form a whitish thick substance, and the grains were well crystallized; in the other process,—which I think preferable, as being the least troublesome,—I waited till the mass was hardened into sugar, and then, piercing the crust in many places, I turned the mass into a cullender, and placed the cullender over a vessel to receive the molasses that drained from the sugar. In the course of the day or two, I frequently stirred the sugar, which thus became perfectly free from moisture, and had acquired a fine sparkling grain, tasting exactly like sugar-candy, free from any taste of the maple-sap, and fit for any purpose.

I observed that in general maple-sugar, as it is commonly made, is hard and compact, showing little grain, and weighing very heavy in proportion to its bulk. Exactly the reverse is the case with that I made, it being extremely light for its bulk, all the heavy molasses having been separated, instead of dried into the sugar. Had the present season been at all a favourable one, which it was not, we should have made a good quantity of excellent sugar.

Vinegar.

By boiling down five gallons of sap to one, and when just a little above the heat of new milk, putting in a cupful of barm (hop-rising will do if it be good), and letting the vessel remain in your kitchen chimney-corner during the summer, and perhaps longer, you will obtain a fine, cheap, pleasant, and strong vinegar, fit for any purpose. This plan I have pursued successfully two years. Care must be taken that the cask or keg be well seasoned and tight before the vinegar is put in; as the dryness of the summer heat is apt to shrink the vessel, and make it leak. If putty well wrought, tar, or even yellow soap, be rubbed over the seams, and round the inner rim of the head of the cask, it will preserve it from opening. The equal temperature of the kitchen is preferred by experienced housewives to letting the vinegar stand abroad; they aver the coldness of the nights in this country is prejudicial to the process, being as speedily perfected as if it underwent no such check. By those well skilled in the manufacture of home-made wines and beer, excellent maple-wine and beer might be produced at a very trifling expense; *i. e.* that of the labour and skill exercised in the making it.

Every settler grows, as an ornament in his garden, or should grow, hops, which form one of the principal components of maple-beer when added to the sap.

Hop-rising.

This excellent, and, I might add, indispensable,

article in every settler's house, is a valuable substitute for ale or beer-yeast, and is made in the following simple manner:—Take two double handfuls of hops, boil in a gallon of soft water, if you can get it, till the hops sink to the bottom of the vessel; make ready a batter formed by stirring a dessert-platefull of flour and cold water till smooth and pretty thick together; strain the hop-liquor while scalding hot into the vessel where your batter is mixed ready; let one person pour the hop-liquor while the other keeps stirring the batter. When cooled down to a gentle warmth, so that you can bear the finger well in it, add a cup or basinful of the former barm, or a bit of leaven, to set it to work; let the barm stand till it has worked well, then bottle and cork it. Set it by in a cellar or cool place if in summer, and in winter it is also the best place to keep it from freezing. Some persons add two or three mealy potatoes boiled and finely bruised, and it is a great improvement during the cool months of the year. Potatoes in bread may be introduced very advantageously; and to first settlers, who have all their flour to buy, I think it must be a saving.

The following method I found made more palatable and lighter bread than flour, mixed in the usual way:—Supposing I wanted to make up about a stone and half of flour, I boiled (having first pared them carefully)—say three dozen—good-sized potatoes in about three quarts or a gallon of water, till the liquor had the appearance of a thin gruel, and the potatoes had become almost entirely incorporated with the water. With this potatoe-gruel the flour was mixed up, no water being required, unless by chance I had not enough of the mixture to moisten my flour sufficiently. The same process of kneading, fermenting with barm, &c., is pursued with the dough, as with other bread. In baking, it turns of a bright light brown, and is lighter than bread made after the common process, and therefore I consider the knowledge of it serviceable to the emigrant's family.

SALT-RISING.

This is a barm much used by the Yanky settlers; but though the bread is decidedly whiter, and prettier to look at, than that raised in any other way, the peculiar flavour it imparts to the bread renders it highly disagreeable to some persons. Another disadvantage is, the difficulty of fermenting this barm in the winter season, as it requires a temperature which is very difficult to preserve in a Canadian winter day. Moreover, after the barm has once reached its height, unless immediately made use of, it sinks, and rises again no more: careful people, of course, who know this peculiarity, are on the watch, being aware of the ill consequences of heavy bread, or having no bread but bannocks in the house.

As near as I can recollect, the salt-rising is made as follows:—For a small baking of two or three loaves, or one large bake-kettle-loaf, (about the size of a London peck loaf,) take about a pint of moderately warm water, (a pleasant heat to the hand,) and stir into the jug or pot containing it as much flour as will make a good batter, not too thick; add to this half a tea-spoonful of salt, not more, and set the vessel in a pan of moderately warm water, within a little distance of the fire, or in the sun: the water that surrounds the pot in which your rising is, must never be allowed to cool much below the original heat, more warm water being added (in the pan, not to the barm) till the whole is in an active state of fermentation, which will be from six to eight hours, when the dough must be mixed with it, and as much warm water or milk as you require. Knead the mass till it is tough, and does not stick to the board. Make up your loaf or loaves, and keep them warmly covered near the fire till they rise: they must be baked directly this second rising takes place. Those that bake what I term a *shanty loaf*, in an iron bake-pot, or kettle, placed on the hot embers, set the dough to rise over a very few embers, or near the hot hearth, keeping the pot or pan turned as the loaf rises; when equally risen all over they put hot ashes beneath and upon the lid, taking care not to let the heat be too fierce at first. As this is the most common method of baking, and the first that a settler sees practised, it is as well they should be made familiar with it beforehand. At first I was inclined to grumble and rebel against the expediency of bake-pans or bake-kettles; but as cooking-stoves, iron ovens, and even brick and clay-built ovens, will not start up at your bidding in the bush, these substitutes are valuable, and perform a number of uses. I have eaten excellent light bread, baked on the emigrant's hearth in one of these kettles. I have eaten boiled potatoes, baked meats, excellent stews, and good soups, all cooked at different times in this universally useful utensil: so let it not be despised. It is one of those things peculiarly adapted to the circumstances of settlers in the bush before they have collected those comforts about their homesteads, within and without, that are the reward and the slow gleaning-up of many years of toil.

There are several other sorts of rising similar to the salt-rising. "Milk-rising," which is mixed with milk, warm from the cow, and about a third warm water; and "bran-rising," which is made with bran instead of flour, and is preferred by many persons to either of the former kinds.

Soft Soap.

Of the making of soft soap I can give little or no correct information, never having been given any *certain* rule myself; and my own experience is too limited. I was, however, given a hint from a professional gentleman, which I mean to act upon forthwith. Instead of boiling the soap, which is some trouble, he assured me the best plan was to run off the ley from a barrel of ashes: into this ley I might put four or five pounds of any sort of grease, such as pot skimmings, rinds of bacon, or scraps from frying down suet; in short any refuse of the kind would do. The barrel with its contents may then be placed in a secure situation in the garden or yard, exposed to the sun and air. In course of time the ley and grease become incorporated: if the grease predominates it will be seen floating on the surface; in such case add more ley; if the mixture does not thicken, add more grease. Now, this is the simplest, easiest, and clearest account I have yet received on the subject of soap-making, which hitherto has seemed a mystery, even though a good quantity was made last spring by one of my servants, and it turned out well: but she could not tell why it succeeded, for want of being able to explain the principle she worked from.

CANDLES.

Every one makes their own candles (*i. e.* if they have any materials to make them from). The great difficulty of making candles—and, as far as I see the only one, is procuring the tallow, which a bush-settler, until he begins to kill his own beef, sheep, and hogs, is rarely able to do, unless he buys; and a settler buys nothing that he can help. A cow, however, that is unprofitable, old, or unlikely to survive the severity of the coming winter, is often suffered to go dry during the summer, and get her own living, till she is fit to kill in the fall. Such an animal is often slaughtered very advantageously, especially if the settler have little fodder for his cattle. The beef is often excellent, and good store of candles and soap may be made from the inside fat. These candles, if made three parts beef and one part hogs'-lard, wil burn better than any store-candles, and cost less than half price. The tallow is merely melted in a pot or pan convenient for the purpose, and having run the cotton wicks into the moulds (tin or pewter moulds for six candles cost three shillings at the stores, and last many, many years), a stick or skewer is passed through the loops of your wicks, at the upper part of the stand, which serve the purpose of drawing the candles. The melted fat, not too hot, but in a fluid state, is then poured into the moulds till they are full; as the fat gets cold it shrinks, and leaves a hollow at the top of the mould: this requires filling up when quite cold. If the candles do not draw readily, plunge the mould for an instant into hot water, and the candles will come out easily. Many persons prefer making dip-candles for kitchen use; but for my own part I think the trouble quite as great, and give the preference, in point of neatness of look, to the moulds. It may be, my maid and I did not succeed so well in making the dips as the moulds.

Pickling.

The great want of spring vegetables renders pickles a valuable addition to the table at the season when potatoes have become unfit and distasteful. If you have been fortunate in your maple-vinegar, a store of pickled cucumbers, beans, cabbage, &c. may be made during the latter part of the summer; but if the vinegar should not be fit at that time, there are two expedients: one is to make a good brine of boiled salt and water, into which throw your cucumbers, &c. (the cabbage, by the by, may be preserved in the root-house or cellar quite good, or buried in pits, well covered, till you want to make your pickle). Those vegetables, kept in brine, must be covered close, and when you wish to pickle them, remove the top layer, which are not so good; and having boiled the vinegar with spices let it stand till it is cold. The cucumbers should previously have been well washed, and soaked in two or three fresh waters, and drained;

then put in a jar, and the cold vinegar poured over them. The advantage of this is obvious; you can pickle at any season. Another plan, and I have heard it much commended, is putting the cucumbers into a mixture of whiskey * and water, which in time turns to a fine vinegar, and preserves the colour and crispness of the vegetable; while the vinegar is apt to make them soft, especially if poured on boiling hot, as is the usual practice.

* In the "Backwoodsman," this whiskey-receipt is mentioned as an abominable compound: perhaps the witty author had tasted the pickles in an improper state of progression. He gives a lamentable picture of American cookery, but declares the badness arises from want of proper receipts. These yeast-receipts will be extremely useful in England; as the want of fresh yeast is often severely felt in country districts.

APPENDIX B.

[In the wish to render this Work of more practical value to persons desiring to emigrate, some official information is subjoined, under the following heads:—]

STATISTICS OF EMIGRATION.

I. The number of Sales and Grants of Crown Lands, Clergy Reserves, Conditions, &c.

II. Information for Emigrants; Number of Emigrants arrived; with extracts from Papers issued by Government Emigration Agents, &c.

III. Abstract of the American Passengers' Act, of Session 1835.

IV. Transfer of Capital.

V. Canadian Currency.

VI. Canada Company.

VII. British American Land Company.

I. *Sales and Grants of Crown Lands.*

The following tables, abstracted from Parliamentary documents, exhibit—

1. The quantity of Crown lands *sold* in Upper and Lower Canada from 1828 to 1833, inclusive, with the average price per acre, &c.

2. Town and park lots sold in Upper Canada during the same period.

3. The quantity of Crown lands granted without purchase, and the conditions on which the grants were given, from 1824 to 1833, inclusive.

4. The amount of clergy reserves sold in each year since the sales commenced under the Act 7 and 8 Geo. IV., c. 62.

Crown Lands sold from 1828 *to* 1833.

LOWER CANADA.

Year.	Number of acres sold.	Average price per acre.		Amount of purchase-money received within the first year.			Amount of purchase-money remitted to military purchasers within the first year.			Amount of quit-rent at 5 per cent. on the purchase-money received within the first year.			Whole amount of the purchase-money.		
		s.	d.	£.	s.	d.	£.	s.	d.	£.	s.	d.	£.	s.	d.
1828	20,011	4	11	1,255	14	10	—			39	12	6	5,044	9	9
1829	31,366	5	2¾	466	2	11	—			307	11	0	7,469	17	7
1830	28,077	5	8¾	273	10	5	—			322	3	0	7,461	13	5
1831	51,357	6	1¾	815	19	8	—			484	14	7	12,442	8	0
1832	24,074	6	9¼	1,013	1	11	555	11	0	119	2	7	6,139	0	10
1833	42,570	4	2	1,975	10	11	1,936	9	3	—			7,549	1	5
Totals .	197,455												46,106	11	0

The conditions on which the land was sold were—on sales on instalments, to be paid within three years; or on sales on quit-rent, at 5 per cent., capital redeemable at pleasure. N.B. Sales on quit-rent ceased in 1832.

Crown Lands sold from 1828 *to* 1833.

UPPER CANADA.

Year.	Number of acres sold.	Average price per acre.		Amount of purchase-money received within the first year.			Whole amount of purchase-money.		
		s.	d.	£.	s.	d.	£.	s.	d.
1829	3,883	15	1¾	760	6	10	2,940	17	3
1830	6,135	13	8½	1,350	16	6	4,209	3	0
1831	4,357	11	3½	1,626	15	0	2,458	1	8
1832	10,323	9	1½	2,503	3	5	4,711	2	9
1833	26,376	8	9¼	5,660	8	3	11,578	19	3
Totals . .	51,074						25,898	3	11

Interest is now exacted on the instalments paid.

Three years is the number within which the whole amount of the purchase-money is to be paid. The sales of town lots, water lots, and park lots, in Upper Canada, are not included in this table, on account of the disproportionate effect which the comparatively large sums paid for these small lots would have on the average price per acre. They are given, therefore, separately, in the following table:—

Town and Park Lots sold in Upper Canada from 1828 *to* 1833.

Year.	Number of acres sold.	Average price per acre.			Amount of purchase-money received within the first year.			Whole amount of purchase money.		
		£.	s.	d.	£.	s.	d.	£.	s.	d.
1828	2	126	0	0	63	0	0	252	0	0
1829	—	—			63	0	0	—		
1830	19	10	10	6¼	55	0	0	200	0	0
1831	3	8	7	6½	*95	12	8	25	2	8
1832	30	15	18	6	81	18	9	327	15	0
1833	114	14	13	9	634	8	6	1,674	9	0
Totals. .	168							2,479	6	8

There were no sales in 1829. The £63 currency paid that year was paid as instalments on lots sold in the previous year.

The whole amount of the purchase-money to be paid within three years.

* *Note.*—It is so given in the Parliamentary Return, but probably the 9 should be 1.

The following exhibits the quantity of Crown Lands granted, and the conditions on which the grants were given, from 1823 to 1833.

LOWER CANADA.

Year.	Number of acres granted to militia claimants.	Number of acres granted to discharged soldiers and pensioners.	Number of acres granted to officers.	Number of acres granted, not coming within the previous descriptions.	Total number of acres granted.
1824	51,810	—	4,100	34,859	90,769
1825	32,620	—	1,000	16,274	49,894
1826	3,525	5,500	—	48,224	57,249
1827	7,640	6,300	800	38,378	53,118
1828	7,300	—	4,504	9,036	20,840
1829	3,200	—	—	5,282	8,482
1830	81,425	—	2,000	10,670	94,095
1831	9,400	8,273	3,408	9,990	30,981
1832	10,116	19,000	4,000	4,000	37,116
1833	5,200	22,500	1,200	—	28,900
Totals .	212,236	61,573	21,012	176,623	471,444

Settler's Conditions.—That he do clear twenty feet of road on his lot within the space of ninety days.

Military and Militia conditions.—That he do, within the space of three years, clear and cultivate four acres of his lot, and build a dwelling-house thereon.

UPPER CANADA.

Year.	Number of acres granted to militia claimants.	Number of acres granted to discharged soldiers and pensioners.	Number of acres granted to officers.	Number of acres granted, not coming within the previous descriptions.	Number of acres granted to U. E. Loyalists.*	Total number of acres granted.
1824	11,800	5,800	5,500	134,500	30,200	187,800
1825	20,300	5,700	8,100	149,060	45,000	228,160
1826	16,600	3,100	4,700	19,390	24,800	68,590
1827	10,900	4,200	7,200	33,600	20,200	76,100
1828	10,800	900	3,000	4,304	30,800	49,804
1829	5,300	7,500	8,400	3,230	22,600	47,030
1830	6,400	12,500	12,600	9,336	27,400	68,236
1831	5,500	58,400	7,200	8,000	34,200	113,300
1832	19,300	97,800	7,600	6,100	62,600	193,400
1833	35,200	46,000	—	9,100	135,600	225,900
Totals .	142,100	241,900	64,300	376,620	433,400	1,258,320

Condition.—Actual settlement.

* U. E. Loyalists means United English Loyalists—individuals who fled from the United States on the breaking out of the American war of independence. The grants in the above column are mostly to the children of these individuals.

The conditions in force in 1824, the time from which the Returns take their commencement, were enacted by Orders in Council of 20th October, 1818, and 21st February, 1820, applied equally to all classes of grantees, and were as follows:—

"That locatees shall clear thoroughly and fence five acres for every 100 acres granted; and build a house 16 feet by 20 in the clear; and to clear one-half of the road, and chop down, without charring, one chain in depth across the lot next to road. These road duties to be considered as part of the five acres per 100. The whole to be completed within two years from date of the location, and upon proof of their fulfilment patents to issue.

"On the 14th of May, 1830, an additional stipulation was made in locations to discharged soldiers, which required an actual residence on their lots, in person, for five years before the issue of their patents.

"On the 14th of November, 1830, the then existing Orders in Council, respecting settlement duties, were cancelled, and it was ordered that in lieu thereof each locatee should clear half the road in front of his lot, and from 10 feet in the centre of the road cut the stumps so low that waggon wheels might pass over them. Upon proof of this, and that a settler had been resident on the lot two years, a patent might issue. Locatees, however, were at liberty, instead of placing settlers on their lands, to clear, in addition to half the road on each lot, a chain in depth across the front, and to sow it and the road with grass seed.

"Upon discharged soldiers and seamen alone, under this order, it became imperative to reside on and improve their lands three years before the issue of the patent.

"On the 24th of May, 1832, an Order in Council was made, abolishing, in all cases except that of discharged soldiers and seamen, the regulations previously existing; and which directed that, upon proof of an actual settler being established on a lot, a patent should issue without the condition of settlement duty."

The following extract is taken from "official information" circulated by Mr. Buchanan, and other Government emigration agents in Canada:—

"Emigrants, wishing to obtain fertile lands in the Canadas in a wild state by purchase from the Crown, may rely on every facility being afforded them by the public authorities. Extensive tracts are surveyed and offered for sale in Upper Canada monthly, and frequently every 10 or 14 days, by the Commissioner of Crown lands, at upset prices, varying according to situation from 10*s.* to 15*s.* per acre, excepting in the townships of Sunnidale and Nottawasaga, where the upset price of Crown lands is 5*s.* only. In Lower Canada, the Commissioner of Crown lands at Quebec puts up land for sale, at fixed periods, in various townships, at from 2*s.* 6*d.* to 12*s.* 6*d.* Halifax currency, per acre, payable by instalments. Wild lands may also be purchased from the Upper Canada Company on very easy terms, and those persons wanting improved farms will find little difficulty in obtaining such from private proprietors. On no account enter into any final engagement for your lands or farms *without personal examination*, and be certain of the following qualifications:—

"1. A healthy situation.

"2. Good land.

"3. A pure spring, or running stream of water.

"4. In the neighbourhood of a good, moral, and religious state of society, and schools for the education of your children.

"5. As near good roads and water transport as possible, saw and grist mills.

"6. A good title."

Clergy Reserves sold in each year since the sales commenced under the Act 7 and 8 Geo. IV. c. 62.

LOWER CANADA.

Year.	Number of acres sold.	Average price per acre.		Amount of purchase-money received within the first year.			Whole amount of the purchase-money.		
		s.	d.	£.	s.	d.	£.	s.	d.
1829	1,100	4	6	10	0	0	230	0	0*
1830	9,956	4	9	543	17	0	1,610	3	0*
1831	11,332	7	2¾	541	7	6	2,665	9	3*
1832	6,873	5	8½	533	2	2	1,278	11	8
1833	37,278	8	2¼	3,454	11	6	12,791	17	5
Totals .	66,539						18,576	1	4

The number of years within which the whole amount of the purchase-money is to be paid is three.

* On sales on quit rent, at 5 per cent., the capital redeemable at pleasure.

N.B. Sales on quit-rent ceased in 1832.

UPPER CANADA.

Year.	Number of acres sold.	Average price per acre.		Amount of purchase-money received within the first year.			Whole amount of the purchase-money.		
		s.	d.	£.	s.	d.	£.	s.	d.
1829	18,014	14	8¼	2,464	14	0	13,229	0	0
1830	34,705	13	6	6,153	5	9	23,452	4	0
1831	28,563	12	1¾	8,010	2	11	17,362	12	1
1832	48,484	13	3¾	10,239	9	7	32,287	19	0
1833	62,282	14	4½	14,080	16	8	44,747	19	9
Totals .	192,049						131,079	14	10

The whole amount of the purchase-money to be paid in nine years. In addition to the purchase-money paid, interest has also been paid with each instalment, a statement of which is as follows:—

Interest received in	1829	£1	7	3	currency.
"	1830	62	16	1	"
"	1831	259	14	9	"
"	1832	473	17	2	"
"	1833	854	4	3	"

II. *Information for Emigrants.*

In the year 1832 a little pamphlet of advice to emigrants was issued by his Majesty's Commissioners for Emigration *, which contained some useful information in a small compass. The Commission no longer exists. In lieu of it, J. Denham Pinnock, Esq., has been appointed by Government His Majesty's agent for the furtherance of emigration from England to the British Colonies. Letters on the subject of emigration should be addressed to this gentleman at the Colonial Office, under cover to the Colonial Secretary of State. One chief object of his appointment is to afford facilities and information to parish authorities and landed proprietors desirous of furthering the emigration of labourers and others from their respective districts, especially with reference to the emigration clause of the Poor Laws Amendment Act. The following Government emigration agents have also been appointed at the respective ports named :—

Liverpool . . .	Lieut. Low, R.N.
Bristol . . .	Lieut. Henry, R.N.
Leith . . .	Lieut. Forrest, R.N.
Greenock . . .	Lieut. Hemmans, R.N.
Dublin . . .	Lieut. Hodder, R.N.
Cork	Lieut. Friend, R.N.
Limerick . . .	Lieut. Lynch, R.N.
Belfast . . .	Lieut. Millar, R.N.
Sligo	Lieut. Shuttleworth, R.N.

And at Quebec, A. C. Buchanan, Esq., the chief Government emigration agent, will afford every information to all emigrants who seek his advice.

The following is an extract from the pamphlet published in 1832 :—

" Passages to Quebec or New Brunswick may either be engaged *inclusive* of provisions, or *exclusive* of provisions, in which case the ship-owner finds nothing but water, fuel, and bed places, without bedding. Children

* " Information published by His Majesty's Commissioners for Emigration, respecting the British Colonies in North America." London, C. Knight, 1832. *Price twopence.*

under 14 years of age are charged one-half, and under 7 years of age one-third of the full price, and for children under 12 months of age no charge is made. Upon these conditions the price of passage from London, or from places on the east coast of Great Britain, has generally been *6l.* with provisions, or *3l.* without. From Liverpool, Greenock, and the principal ports of Ireland, as the chances of delay are fewer, the charge is somewhat lower; this year [1832] it will probably be from *2l.* to *2l. 10s.* without provisions, or from *4l.* to *5l.* including provisions. It is possible that in March and April passages may be obtained from Dublin for *1l. 15s.*, or even *1l. 10s.*; but the prices always grow higher as the season advances. In ships sailing from Scotland or Ireland, it has mostly been the custom for passengers to find their own provisions; but this practice has not been so general in London, and some shipowners, sensible of the dangerous mistakes which may be made in this matter through ignorance, are very averse to receive passengers who will not agree to be victualled by the ship. Those who do resolve to supply their own provisions, should at least be careful not to lay in an insufficient stock; fifty days is the shortest period for which it is safe to provide, and from London the passage is sometimes prolonged to seventy-five days. The best months for leaving England are certainly March and April; the later emigrants do not find employment so abundant, and have less time in the colony before the commencement of winter."

From a printed paper, issued by Mr. Buchanan at Quebec, the following statements are taken: (the paper is dated July, 1835).

"There is nothing of more importance to emigrants, on arrival at Quebec, than correct information on the leading points connected with their future pursuits. Many have suffered much by a want of caution, and by listening to the opinions of interested, designing characters, who frequently offer their advice unsolicited, and who are met generally about wharfs and landing-places frequented by strangers: to guard emigrants from falling into such errors, they should, immediately on arrival at Quebec, proceed to the office of the chief agent for emigrants, Sault-au-Matelot Street, Lower Town, where every information requisite for their future guidance in either getting settlements on lands, or obtaining employment in Upper or Lower Canada, will be obtained *gratis*. On your route from Quebec to your destination you will find many plans and schemes offered to your consideration, but turn away from them unless you are well satisfied of the purity of the statements: on all occasions when you stand in need of advice, apply only to the Government agents, who will give every information required, *gratis*.

"Emigrants are informed that they may remain on board ship 48 hours after arrival, nor can they be deprived of any of their usual accommodations for cooking or berthing during that period, and the master of the ship is bound to disembark the emigrants and their baggage *free of expense*, at the usual landing places, and at seasonable hours. *They should avoid drinking the water of the river St. Lawrence, which has a strong tendency to produce bowel complaints in strangers*.

"Should you require to change your English money, go to some respectable merchant or dealer, or the banks: the currency in the Canadas is at the rate of 5*s*. the dollar, and is called Halifax currency; at present the gold sovereign is worth, in Quebec and Montreal, about 1*l*. 4*s*. 1*d*. currency. In New York 8*s*. is calculated for the dollar, hence many are deceived when hearing of the rates of labour, &c.—5*s*. in Canada is equal to 8*s*. in New York; thus 8*s*. New York currency is equivalent to 5*s*. Halifax currency.

"Emigrants who wish to settle in Lower Canada or to obtain employment, are informed that many desirable situations are to be met with. Wild lands may be obtained by purchase from the Commissioner of Crown Lands in various townships in the province, and the British American Land Company are making extensive preparations for selling lands and farms in the Eastern Townships to emigrants.

"Farm labourers are much wanted in all the districts

of Upper Canada, and, if industrious, they may be sure of obtaining very high wages; mechanics of almost every description, and good servants, male and *female*, are much in request.

"Emigrants proceeding to Upper Canada, either by the Ottawa or St. Lawrence route, are advised to supply themselves with provisions at Montreal, such as bread, tea, sugar, and butter, which they will purchase cheaper and of *better quality*, until they reach Kingston, than along the route. They are also particularly cautioned against the use of *ardent spirits or drinking cold river water*, or lying on the banks of the river exposed to the night dews; they should proceed at once from the steam-boat at Montreal to *the entrance of the Canal* or Lachine, from whence the Durham and steam-boats start for Prescott and Bytown daily. The total expense for the transport of an adult emigrant from Quebec to Toronto and the head of Lake Ontario, by steam and Durham-boats, will not exceed 1*l*. 4*s*. currency, or 1*l*. 1*s*. sterling. Kingston, Belleville, up the Bay of Quinte, Cobourgh, and Port Hope, in the Newcastle district, Hamilton and Niagara at the head of Lake Ontario, will be convenient stopping-places for families intending to purchase lands in Upper Canada.

"There is considerable competition among the Forwarding Companies at Montreal; emigrants therefore had better exercise a little caution before agreeing for their transport to Prescott or Kingston, and they should avoid those persons that crowd on board the steam-boats on arrival at Montreal, offering their services to get passages, &c. Caution is also necessary at Prescott or Kingston, in selecting regular conveyances up Lake Ontario. I would particularly advise emigrants destined for Upper Canada, not to incur the expense of lodging or delay at Montreal, but to proceed on arrival of the steam-boat to the barges for Bytown or Prescott.

"Labourers or mechanics dependent on immediate employment, are requested to proceed immediately on arrival into the country. The chief agent will consider such persons as may loiter about the ports of landing beyond *four days* after their arrival, to have no further claims on the protection of his Majesty's agents for assistance or employment, unless they have been detained by sickness or some other satisfactory cause."

Comparative Statement of the number of Emigrants arrived at Quebec from 1829 *to* 1834 *inclusive:—*

	1829.	1830.	1831.	1832.	1833.	1834.
England and Wales . .	3,565	6,799	10,343	17,481	5,198	6,799
Ireland . . .	9,614	18,300	34,133	28,204	12,013	19,206
Scotland . . .	2,643	2,450	5,354	5,500	4,196	4,591
Hamburg and Gibraltar .	—	—	—	15	—	—
Nova Scotia, Newfoundland, West Indies, &c.	123	451	424	546	345	339
Totals .	15,945	28,000	50,254	51,746	21,752	30,935

The total number of emigrants arrived at Quebec, from 1829 to 1834, is 198,632. It will be remarked, that the number rose high in 1831 and 1832, and fell very low in 1833.

Distribution of the 30,935 *Emigrants who arrived at Quebec during* 1834:—

LOWER CANADA.

City and District of Quebec	1,500
District of Three Rivers	350
District of St. Francis and Eastern Townships .	640
City and District of Montreal	1,200
Ottawa District	400
Total to Lower Canada . . .	4,090

UPPER CANADA.

Ottawa, Bathurst, Midland and Eastern Districts, as far as Kingston, included	1,000
District of Newcastle, and Townships in the vicinity of the Bay of Quinte	2,650
Toronto and the Home District, including Settlements round Lake Simco	8,000

x 2

Hamilton, Guelph, and Huron Tracts, and situations adjacent	2,660
Niagara Frontier and District, including the line of the Welland Canal, and round the head of Lake Ontario, to Hamilton	3,300
Settlements bordering on Lake Erie, including the London District, Adelaide Settlement, and on to Lake St. Clair	4,600
Total to Upper Canada . . .	22,210

Died of cholera in Upper and Lower Canada .	800
Returned to United Kingdom	350
Went to United States	3,485
	4,635

Of the number of 30,935 *Emigrants who arrived at Quebec in* 1834, *there were of*—

Voluntary emigrants	29,041
Assisted by parochial aid	1,892
Number of males	13,565
Number of females	9,685
Number of children under fourteen years of age .	7,681

Emigrants who prefer going into Canada by way of New York will receive advice and direction by applying to the British Consul at New York (James Buchanan, Esq.) Formerly this gentleman could procure for emigrants who were positively determined to settle in the Canadas, permission to land their baggage and effects free of custom-house duty; but in a letter dated 16th March, 1835, he says:—

"In consequence of a change in the truly liberal course heretofore adopted at this port, in permitting, without unpacking or payment of duty, of the personal baggage, household, and farming utensils of emigrants landing here to pass in transit through this state to his Majesty's provinces, upon evidence being furnished of the fact, and that such packages alone contained articles of the foregoing description, I deem it my duty to make known that all articles arriving at this port accompanying emigrants in transit to Canada, will be subject to the same inspection as if to remain in the

United States, and pay the duties to which the same are subjected. I think it proper to mention, that all articles suited to new settlers are to be had in Canada on better terms than they can be brought out—and such as are adapted to the country."

The difference between proceeding to Upper Canada by way of Quebec and New York, consists chiefly in the circumstance that the port of New York is open all the year round, while the navigation of the St. Lawrence up to Quebec and Montreal is tedious, and the river is only open between seven and eight months of the year. The latter is, however, the cheapest route. But to those who can afford it, New York is the most comfortable as well as the most expeditious way of proceeding to Upper Canada.

The route, as given in a printed paper, distributed by the British consul at New York, is as follows:—

"Route from New York and Albany by the Erie Canal to all parts of Upper Canada, west of Kingston, by the way of Oswego and Buffalo:—

New York to Albany,	160	miles by steam-boat.		
Albany to Utica,	110	do. by canal or stage.		
Utica to Syracuse,	55	"	"	"
Syracuse to Oswego,	40	"	"	"
Syracuse to Rochester,	99	"	"	"
Rochester to Buffalo,	93	"	"	"

Total expense from Albany to Buffalo, by canal, exclusive of victuals for an adult steerage passenger—time going about 7 or 8 days—3 dollars 63 cents; ditto by packet-boats, and found, 12¼ dollars, 6 days going.

"Ditto do. by stage, in 3½ and 4 days—13 to 15 dollars.

"Ditto do. from Albany to Oswego by canal, 5 days going, 2½ dollars.

"Ditto do. by stage, 2 days—6½ to 7 dollars.

"No extra charge for a moderate quantity of baggage.

"Route from New York to Montreal, Quebec, and all parts of Lower Canada:—

"New York to Albany, 160 miles by steam-boat, 1 to 3 dollars, exclusive of food.

' Albany to Whitehall, by canal, 73 miles, 1 dollar; stage 3 dollars.

"Whitehall to St. John's, by steam-boat, board included, cabin 5 dollars; deck passage 2 dollars without board.

"St. John's to Laprairie, 16 miles per stage, 5*s.* to 7*s.* 6*d.*

"Laprairie to Montreal, per ferry steam-boat, 8 miles, 6*d.*

"Montreal to Quebec, by steam-boat, 180 miles, cabin, found, 1*l.* 5*s.*; deck passage, not found, 7*s.* 6*d.*

"Those proceeding to the eastern townships of Lower Canada, in the vicinity of Sherbrooke, Stanstead, &c., &c., will proceed to St. John's, from whence good roads lead to all the settled townships eastward. If they are going to the Ottawa River, they will proceed from Montreal and Lachine, from whence stages, steam-boats, and batteaux go daily to Grenville, Hull, and Bytown, as also to Chateauguay, Glengary, Cornwall, Prescott, and all parts below Kingston.

"Emigrants can avail themselves of the advice and assistance of the following gentlemen:—at Montreal, Carlisle Buchanan, Esq.; Prescott, John Patton, Esq."

Number of Emigrants who arrived at New York from the United Kingdom for six years, from 1829 *to* 1834:—

Year.	England.	Ireland.	Scotland.	Total.
1829	8,110	2,443	948	11,501
1830	16,350	3,497	1,584	21,433
1831	13,808	6,721	2,078	22,607
1832	18,947	6,050	3,286	28,283
1833	—	—	—	16,000
1834*	—	—	—	26,540
			Total . .	126,464

* The returns for 1834 are made up to the 20th November of that year.

III. *American Passengers' Act.*

The 9th Geo. IV., c. 21, commonly called the " American Passengers' Act," was repealed during the Session of 1835, by an Act then passed, the 5 and 6 Will. IV., c. 53. The intention of the new Act is, of course, to secure, as effectually as possible, and more effectually than the previous Act did, the health and comfort of emigrants on board of passenger ships. By a clause of the Act, copies or abstracts are to be kept on board ships for the perusal of passengers, who may thus have an opportunity of judging whether the law has been complied with; but the discovery of any infractions of the Statute may be made at a time when, in the particular instance, it may be too late to remedy it, so far as the comfort and even the health of the passengers are concerned. It is to be hoped, therefore, that the humane intentions of the legislature will not be frustrated by any negligence on the part of those (especially of the officers of customs) whose business it is to see that the regulations of the Act have been complied with before each emigrant ship leaves port.

No passenger ship is to sail with more than three persons on board for every five tons of registered burthen. Nor, whatever may be the tonnage, is there to be a greater number of passengers on board than after the rate of one person for every ten superficial feet of the lower deck or platform unoccupied by goods or stores, not being the personal luggage of the passengers.

Ships with more than one deck to have five feet and a half, at the least, between decks; and where a ship has only one deck, a platform is to be laid beneath the deck in such a manner as to afford a space of the height of at least five feet and a half, and no such ship to have more than two tiers of berths. Ships having two tiers of berths to have an interval of at least six inches between the deck or platform, and the floor of the lower tier throughout the whole extent.

Passenger ships are to be provisioned in the following proportion :—pure water, to the amount of five gallons, to every week of the computed voyage, for each passenger—the water to be carried in tanks or sweet casks; seven pounds' weight of bread, biscuit, oatmeal, or bread stuffs, to every week for each passenger; potatoes may be included to one-third of the extent of supply, but seven pounds' weight of potatoes are to be reckoned equal to one pound of bread or bread stuffs. The voyage to North America is to be computed at ten weeks, by which each passenger will be secured fifty gallons of water, and seventy pounds weight of bread or bread stuffs for the voyage.

Where there are 100 passengers, a medical practitioner is to be carried; if under 100, medicines of sufficient amount and kind are to be taken out as part of the necessary supplies.

Passenger ships are not to be allowed to carry out ardent spirits as merchandise beyond one-tenth of the quantity as would, but for this restriction, be allowed by the officers of the customs upon the victualling bill of such ship for the outward voyage only, according to the number of passengers.

[An important restriction, which ought to be enforced to the letter of the law. The strong temptation which the tedium of a voyage presents to numbers pinned up in a small space to resort to drinking, has frequently made sad havoc of the money, comfort, and health of emigrants, when, especially, the ship steward has contrived to lay in a good stock of strong waters.]

In the enumeration of passengers, *two* children above seven, but under fourteen, or *three* under seven years of age, are to be reckoned as one passenger. Infants under 12 months are not to be included in the enumeration.

Passengers are entitled to be maintained on board for 48 hours after the ship has arrived at her destination. [Emigrants whose means are limited may thus avoid much inconvenience and expense, by planning and executing with promptitude the route which they mean to take, instead of landing, and loitering in the expensive houses of entertainment of a sea-port.]

Masters of ships are to enter into bonds of 1,000*l.* for the due performance of the provisions of the Act. The penalty on any infraction of the law is to be not less than 5*l*., nor more than 20*l*. for each offence.

[The government emigration agents at the various ports, or the officers of customs, will doubtless give every facility to passengers who seek their advice relative to any violation of the provisions of the Act, and point out the proper course to be taken.]

If there be any doubt that a ship about to sail is not sea-worthy, the collector and comptroller of the customs may cause the vessel to be surveyed. Passengers detained beyond the time contracted for to sail, are to be maintained at the expense of the master of the ship; or, if they have contracted to victual themselves, they are to be paid 1*s*. each for each day of detention not caused by stress of weather or other unavoidable cause.

IV. *Transfer of Capital.*

It is, of course, of the greatest importance to emigrants that whatever capital they may possess, over the necessary expenses of the voyage, &c., should be remitted to Canada in the *safest* and most *profitable* manner. Both the British American Land Company and the Canada Company afford facilities to emigrants, by receiving deposits and granting letters of credit on their agents in Canada, by which the emigrants obtain the benefit of the current premium of exchange. It is unsafe and injudicious to carry out a larger amount of specie than what will defray the necessary expenses of the voyage, because a double risk is incurred,—the danger of losing, and the temptation of squandering. The emigrant, therefore, who does not choose to remit his money through either of the before-mentioned companies, should procure a letter of credit from some respectable bank in the United Kingdom on the Montreal bank.

V. *Canadian Currency.*

In all the British North American colonies accounts are kept and prices are quoted in pounds, shillings, and pence, as in England. The accounts are contradistinguished by calling the former currency, or Halifax currency, and the latter sterling, or British sterling.

The one pound Halifax currency, or currency, as it is more commonly called, consists of four Spanish dollars. The dollar is divided into five parts—called in Spanish pistoreens—each of which is termed a shilling. Each of these shillings or pistoreens is again subdivided into twelve parts, called pence, but improperly, for there is no coin answering to any such subdivision. To meet the want a great variety of copper coins are used, comprising the old English halfpenny, the halfpenny of later coinage, the penny, the farthing, the American cent.; all and each pass as the twenty-fourth part of the pistoreen or colonial shilling. Pence in fact are not known, though almost anything of the copper kind will be taken as the twenty-fourth part of the pistoreen.*

At a time when the Spanish dollar, the piece of eight, as it was then called, was both finer and heavier than the coin now in circulation, its value at the mint price of silver† was found to be 4*s.* 6*d.* sterling. Accordingly, the pound currency was fixed at 18*s.* sterling, and £90 sterling was equal to £100 currency, the rules of conversion being, *add one-ninth to sterling to obtain currency, and deduct one-tenth from currency to find the sterling.* This was called the par of exchange, and was so then. So long as it continued correct, fluctuations were from a trifle above, to a trifle below par,

* The Americans also have their 1*s.*, which is the eighth part of a dollar, or 12½ cents. It is no uncommon thing to hear the emigrant boast that he can get 10*s.* per day in New York. He knows not that a dollar, which is equal to eight of these shillings, is in England equivalent but to 4*s.* 2*d.*, and that the American shilling is, therefore, when compared with the English shilling in value, only 6¼*d.*, and consequently, that 10*s.* a-day is, in fact, but ten 6¼*d.*, or 5*s.* 2*d*½. This rate of payment it may be said is still great; so it is, but it is not often obtained by the labourer; when it is, it is for excessive labour, under a burning sun in sea-port towns, during the busy shipping season.

† The mint price then coincided more nearly with the market price than at present.

and this fluctuation was a real *premium* or *discount*, governed by the cost of the transportation of bullion from the one to the other side of the Atlantic, an expense which now does not exceed, and rarely equals, 2 per cent. 4*s*. 6*d*. has long ceased to be the value of the dollar. Both the weight and purity of the coin have been reduced, until its value in the London market * is not more than 4*s*. 2*d*., the pound currency being consequently reduced to 16*s*. 8*d*. sterling, and 100*l*. sterling become equivalent to 120*l*. currency, or 480 dollars, the common average rate now given for the 100*l*. sterling bill of exchange in England.

The Government, however, still sanction, nay, will not change, the old language, so that the difference is made up by adding what is commonly termed a *premium*. The difference between the *real* par, 4*s*. 2*d*., and the nominal par, 4*s*. 6*d*., is 4*d*. or eight per cent. Thus the fluctuations, instead of being from 1 or 2 per cent. below, to 1 or 2 per cent. above the *real* par, are from 1 to 2 per cent. below, to 1 to 2 per cent. above 8 per cent. *premium* as it is called on the *nominal* par, or from 6 or 7 to 9 or 10 per cent. *premium* on the par. This leads to gross deception, and the emigrant in consequence is not unfrequently outrageously cheated by parties accounting to him for money obtained by sale of bills, minus this or some portion of this nominal premium. Nothing is more common than to hear the new comer boast that he has sold his bill on England for 8 per cent. premium, while in fact he has not received *par* value. As by the above changes 100*l*. sterling is shewn to be equal to 120 currency, or 480 dollars, the rule of conversion, in the absence of a law, where no understanding to the contrary existed, should be, *add one-fifth to sterling money, and currency is obtained, or deduct one-sixth from currency, and sterling is found*. An examination of the exchanges for ten years has proved this to be correct.

* It is necessary to use the market price, as the difference between the mint and the market price is 4 per cent., and as the Spanish dollar possesses no conventional value, it is only worth what it will bring as an article of traffic.

VI. *The Canada Company.*

The Canada Company was incorporated by royal charter and Act of Parliament in 1826. The following are extracts from the prospectus of the Company:—

"The Canada Company have lands for sale in almost every part of the province of Upper Canada, on terms which cannot fail to be highly advantageous to the emigrant, as from the Company requiring only one-fifth of the purchase-money to be paid in cash, and allowing the remainder to be divided into five annual payments, bearing interest, the settler, if industrious, is enabled to pay the balance from the produce of the land.

"The lands of the Canada Company are of three descriptions, viz.—

Scattered reserves;

Blocks or tracts of land, of from 1,000 to 40,000 acres each;

The Huron tract, containing upwards of 1,000,000 acres.

"*Scattered reserves.* The scattered crown reserves are lots of land of from 100 to 200 acres each, distributed through nearly every township in the province, and partaking of the soil, climate, &c., of each particular township. These lands are especially desirable for persons who may have friends settled in their neighbourhood, and can be obtained at prices varying from 8*s*. 9*d*. to 25*s*. currency an acre.

"*Blocks of Land.* The blocks or tracts lie entirely in that part of the province situated to the westward of the head of Lake Ontario, and contain lands which, for soil, climate, and powers of production, are equal, and perhaps superior, to any on the continent of America. These are worthy the attention of communities of emigrants, who from country, relationship, religion, or any other bond, wish to settle together.

"The largest block of this kind in the Company's possession is the township of Guelph, containing upwards of 40,000 acres, of which the greater part has been already sold, and, in the space of a few years only, a town has been established, containing churches, schools, stores, taverns, and mills, and where there are mechanics of every kind, and a society of a highly respectable description.

" *The Huron Territory.* This is a tract of the finest land in America, through which the Canada Company have cut two roads of upwards of 100 miles in extent, of the best description of which a new country admits. The population there is rapidly on the increase.

"The town of Goderich, at the mouth of the river Maitland, on Lake Huron, is very flourishing, and contains several excellent stores, or merchants' shops, in which any article usually required by a settler is to be obtained on reasonable terms. There is a good school established, which is well attended; a Church of England and a Presbyterian clergyman are appointed there; and as the churches in Upper Canada are now principally supported by the voluntary subscriptions of their respective congregations, an inference may be drawn of the respectable character of the inhabitants of this settlement and the neighbourhood. The town and township of Goderich contain about 1,000 inhabitants; and since the steam-boat, built by the Company for the accommodation of their settlers, has commenced running between Goderich and Sandwich, a great increase has taken place in the trade and prosperity of the settlement. In this tract there are four good saw-mills, three grist-mills, and in the neighbourhood of each will be found stores well supplied. And as the tract contains a million acres, the greater portion of which is open for sale, an emigrant or body of emigrants, however large, can have no difficulty in selecting eligible situations, according to their circumstances, however various they may be. The price of these lands is from 11*s*. 3*d*. to 15*s*. provincial currency, or about from 11*s*. to 13*s*. 6*d*. sterling per acre."

Emigrants wishing to communicate with the Company should address the secretary, John Perry, Esq., St. Helen's-place, Bishopsgate-street, London, or the Company's agents at outports.

VII. *The British American Land Company.*

The British American Land Company state, in their prospectus, that they have purchased from the British Government "nearly 1,000,000 of acres in the counties of Shefford, Stanstead, and Sherbrooke," in what are termed "the Eastern Townships of Lower Canada." These townships comprise "a tract of country, lying inland, on the south side of the St. Lawrence, between 45° and 46½° north latitude, and 71° and 73° west longitude. This tract, containing between five and six millions of acres, is divided into eight counties, and these again are subdivided into about one hundred townships. These townships enjoy an important advantage in their geographical position. On the one side, they are of easy access from Montreal, Quebec, and Three Rivers, the shipping ports and great markets of the Canadas; on the other, from New York up the Hudson River and through Lake Champlain, as well as from Boston and other parts on the seaboard of the Atlantic. By their compact and contiguous position, facility of intercourse and mutual support are ensured throughout the whole, as well as a general participation in all local improvements."

The terms on which the Company propose to dispose of these lands "vary according to the situation, quality, and advantages which the different lots may possess; but in the first instance they will generally range from 4*s*. to 10*s*. currency per acre, and in all cases a deposit of part of the purchase-money will be required, viz.:—On the higher priced lots one-fifth; on the lower priced lots one-fourth.

"The terms of payment for the balance will be six annual instalments, bearing the legal interest of the province from the date of sale; but should purchasers prefer anticipating the payments, they will have the option at any time of doing so.

"The price of a building lot at Port St. Francis, for the present season (1835), is 12*l*. 10*s*., payable 5*l*. cash down, and the balance in one year, with interest.

"Deposits of purchase-money may be made with the

Company in London for lands to be selected by emigrants on their arrival in the country.

"By the agreement between his Majesty's Government and the Company, upwards of 50,000*l*. of the purchase-money paid by the latter are to be expended by them in public works and improvements, such as high roads, bridges, canals, school-houses, market-houses, churches, and parsonage-houses. This is an extremely important arrangement, and must prove highly beneficial to settlers, as it assures to them the improvement and advancement of this district. The formation of roads and other easy communications are the great wants of a new country; and the application of capital on works of this nature, which are beyond the means of private individuals, is the best mode by which the successful settlement may be promoted and accomplished.

"The expenditure of the large sum above mentioned, will offer at the same time an opportunity of employment to honest and industrious labourers, immediately on arrival."

The office of the British American Land Company is at 4, Barge-yard, Bucklersbury, London; they have also agents at the various outports.

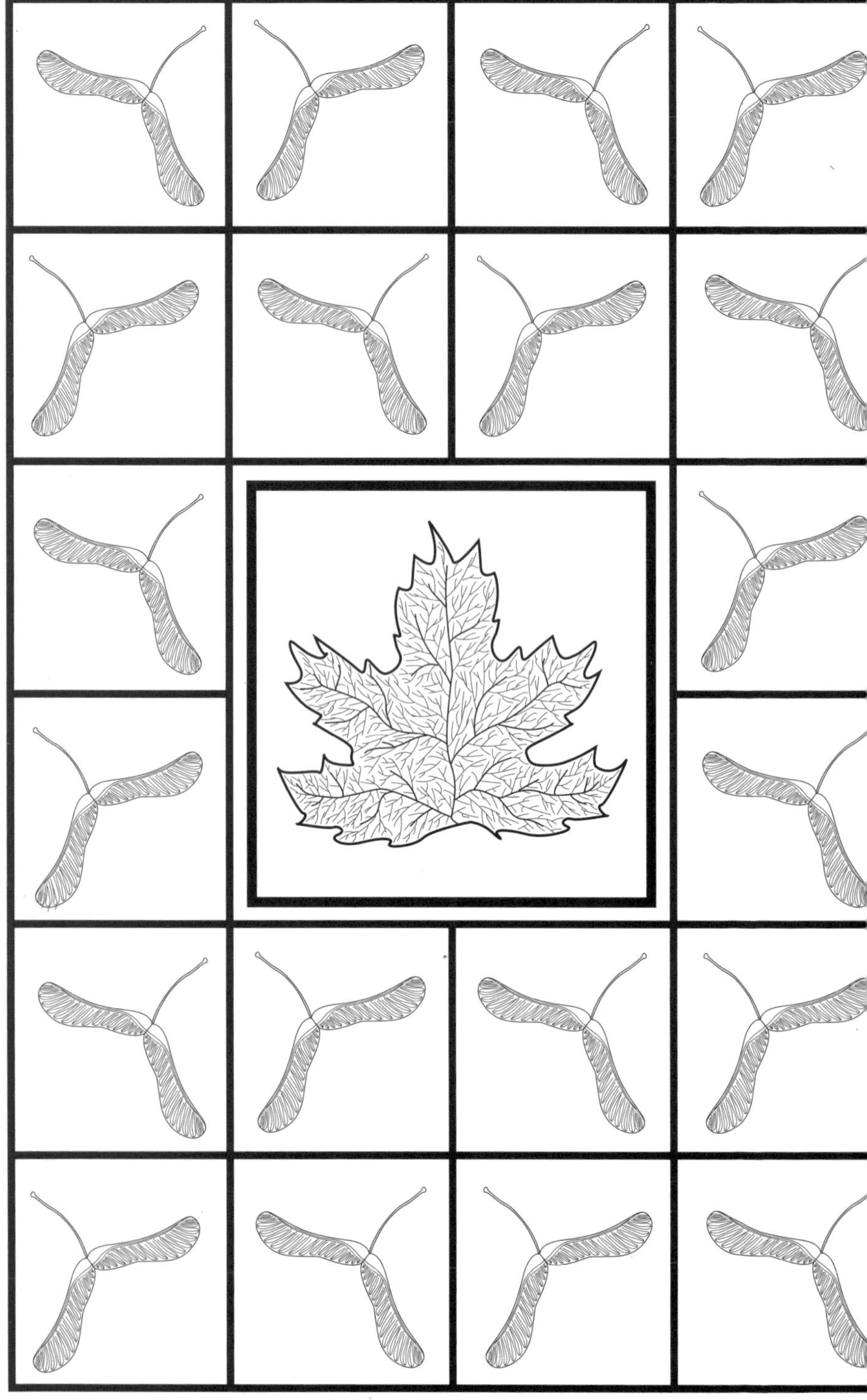